Charles King

Two Soldiers and Dunraven Ranch

Charles King

Two Soldiers and Dunraven Ranch

ISBN/EAN: 9783337133023

Printed in Europe, USA, Canada, Australia, Japan

Cover: Foto ©ninafisch / pixelio.de

More available books at **www.hansebooks.com**

TWO SOLDIERS,

AND

DUNRAVEN RANCH.

TWO NOVELS.

CAPT. CHARLES KING, U.S.A.,

AUTHOR OF "THE COLONEL'S DAUGHTER," "MARION'S FAITH," "KITTY'S CONQUEST," ETC., ETC.

PHILADELPHIA:
J. B. LIPPINCOTT COMPANY.
1891.

TWO SOLDIERS.

TWO SOLDIERS.

I.

THE rain was plashing dismally on the grimy window-sill and over the awning of the shops below. The street-cars went jingling by with a dripping load of outside passengers on both platforms. Wagons and drays, cabs and closed carriages, that rattled or rumbled along the ordinarily busy thoroughfare, looked as though they had been dipped in the river before being turned loose on the street, and their Jehus, a bedraggled lot, must needs have had something amphibious in their composition, else they could not have borne up against the deluge that had been soaking the city for two days past. The policeman, waddling aimlessly about at the opposite corner, enveloped in rubber cap and overcoat, cast occasional wistful glances into the bar-room across the way, wherein the gas was burning in deference to the general gloom that overhung the neighborhood, and such pedestrians as had to be abroad hurried along under their umbrellas as though they half expected to have to swim before they could reach their destination. The dense cloud of sooty smoke that had overhung the metropolis for weeks past, and that wind from any direction could never entirely dissipate, for the simple reason that smoke-stacks by the score shot up in the outskirts on every side, now seemed to be hurled upon the roofs and walls, the windows and the pavement, in a black, pasty, carboniferous deposit, and every object out of doors that one could touch would leave its inky response upon the hand. A more depressing "spell of weather" had not been known for a year, and every living being in sight seemed saturated with the general gloom,—every living being except one: Captain Fred Lane, of the Eleventh Cavalry, was sitting at the dingy window of his office in the recruiting rendezvous on Sycamore Street and actually whistling softly to himself in supreme contentment.

Two missives had reached him that ghastly morning that had served to make him impervious to wind or weather. One—large, formal, impressive, and bearing the stamp of the War Department in heavy type across its upper corner—had borne to him the notification of his promotion to the rank of Captain (Troop D) Eleventh Cavalry, *vice* Curran, retired. The other—a tiny billet—had given him even greater happiness. It might be hard to say how many times he had read and re-read it since he found it on the snowy cloth of his particular breakfast-table in his particular corner of the snug refectory of "The Queen City," on the books of which most respectable if somewhat venerable club his name had been borne among the list of Army or Navy Members ever since his "graduation-leave," fifteen years before.

All his boyhood, up to the time of his winning his cadetship at West Point, had been spent in the city where for the past sixteen months he had considered himself fortunate in being stationed on recruiting-service. During the second year of his term at the Academy he was startled by the receipt of a sad letter from his mother, telling him briefly that his father, long one of the best-known among the business-men of the city, had been compelled to make an assignment. What was worse, he had utterly broken down under the strain, and would probably never be himself again. Proud, sensitive, and honorable, Mr. Lane had insisted on paying to the uttermost farthing of his means. Even the old homestead went, and the broken-hearted man retired with his faithful wife to a humble roof in the suburbs. There, a few months afterwards, he breathed his last, and there, during Fred's graduating year, she followed him. When the boy entered on his career in the army he was practically alone in the world. Out of the wreck of his father's fortune there came to him a little sum that started him in the service free from debt and that served as a nest-egg to attract future accumulations. This he had promptly banked until some good and safe investment should present itself, and, once with his regiment on the frontier, Mr. Lane had found his pay ample for all his needs.

It is unnecessary to recount the history of his fifteen years' service as a subaltern. Suffice it to say that, steering clear of most of the temptations to which young officers were subjected, he had won a reputation as a capital "duty-officer," that was accented here and there by some brilliant and dashing exploits in the numerous Indian campaigns through which the Eleventh had passed with no small credit. Lane was never one of the jovial souls of the regiment. His mood was rather taciturn and contemplative. He read a good deal, and spent many days in the saddle exploring the country in the neighborhood of his post and in hunting and fishing.

But, from the colonel down, there was not a man in the Eleventh who did not thoroughly respect and like him. Among the ladies, however, there were one or two who never lost an opportunity of giving the lieutenant a feline and not ineffective clawing when his name came up for discussion in the feminine conclaves occasionally held in the regiment. Sometimes, too, when opportunity served, he was made the victim of some sharp or sarcastic speech that was not always easy to bear in silence. Mrs. Judson, wife of the captain of B Troop, was reputed to be "down on Lane," and the men had no difficulty whatever in locating the time when her change of heart took place.

The truth of the matter was that, thanks to simple habits and to his sense of economy, Lane had quite a snug little balance in the bank, and the ladies of the regiment believed it to be bigger than it really was; and, having approved the furnishing and fitting up of his quarters, the next thing, of course, that they essayed to do was to provide him with a wife. There the trouble began. Simultaneously with the arrival of his first bar as a first lieutenant there came from the distant East Mrs. Judson's younger sister "Emmy" and Mrs. Loring's pretty niece Pansy Fletcher. Lane was prompt to call on both, to take the young ladies driving or riding, to be attentive and courteous in every way; but, while he did thus "perceive a divided duty," what was Mrs. Loring's horror on discovering that pretty Pansy had fallen rapturously in love with "Jerry" Lattimore, as handsome, reckless, and impecunious a young dragoon as ever lived, and nothing but prompt measures prevented their marriage! Miss Fletcher was suddenly re-transported to the East, whither Jerry was too hard up to follow; and then, in bitterness of heart, Mrs. Loring blamed poor Fred for the whole transaction. "Why had he held aloof and allowed that—that scamp—that ne'er-do-weel—to cut in and win that innocent child's heart, as he certainly did do?" Against Lattimore the vials of her wrath were emptied *coram publico*, but against Lane she could not talk so openly.

Mrs. Judson had beheld the sudden departure of Miss Pansy with an equanimity she could barely disguise. Indeed, there were not lacking good Christians in the garrison who pointed significantly to the fact that she had almost too hospitably opened her doors to Miss

Fletcher and her lover during that brief but volcanic romance. Certain it is, however, that it was in her house and in a certain little nook off the sitting-room that their long, delicious meetings occurred almost daily, the lady of the house being busy about the dining-room, the kitchen, or the chambers overhead, and Emmy, who was a good girl, but densely uninteresting, strumming on the piano or yawning over a book at the front window.

"What Mr. Lane needs is a gentle, modest, domestic little woman who will make his home a restful, peaceful refuge always," said Mrs. Judson; and, inferentially, Emmy was the gentle and modest creature who was destined so to bless him. The invitations to tea, the lures by which he was induced to become Emmy's escort to all the hops and dances, redoubled themselves after Miss Fletcher's departure; but it was all in vain. Without feeling any particular affinity for Mr. Lane, Emmy stood ready to say "Yes" whensoever he should ask; but weeks went on, he never seemed to draw nearer the subject, and just as Mrs. Judson had determined to resort to heroic measures and point out that his attentions to Emmy had excited the remark of the entire garrison, and that the poor child herself was looking wan and strange, there was a stage-robbery not twenty miles from the post. Lane, with fifteen troopers, was sent in pursuit of the desperadoes, and captured them, after a sharp fight, ninety miles up the river and near the little infantry cantonment at the Indian reservation; and thither the lieutenant was carried with a bullet through his thigh. By the time he was well enough to ride, the regiment was again in the field on Indian campaign, and for six months he never saw Fort Curtis again. When he did, Emmy had gone home, and Mrs. Judson's politeness was something awful.

Lane was out with the Eleventh again in three more sharp and severe campaigns, received an ugly bullet-wound through the left shoulder in the memorable chase after Chief Joseph, was quartermaster of his regiment a year after that episode, then adjutant, and finally was given the recruiting-detail as he neared the top of the list of first lieutenants, and, for the first time in fifteen years, found himself once more among the friends of his youth,—and still a bachelor.

Securing pleasant quarters in the adjoining street, Mr. Lane speedily made himself known at the club to which he had been paying his moderate annual dues without having seen anything of it but its bills for years past, yet never knowing just when he might want to drop in.

Then he proceeded, after office hours, to hunt up old chums, and in the course of the first week after his arrival he had found almost all of them. Bailey, who sat next him in school, was now a prominent and prosperous lawyer. Terry, who sat just behind him and occasionally inserted crooked pins in a convenient crack in his chair, was thriving in the iron business. Warden had made a fortune "on 'Change," and was one of the leading brokers and commission-merchants of the metropolis. He had always liked Warden: they lived close together, and used to walk to and from school with each other almost every day. Mr. Lane had started on his quest with a feeling akin to enthusiasm. Calm and reticent and retiring as he generally was, he felt a glow of delight at the prospect of once more meeting "the old crowd;" but that evening he returned to his rooms with a distinct sense of disappointment. Bailey had jumped up and shaken hands with much effusion of manner, and had "my-dear-fellow"-ed him for a minute or two, and then, "Now, where are you stopping? I'll be round to look you up the very first evening I can get away, and —of course we'll have you at the house;" but Lane clearly saw he was eager to get back to his desk, and so took his leave. Terry did not know him at all until he began to laugh, and then he blandly inquired what he'd been doing with himself all these years. But the man who rasped him from top to toe was Warden. Business hours were over, and their meeting occurred at the club. Two minutes after they had shaken hands, Warden was standing with his back to the log fire, his thumbs in the arm-holes of his waistcoat, tilting on his toes, his head well back, and most affably and distinctly patronizing him.

"Well, Fred, you're still in the army, are you?" he asked.

"Still in the army, Warden."

"Well, what on earth do you find to do with yourself out there? How do you manage to kill time?"

"Time never hung heavily on my hands. It often happened that there wasn't half enough for all we had to do."

"You don't tell me! Why, I supposed that about all you did was to drink and play poker."

"Not an unusual idea, I find, Warden, but a very unjust one."

"Oh, yes, I know, of course, you have some Indian-fighting to do once in a while; but that probably amounts to very little. I mean when you're in permanent camp or garrison. I should think a man of your temperament would just stagnate in such a life. I wonder you hadn't resigned years ago and come here and made a name for yourself."

"The life has been rather more brisk than you imagine," he answered, with a quiet smile, "and I have grown very fond of my profession. But you speak of making a name for myself. Now, in what would that have consisted?"

"Oh, well, of course, if you really like the army and living in a desert and that sort of thing, I've nothing to say," said Warden; "but it always struck me as such a—such a—well, Fred, such a wasted life, all very well for fellows who hadn't brains or energy enough to achieve success in the real battle of life" (and here Warden was "swelling visibly"), "but not at all the thing for a man of your ability. We all conceded at school that you were head and shoulders above the rest of us. We were talking of it some years ago here in this very room: there'd been something about you in the papers,—some general or other had mentioned you in a report. Let's see: didn't you get wounded, or something, chasing some Indians?" Lane replied that he believed that "something like that had happened," but begged his friend to go on; and Warden proceeded to further expound his views:

"Now, you might have resigned years ago, taken hold of your father's old business, and made a fortune. There's been a perfect boom in railroad iron and every other kind of iron since that panic of '73. Look at Terry: he is rolling in money,—one of our most substantial men; and you know he was a mere drone at school. Why, Fred, if your father could have held on six months longer he'd have been the richest man in town to-day. It always seemed to me that he made such a mistake in not getting his friends to help him tide things over."

"You probably are not aware," was the reply, "that he went to friend after friend,—so called,—and that it was their failure or refusal to help that broke him down. The most active man in pushing him to the wall, I am told, was Terry's father, who had formerly been his chief clerk."

"Well," answered Warden, in some little confusion, for this and other matters in connection with the failure of Samuel Lane & Co., years before, were now suddenly recalled to mind, "that's probably true. Business is business, you know, and those were tough times in the money market. Still, you could have come back here when you left West Point, and built up that concern again, and been a big man to-day,—had your own establishment here, married some rich girl—you're not married, are you?"

Lane shook his head.

"On the other hand, then, you've been fooling away all this time in the army, and what have you got to show for it?"

"Nothing—to speak of," was the half-whimsical, half-serious answer.

"Well, there! Now don't you see? That's just what I'm driving at. You've thrown away your opportunities.—All right, Strong: I'll be with you in a minute," he called to a man who was signalling to him from the stairway. "Come in and see us, Fred. Come and dine with us,—any day. We're always ready for friends who drop in. I want you to meet Mrs. Warden and see my house. Now excuse me, will you? I have to take a hand at whist." And so away went Warden, leaving Lane to walk homeward and think over the experiences of the day.

He had "made a name for himself" that was well known from the Yellowstone to the Colorado. Thrice had that name been sent to the President with the recommendation of his department commander for brevets for conspicuous and gallant conduct in action against hostile Indians. The Pacific coast had made him welcome. Busy San Francisco had found time to read the *Alta's* and the *Chronicle's* correspondence from the scene of hostilities, and cordially shook hands with the young officer who had been so prominent in more than one campaign. Santa Fé and San Antonio, Denver, Cheyenne, and Miles City, were points where he could not go without meeting "troops of friends." It was only when he got back to his old home in the East that the lieutenant found his name associated only with his father's failure, and that his years of honorable service conveyed no interest to the friends of his youth. "Money makes the mare go," said Mr. Warden, in a subsequent conversation; and money, it seems, was what he meant in telling Lane he should have come home and "made a name for himself."

Lane had been on duty a year in the city when a rumor began to circulate, to the effect that investments of his in mining stocks had brought him large returns, and men at the club and matronly women at the few parties he attended began asking significant questions which now it pleased him to parry rather than answer directly. His twelve months' experiences in society had developed in him a somewhat sardonic vein of humor and made him, if anything, more reticent than before. And then—then all of a sudden there came over the spirit of his dream a marked and wondrous change. He no longer declined invitations to balls, parties, or dinners when he knew that certain persons were to be present. Mabel Vincent had just returned from a year's tour abroad, and Lieutenant Fred Lane had fallen in love at first sight.

It was a note from her that made even that dingy old office, on this most dismal of days, fairly glow and shine with a radiance of hope, with a halo of joy and gladness such as his lonely life had never known before. The very first time he ever saw himself addressed as Captain Fred Lane, Eleventh Cavalry, was in her dainty hand. He turned his chair to the window to read once again the precious words; but there entered, dripping, a Western Union messenger with a telegram.

Tearing it open, Lane read these words: "All join in congratulations on your promotion and in wonderment at the colonel's selection of your successor. Noel is named."

Lane gave a long whistle of amazement. "Of all men in the regiment!" he exclaimed. "Who would have thought of Gordon Noel?"

II.

The colonel of the Eleventh Cavalry was a gentleman who had some peculiarities of temperament and disposition. This fact is not cited as a thing at all unusual, for the unbiassed testimony of the subalterns and even the troop commanders of every cavalry regiment in service would go far towards establishing the fact that all colonels of cavalry are similarly afflicted. One of the salient peculiarities of the commanding officer of the Eleventh was a conviction that nothing went smoothly in the regiment unless the captains were all on duty with their companies; for, while at any time Colonel Riggs would approve an application for a lieutenant's leave of absence, it was worse than pulling teeth to get him to do likewise for a gentleman with the double bars on his shoulder. "Confound the man!" growled Captain Greene, "here I've been seven years with my troop, saving up for a six months' leave, and the old rip disapproves it! What on earth can a fellow say?"

"You didn't go about it right, Greeney," was the calm rejoinder of a comrade who had been similarly "cut" the year previous. "You should have laid siege to him through Madame a month or so. What she says as to who goes on leave and who doesn't is law at head-quarters, and I know it. Now, you watch Noel. That fellow is wiser in his generation than all the rest of us put together. It isn't six months since he got back from his staff detail, and you see how constant he is in his attentions to the old lady. Now, I'll bet you anything you like the next plum that tumbles into the regiment will go to his maw and nobody else's."

"Riggs wouldn't have the face to give anything to Noel,—in the way of detached duty, I mean. I heard him say when 'Gordy' was coming back to the regiment that he wished he had the power to transfer subs from troop to troop: he'd put Noel with the most exacting captain he knew and see if he couldn't get a little square service out of the fellow."

"That's all right, Greene. That's what he said six months ago, before Noel was really back, and before he had begun doing the devoted to her ladyship at head-quarters. Riggs wouldn't say so now, —much less do it. She wouldn't let him, comrade mine; and you know it."

"Noel has been doing first-rate since he got back, Jim," said Captain Greene, after a pause.

"Oh, Noel's no bad soldier in garrison,—at drill or parade. It's field-work and scouting that knocks him endwise; and if there's an Indian within a hundred miles—— Well, you know as much as I do on that subject."

Greene somewhat gloomily nodded assent, and his companion, being wound up for the day, plunged ahead with his remarks:

"Now, I'm just putting this and that together, Greene, and I'll make you a bet. Riggs has managed things ever since he has been colonel so that a lieutenant is ordered detached for recruiting-service and never a captain. It won't be long before Lane gets his promotion; and I'll bet you that even before he gets it Riggs will have his letter skimming to Washington begging his immediate recall and nominating a sub to take his place. I'll give you odds on that; and I'll bet you even that the sub he names will be Gordy Noel."

But, though he scouted the idea, Greene would not bet, for at that instant the club-room was invaded by a rush of young officers just returning from target-practice, and the jolliest laugh, the most all-pervading voice, the cheeriest personality, of the lot were those of the gentleman whose name Captain Jim Rawlins had just spoken.

"What you going to have, fellows?" he called. "Here, Billy, old man, put up that spelter: I steered the gang in here, and it's my treat.

Don't go, Forbes; come back, old fellow, and join us. Captain, what shall it be? Say, you all know Dick Cassidy of the Seventh? I heard such a good rig on him this morning. I got a letter from Tommy Craig, who's on duty at the War Department, and he told me that Dick was there trying to get one of these blasted college details. What d'ye suppose a cavalryman wants to leave his regiment for, to take a thing like that?"

"Perhaps his health is impaired, Noel," said Wharton, with a humorous twinkle in his handsome eyes. "Even cavalrymen have been known to have to quit their beloved profession on that account and get something soft in the East for a year or so."

The color mounted to Noel's cheeks, but he gave no other sign of understanding the shaft as aimed at him. Promptly and loudly as ever he spoke out:

"Oh, of course, if he's used up in service and has to go in to recuperate, all well and good; but I always supposed Cassidy was a stalwart in point of health and constitution. Who's going to the doctor's to-night?—you, Jack?"

Jack—otherwise Lieutenant John Tracy—shook his head as he whiffed at the cigarette he had just lighted and then stretched forth his hand for the foaming glass of beer which the attendant brought him, but vouchsafed no verbal reply. Lee and Martin edged over to where the two captains were playing their inevitable game of seven-up. Two of the juniors,—young second lieutenants,—despite the extreme cordiality of Noel's invitation, begged to be excused, as they did not care to drink anything,—even a lemonade; and no sooner had the party finished their modest potation than there was a general move. Wallace and Hearn went in to the billiard-room; Wharton and Lee started in the direction of their quarters; and presently Mr. Noel was the only man in the club-room without an occupation of some kind or a comrade to talk to.

Now, why should this have been the case? Noel's whole manner was overflowing with jollity and kindliness; his eyes beamed and sparkled as he looked from one man to the other; he hailed each in turn by his Christian name and in tones of most cordial friendship; he chatted and laughed and had comical anecdotes to tell the party; he was a tall, stylish, fine-looking fellow, with expressive dark eyes and wavy dark-brown hair; his moustache was the secret envy of more than half his associates; his figure was really elegant in its grace and suppleness; his uniforms fitted him like a glove, and were invariably of Hatfield's choicest handiwork. Appearances were with him in every sense of the word; and yet there was some reason why his society was politely but positively shunned by several of his brother officers and "cultivated" by none.

It was only a few years after the great war when Gordon Noel joined the Eleventh from civil life. He came of an old and influential family, and was welcomed in the regiment as an acquisition. He made friends rapidly, and was for two or three years as popular a youngster as there was in the service. Then the troop to which he was attached was ordered to the Plains, *via* Leavenworth. It was a long journey by boat, and by the time they reached the old frontier city orders and telegrams were awaiting them, one of which, apparently to Mr. Noel's great surprise, detached him from his company and directed him to report for temporary duty at the War Department in the city of Washington. He was there eighteen months, during which time his regiment had some sharp battles with the Cheyennes and Kiowas in Kansas and the Indian Territory. Then a new Secretary of War gave ear to the oft-repeated appeals of the colonel of the Eleventh to have Mr. Noel and one or two other detached gentlemen returned to duty with their respective companies, and just as they were moving to the Pacific coast the absentees reported for duty and went along. At Vancouver and Walla Walla Noel seemed to regain by his joviality and good-fellowship what he had lost in the year and a half of his absence, though there were out-and-out soldiers in the Eleventh who said that the man who would stay on "fancy duty" in Washington or anywhere else while his comrades were in the midst of a stirring campaign against hostile Indians couldn't be of the right sort.

Up in Oregon the Modoc troubles soon began, and several troops were sent southward from their stations, scouting. There were several little skirmishes between the various detachments and the agile Indians, with no great loss on either side; but when "Captain Jack" retired to the natural fastness of the lava-beds, serious work began, and here Mr. Noel was found to be too ill to take part in the campaign, and was sent in to San Francisco to recuperate. The short but bloody war was brought to a close without his having taken part in any of its actions, but he rejoined after a delightful convalescence in San Francisco (where it was understood that he had broken down only after riding night and day and all alone some three hundred miles through the wilderness with orders to a battalion of his regiment that was urgently needed at the front), and was able to talk very glibly of what had occurred down in the Klamath Lake country. Then came his promotion to a first-lieutenancy, and, as luck would have it, to a troop stationed at the Presidio. For three months he was the gayest of the gay, the life of parties of every kind both in town and in garrison; he was in exuberant health and spirits; he danced night after night, and was the most popular partner ever welcomed in the parlors of hospitable San Francisco. And then all of a sudden there came tidings of an outbreak among the Arizona Apaches of so formidable a character that the division commander decided to send his Presidio troopers to reinforce the one regiment that was trying to cover a whole Territory. There was pathetic parting, with no end of lamentation, when Mr. Noel was spirited away with his lynx-eyed captain; but they need not have worried,—those fair dames and damsels; not a hair of his handsome head was in danger, for the —th had grappled with and throttled their foes before the detachment from the Eleventh were fairly in the Territory, and the latter were soon ordered to return and to bring with them, as prisoners to be confined at Alcatraz, the leaders of the outbreak, who would be turned over to them by the —th. To hear Noel tell of these fierce captives afterwards was somewhat confusing, as, from his account, it would appear that they had been taken in hand-to-hand conflict by himself and a small detachment of his own troop; but these were stories told only to over-credulous friends.

The Eleventh came eastward across the Rockies in time to participate in the great campaign against the Sioux in '76, and was on the Yellowstone when Custer and his favorite companies were being wiped out of existence on the Little Horn. The news of that tragedy made many a heart sick, and Mr. Noel was so much affected that when his comrades started to make a night ride to the front to join what was left of the Seventh, he was left behind, ostensibly to sleep off a violent headache. He promised to ride after and catch them the next day, but, through some error, got aboard General Terry's steamer, the Far West, and made himself so useful looking after the wounded that the surgeon in charge was grateful, and, knowing nothing of his antecedents, gave him a certificate on which he based an application for leave on account of sickness, and went to Bismarck with the wounded, and thence to the distant East, where he thrilled clubs and dinner-tables with graphic accounts of the Custer battle and of how we got up just in time to save the remnant of the Seventh. The Eleventh fought all through the campaign of '76 and the chase after Chief Joseph in '77; but Noel was again on temporary duty at the War Department, and there he stayed until '78, by which time various officials had become acquainted with some of the facts in the case. The Eleventh "cold-shouldered" him for a while after he got back; but they happened to be now in a region where there were no "hostiles," and where hops, germans, theatricals, tableaux, and entertainments of all kinds were the rage. No other man could be half so useful to the ladies as Gordon Noel. He had just come from Washington, and knew *everything;* and when *they* took him up and made much of him 'twas no use for the men to stand aloof; they had to take him up too. Lane was adjutant of the regiment at this time; and he, having seen every report and letter with reference to Mr. Noel that had been filed in the office, would hardly speak to him at all except when on duty, and this feeling was intensified when, a year or so later, they were suddenly hurried to Arizona on account of a wild dash of the Chiricahuas, and as the different companies took the field and hastened in the pursuit Mr. Noel was afflicted with a rheumatic fever of such alarming character that the youthful "contract" surgeon who had accompanied his troop held him back at the railway and speedily sent him East on a three months' sick-leave, which family influence soon made six. And this was about the record and reputation that Mr. Noel had succeeded in making when Captain Rawlins was ready to bet Captain Greene that, despite it all, the regimental Adonis would get the recruiting-detail, *vice* Lane, for everybody knew Fred Lane so well as to prophesy that he would apply to be relieved and ordered to rejoin his regiment, and everybody was eager to see him take hold of poor old Curran's troop, for if anybody could "straighten it out" Lane could.

The news that Noel was named by the colonel caused a sensation at regimental head-quarters which the Eleventh will probably not soon forget. "Old Riggs" had become the commander of the regiment after it seemed that the Indian wars were over and done with, and, thanks to our peculiar system of promotion, was now at the head of an organization with which he had never served as subaltern, captain, or junior field-officer. Discipline forbade saying anything to his face,—for which the colonel was devoutly thankful,—but everybody said to everybody else that it was all Mrs. Riggs's doing, a fact which the colonel very well knew.

2*

So did Noel, though he rushed into the club-room apparently overwhelmed with amazement and delight:

"I supposed of *course* it would be Follansbee. I never dreamed he would give it to me. Come up, crowd! come up everybody! It's champagne to-day," he jovially shouted; and there were men who could not bear to snub him openly. Nothing had really ever been proved against him: why should they judge him? But there were several who declined, alleging one excuse or another, and even those who drank with him did so while applauding Wharton's toast:

"Well, Noel, here's to you! It ought to have been Follansbee but I wish you the joy of it."

III.

Never before had Fred Lane known the sensation of being reluctant to rejoin his regiment. When the colonel wrote a personal letter to him some eight or ten weeks previous, telling him that Curran would almost surely get the next vacancy on the retired list and that he would expect his old adjutant to come back to them at once and restore efficiency and discipline to Troop D, Mr. Lane replied with the utmost readiness; but this was before Mabel Vincent came into his life and changed its whole current. How much and how devotedly he loved her, Lane himself never realized until the day his promotion reached him, and with it the news that his successor was already designated. He knew that within the week he might expect orders from the War Department to join his troop at Fort Graham as soon as he had turned over his funds and property to the officer designated to relieve him; he knew Noel so well as to feel assured that he would not wait for the arrival of formal orders, but, if the colonel would permit, would start the instant he received telegraphic notification from Washington that "Old Riggs's" nomination had been approved. "This is Wednesday," he mused; "and by a week from to-day I can count on his being here; and in ten days I must go."

There was a large party that night, and, fully a week before, he had asked that he might have the honor of being Miss Vincent's escort. It was with great disappointment that he received her answer, which was spoken, however, in a tone of such sorrow that poor Lane felt that the barbs, at least, of the arrow had been removed.

"I don't know how to tell you how I regret having to say 'No,'

Mr. Lane," she said, and there was a tremor in her voice and a little quiver at the corners of her pretty mouth. "I have almost felt confident that you were going to ask me,—is that a very bold thing to say?—for you have been so—so kind to me since our first meeting, and indeed I wanted in some way to let you know that there were other arrangements already made. But how could I say anything? Mr. Rossiter, the eldest son of father's former partner, comes to pay us a visit of four or five days before he goes abroad again. And he is a great friend of the Chiltons, and, being our guest, he goes with me. Indeed, I'm *very* sorry, Mr. Lane, if you are disappointed."

Fred, of course, begged that she should give herself no uneasiness. There was no other girl whom he had thought of taking. Mr. Rossiter was very much to be envied, and he would like to call and pay his respects to that gentleman when he arrived. "By all means do," said Miss Vincent; and, if not asking too much, would Mr. Lane get him a card at the club? Brother Rex was away, or she wouldn't trouble him. But Lane was delighted to be troubled. Anything she asked—any service he could render her—he flew with untold eagerness to accomplish; and, though properly jealous of the coming man, —this Mr. Rossiter, of whom he had never before heard mention,—he was eager to meet and entertain him. The gentleman was to arrive on Monday, and Lane spent a delightful evening at the Vincents', wondering why he hadn't come. Tuesday would surely bring him, or an explanation, said Miss Mabel; and on Tuesday Lane was prompt to call, and glad to spend another long evening at the hospitable old homestead, and stoutly did he hold his ground through three successive relays of visitors, encouraged to do so by a certain look in his lady's bright eyes that spoke volumes to his throbbing heart, and that very next morning at the club he found her dainty missive on his breakfast-table. How early she must have risen to write it!—and to have seen the announcement of his promotion in the Washington despatches! True, he remembered that it was frequently her pleasure to be up betimes to give her father his coffee; for Vincent *père* was a business-man of the old school, who liked to begin early in the day. Of course he had seen the name in the Washington news and had read the paragraph to her: that was the way to account for it. But her note was a joy to him in its sweet, half-shy, half-confidential wording. She merely wrote to say that Mr. Rossiter had wired that he would be detained in New York until the end of the week; and now, if Captain Lane had *really* made no engagement, she would be glad indeed if he cared to renew the invitation which with such regret she was compelled a week ago to decline. Lane totally forgot his breakfast in his haste to rush to the writing-room and send her a reply.

All "The Queen City" had been quick to see or hear of his "sudden smite" and consequent devotion to Mabel Vincent, and great was the speculation as to the probable result.

"How can she encourage him as she does? What can she see in that solemn prig?" indignantly demanded Miss Fanny Holton, who had shown a marked interest in Mr. Lane during his first six months in society and had danced with him all through the season. "He is one of the forlornest, stupidest men I ever knew,—utterly unlike what I supposed a cavalry officer to be."

"And yet, Fanny dear, you were very much taken up with him the first winter,—last year, I mean," was the reply of her most devoted and intimate friend.

"What an outrageous fib! I wasn't; and if I was, it was because I wanted to draw him out,—do *something* to enliven him. Of course I danced with him a great deal. There isn't a better dancer in town, and you know it, Maud: you've said so yourself time and again."

"Well, *you* didn't draw him out,—nor on. But the moment he sees Mabel Vincent he falls heels over head in love with her. Why, I never saw a man whose every look and word so utterly 'gave him away,'" was Miss Maud's characteristic and slangy reply. "And it's my belief she'll take him, too. She likes him well, and she says he knows more than any other man she has ever met.

"He has money, too, and can resign and live here if she wants him to," went on Miss Maud, after a pause which, oddly enough, her friend had not taken advantage of.

"You don't know anything about what Mabel Vincent will or won't do, Maud. I've known her years longer than you have, and, though I'm awfully fond of her, and wouldn't have this repeated for the world,—and you must swear never to repeat it to anybody,—I know her so well that I can say she doesn't know her own mind now and would change it in less than six months if she did. She is as fickle in love as in her friendships; and you can't have forgotten how inseparable you and she were for three months at Madame Hoffman's, and then how she fastened on Katherine Ward. I don't care a snap of my finger whom Mr. Lane chooses to fall in love with, but if it's

Mabel Vincent he'd better insist on a short engagement and stand guard over her with his sword in the mean time. It's 'out of sight out of mind' with her, and has been ever since she was four years old."

And so in the smoking-room at the club and in the feminine cliques and coteries in society the probability of Mabel Vincent's accepting Lieutenant Lane was a matter of frequent discussion. But of all this chit-chat and speculation Captain Lane stood in profound ignorance as he entered his dark office that drenching Wednesday morning with her precious note in his waistcoat-pocket. He neither knew nor cared what old Vincent was worth: all he wanted was Mabel's own sweet self, for he loved her with his whole heart and soul, with all the strength and devotion of his deep and loyal nature. He could hardly control his voice so as to speak in the conventional official tone to the sergeant in charge as the latter saluted him at the door-way and made the customary report of the presence of the detachment. Lane stepped into his little dressing-room and quickly appeared in his neat fatigue uniform. There wasn't a ghost of a chance of would-be recruits wandering in that day; but he was a stickler for discipline. He required his men to be always in their appropriate uniform, and never neglected wearing his own while in the office; yet in all the Queen City no one but his little party, the applicants for enlistment, and the few citizens who came in on business had ever seen him except in civilian dress.

"These reports and returns all go in to-morrow, I believe?" said Lane to his sergeant.

"They do, sir."

"Well, will you take them in to the clerk again," said Lane, blushing vividly, "and tell him to alter that 'First Lieutenant' to 'Captain' wherever it occurs? The—official notification is just here," he added, almost apologetically.

"Sure I'm glad to hear it, sir. All the men will be glad, sir; and I'm proud to think that I was the first man to salute the captain to-day," was the sergeant's delighted answer. "I'll call Taintor in at once."

But Lane was blissfully thinking of the little note, now transferred to the breast-pocket of his uniform blouse, and of how not his honest old sergeant but sweet Mabel Vincent was the first to hail him by his new title; and in thinking of the note and of her he failed to notice that, so far from coming at once, it was fully ten or fifteen minutes before Taintor, the clerk, put in an appearance, and when he did that his face was ashen-gray and his hand shook as though with palsy.

"The sergeant will tell you what is to be done with the papers, Taintor," said Lane, conscious that he was blushing again, and consequently striving to appear engrossed in the morning paper. The man picked them up one after another and without a word; he dropped one to the floor in his nervousness, but made a quick dive for it, and then for the door, as though fearful of detention. He hurried through the room in which the sergeant and one or two men were seated, and, reaching his big desk at a rear window, where he was out of sight, dropped the papers on the floor and buried his face in his shaking hands.

A few minutes later the sergeant, coming into the little cubby-hole of a room in which Taintor had preferred to do his work, found him with his arms on the desk and his face hidden in them, and the soldier clerk was quivering and twitching from head to foot.

"What's the matter with you, Taintor?" growled the old soldier. "Didn't you promise me you'd quit drinking?"

The face that looked up into his was ghastly.

"It isn't drink, sergeant," moaned the man. "At least, I haven't exceeded for a month. I've got a chill,—an ague of some kind. Just let me run down to the drug-store and get some quinine,—with perhaps a little brandy. Then I can do this work. *Do*, sergeant. I won't abuse your kindness."

"Well, go, then," was the reluctant answer; "but get back quick. And only one drink, mind you."

Taintor seized his cap and fairly tottered through the adjoining room to the stairway, down which he plunged madly, and, heedless of the pelting rain, darted across the street to the gas-lighted bar-room.

"By G—d," muttered the veteran sergeant, "there's something worse than either whiskey or ague back of this; and I could swear to it."

IV.

Captain Lane, as has been said, allowed until the following Wednesday for the arrival of his regimental comrade Mr. Noel. He was not a little surprised, however, on the following Tuesday morning, as he sat at breakfast at the club, glancing over the morning paper, to come upon the following announcement:

"DISTINGUISHED ARRIVAL.

"Our readers will be interested in knowing that Captain Gordon Noel, of the Eleventh U.S. Cavalry, has been ordered on duty in the city, in charge of the cavalry rendezvous on Sycamore Street. Captain Noel comes to us with a reputation that should win instant recognition and the heartiest welcome from the Queen City. For nearly fifteen years he has served with his gallant regiment, and has been prominent in every one of the stirring campaigns against the hostile Indians of our Western frontier. He has fought almost every savage tribe on the continent; was disabled in the Modoc campaign in '73, commanded the advance-guard of his regiment that reached the scene of the Custer massacre only just in time to rescue the remnant of the regiment from a similar fate, and for his services on that campaign was awarded the compliment of staff duty in the city of Washington. At his own request, however, he was relieved from this, and rejoined his regiment when hostilities were threatened in Arizona two years ago. And now, as a reward for gallant and distinguished conduct in the field, he is given the prized recruiting-detail. Captain Noel is the guest of his cousin, the Hon. Amos Withers, at his palatial home on the Heights; and our fair readers will be interested in knowing that he is a bachelor, and, despite his years of hardship, danger, and privation, is a remarkably fine-looking man.

"It is understood that Lieutenant Lane, the present recruiting officer, has been ordered to return to his regiment at once, although the time has not yet expired."

In the expression on Captain Lane's face as he finished this item there was something half vexed, half comical.

A few hours afterwards, while he was seated in his office, the orderly entered, and announced two gentlemen to see the captain. Lane turned to receive his visitors, but before he could advance across the dark room the taller of the two entering the door made a spring towards him, clapped him cordially on the back, and, with the utmost delight, shouted, "How are you, old fellow? How well you're looking! Why, I haven't set eyes on you since we were out on the field hunting up old Geronimo's trail! By Jove! but I'm glad to see you!" And Lane had no difficulty in recognizing at once his regimental comrade Gordon Noel.

"Let me present you to my cousin, Mr. Withers," said Noel.

And a stout, florid man, whom Lane had often seen at the club, but to whom he had never hitherto been made known, bowed with much cordiality and extended his hand.

"I didn't know," said he, "that you were a friend of Noel's, or I'd have come to see you before, and invited you to my house."

"Friend!" exclaimed Noel. "*Friend!* Why, we've been partners and chums! Why, we've been all over this continent together, Withers! Fred, do you remember the time we were up on the Sioux campaign?—the night I went over with those fellows to hunt up the trail to the Custer ground? Let's see, you were acting adjutant then, if I recollect right. Oh, yes; you were back with the colonel."

Lane received his guests with perfect courtesy, but without that overweening cordiality which distinguished the other's manner, and then Mr. Withers entered into the conversation. Turning to Captain Lane, he said,—

"I didn't know that you had been on the Sioux campaign. Were you there too?"

Lane replied quietly that he had been with his regiment through that year,—in fact, had never been away from it for any length of time, except on this detail which had brought him to his old home.

"Oh, yes; I remember having heard that this was your home. I am very sorry indeed that you did not make yourself known to me before," said Mr. Withers. "You know that I am a very busy man and don't get around much. Now you can come and dine with us this evening, can you not? Mrs. Withers will certainly expect you, now that Noel is here."

"I am very sorry indeed, Mr. Withers, but I am already engaged."

"You must make early bids if you want to get this young man, Amos," put in Mr. Noel, affectionately patting Lane on the shoulder. "It was just so in the regiment. He was always in demand.—Well, when *can* you come, Fred? What evening shall we say?"

"It will depend, perhaps, on the day I turn over the property to you. How soon do you wish to take hold?"

"Oh, any time. Any day. Whenever you're ready."

"I'm ready now, to-day, if you choose," was Lane's prompt response. "I fancied you might be here by to-morrow."

"Yes, you bet I didn't let the grass grow under my feet. The moment we got the telegraphic notification that the colonel's nomination was approved, I lit out for the railroad," said Noel, laughing gleefully.

"And when will you come in and take over the property? There's a good deal of clothing to be counted. As for the funds, they, of course, are all in the bank."

"Suit yourself about that, Freddy, old boy. I'm going down street with Amos now. How'll to-morrow morning do?"

"Very well indeed. You will find me here any time you come in."

"All right. Now get out of your yellow stripes and come along down town with us. The carriage is right here at the door. We're going over to see the works,—Mr. Withers's foundries, you know. Come."

"Yes, come with us. I think I have heard it was your father who—ah—who was in the same line of business at one time, Mr. Lane," said Mr. Withers.

"*Captain* Lane, Amos!—*Captain* Lane! Great Scott! you mustn't 'mister' a man who has been through the years of service he has."

"I beg pardon. I did not so understand you, Gordon, when we were talking last night with the—when we were having our smoke and chat after dinner.—You will come with us, won't you, captain?"

"I wish I could, Mr. Withers, but my office-hours have to be observed, and I cannot leave in the morning. Thank you heartily none the less.—Then you will be here to-morrow, Noel?"

"To-morrow be it, Fred: so *au revoir*, if you can't join us. I mustn't keep Withers waiting,—business-man, you know. God bless you, old fellow, you don't begin to realize how delighted I am to see you! So long."

"But about dining with us, Captain——"

"Oh, Lord, yes!" burst in Noel. "What evening, now? I'd almost forgotten. Getting in among bricks and mortar addles my head. 'Tisn't like being out in the saddle with the mountain breezes all around you: hey, Fred? Gad! I don't know whether I can stand this sort of thing, after our years of campaigning." And the lieutenant looked dubiously around upon the dark and dingy walls and windows.

"Suppose we say Thursday evening, captain," suggested Mr. Withers; "and I'll have just a few friends to meet you two army gentlemen."

"I shall be very happy, Mr. Withers."

"Good! That's the talk, Fred!" heartily shouted the lieutenant, bringing his hand down with a resounding whack between Lane's shoulder-blades. "Now we *are* off! Come along, Amos." And the cousins disappeared down the dark stairway and popped into the carriage.

"Not a very demonstrative man, your friend the captain, but seems to be solid," was Mr. Withers's remark.

"Oh, yes. He is about as solid as they make them," answered Noel, airily. "Lane has his faults, like most men. It is only those who really know him, who have been associated with him for years, and whom he trusts and likes, that are his friends. Now, *I'd* go through fire and water for him, and he would for me,—but of course you wouldn't think it, to see his perfectly conventional society manner this morning. If I had left you down at the foot of the stairs and had stolen up on tiptoe and gone over and put my arms round his neck, you would probably have found us hugging each other and dancing about that room like a couple of grizzly bears when you came up, and the moment he caught sight of you he would have blushed crimson and got behind his ice screen in a second. You just ought to have seen him the night we met each other with our detachments down near Guadalupe Cañon when we were hunting Geronimo. Some d—d fool of a ranchman had met him and said I was killed in the little affair we had with the Apache rear-guard. Why, I was perfectly amazed at the emotion he showed. Ever since then I've sworn by Fred Lane; though, of course, he has traits that I wish he could get rid of."

"Good officer, isn't he?"

"Ye—es, Lane isn't half a bad soldier. Of course it remains to be seen what sort of captain he will make. He has only just got his troop."

"But I mean he—well—is a brave man,—has shown up well in these Indian fights you were telling us about?"

"H'm!" answered Noel, with a quiet little chuckle: "if he wasn't, you bet he wouldn't have been all these years in the Eleventh. A shirk of any kind is just the one thing we *won't* stand. Why, Amos, when old Jim Blazer was our colonel during those years of the Sioux and Cheyenne and Nez Percé wars he ran two men out of the regiment simply because they managed to get out of field duty two successive years. Oh, no! Lane's all right as a soldier, or he wouldn't be wearing the crossed sabres of the Eleventh."

Mr. Withers listened to these tales of the doings and sayings of the regiment with great interest. "Lane might have been here a dozen years," said he to himself, "and no one in our community would have known anything at all about the dangers and hardships his comrades and he had encountered in their frontier service. It's only when some fellow like Noel comes to us that we learn anything whatever of our army and its doings."

He took his cousin to the great moulding-works of which he was the sole head and proprietor, and presented his foremen and his clerks to the captain, and told them of his career in the Indian wars on the frontier, and then up on 'Change and proudly introduced " my cousin Captain Noel" to the magnates of the Queen City; and, though not one out of a dozen was in the least degree interested in "the captain" or cared a grain of wheat what the army had done or was doing on the frontier, almost every man had time to stop and shake hands cordially with the handsome officer, for Amos Withers was said to be a man whose check for a round million would be paid at sight, and anybody who was first-cousin to that amount of "spot cash" was worth stopping to chat with, even in the midst of the liveliest tussle 'twixt bull and bear on the floor of the Chamber of Commerce. A tall, gray-haired gentleman, with a slight stoop to his shoulders and rather tired, anxious eyes, who listened nervously to the shouts from "the pit" and scanned eagerly the little telegraphic slips thrust into his hand by scurrying messenger-boys, was introduced as Mr. Vincent, and Mr. Vincent inquired if Noel knew Lieutenant—or rather Captain—Lane.

"Know Fred Lane? He is the best friend I have in the world," was the enthusiastic answer, "and one of the best men that ever lived."

"Ah! I'm glad to know you,—glad to know what you say. The captain is a constant visitor at our house, a great friend of ours, in fact. Ah! excuse me a moment." And Mr. Vincent seized a certain well-known broker by the arm and murmured some eager inquiries in his ear, to which the other listened with ill-disguised impatience.

Withers and, of course, "the captain" were the centre of a cordial —not to say obsequious—group so long as they remained upon the floor, and the secretary presently came to them with the compliments of the president and a card admitting Captain Gordon Noel to the floor of the Chamber at any time during business hours, which that officer most gracefully acknowledged and then went on replying to the questions of his new friends about the strange regions through which he had scouted and fought, and the characteristics of the Indian tribes with whom he had been brought in contact. And by the time Cousin Amos declared they must go up to the club for luncheon, everybody was much impressed by the hearty, jovial manner of the dashing cavalryman, and there were repeated hand-shakes, promises to call, and prophecies of a delightful sojourn in their midst as he took his leave.

"Has Captain Lane come in yet to lunch?" inquired Mr. Withers of the liveried attendant at "The Queen City," as his cousin inscribed his name and regiment in the visitors' book, as introduced by "A. W.," in ponderous strokes of the pen.

"No, sir. It's considerably past the time the gentleman generally comes. I don't think he'll be in to-day, sir."

"Then we won't wait, Gordon. We'll order for two. What wine do you like?"

*   *   *   *   *   *   *   *   *

Over at the dingy recruiting-office Captain Lane had forgotten about luncheon. There were evidences of carelessness on the part of the clerk who had made out his great batch of papers, and the further he looked the more he found. The orderly had been sent for Taintor, and had returned with the information that he was not at his desk. Sergeant Burns, when called upon to explain how it happened that he allowed him to slip away, promptly replied that it was half-past eleven when he came out of the captain's office and said that the captain would want him all the afternoon, so he had best go and get his dinner now. Half-past twelve came, and he did not return. The sergeant went after him, and came back in fifteen minutes with a worried look about his face to say that Taintor had not been to dinner at all, and that the door of the little room he occupied was locked. He had not been in the house since eight that morning.

"I'm afraid, sir, he's drinkin' again," said Burns; "but he's so sly about it I never can tell until he is far gone."

"You go out yourself, and send two of the men, and make inquiries at all his customary haunts," ordered Lane. "I will stay here and go through all these papers. None are right, so far. He never failed me before; and I do not understand it at all."

But when night came Taintor was still missing,—had not been seen nor heard of,—and Captain Lane had written a hurried note to the lady of his love to say that a strange and most untoward case of desertion had just occurred which necessitated his spending some time with the Chief of Police at once. He begged her to make his excuses to her good mother for his inability to come to dinner. Later in the evening he hoped to see her.

"P.S.—Gordon Noel, who is to relieve me, has arrived. I have only three or four days more."

"Gordon Noel!" said Miss Vincent, pensively. "Where have I heard of Gordon Noel?"

V.

And now a matter has to be recorded which will go far to convince many of our readers that Captain Lane was even more of an old-fashioned prig than he has hitherto appeared to be. After leaving the Vincents' late on the previous day, he had come to his rooms, and sat there for fully two hours in the endeavor to compose a brief, manly letter addressed to Vincent *père*. It was nothing more nor less than the old style of addressing a gentleman of family and requesting permission to pay his addresses to his daughter Mabel. A very difficult task was the composition of this letter for our frontier soldier. He was desperately in earnest, however; time was short, and after several attempts the missive was completed. His first duty in the morning was to send that letter by an orderly to Mr. Vincent's office. Then he turned to his sergeant and asked for news of the deserter. Not a word had been heard,—not a single word.

"I have been everywhere I could think of, sir," said the sergeant, "and both the men have been around his customary haunts last night and this morning making inquiries, but all to no purpose. The detectives came and burst into his trunk, and there was nothing in it worth having. He had been taking away his clothing, etc., from time to time in small packages and secreting them we don't where. One thing I heard, sir, that I never knew before, and that was that after he had gone to bed at night he would frequently steal out of his room and go away and never reappear until breakfast-time in the morning. And now will the lieutenant—the captain pardon me for asking the question, Are the check-books all right, sir?"

"What put that idea into your head?" asked Lane.

"Well, sir, some of the men tell me that he was always writing at his desk, and once Strauss said that he had picked up a scrap of paper that he hadn't completely destroyed, and the handwriting on it didn't look like Taintor's at all; he said it more resembled that of the captain; and it made me suspicious. I never heard this until late last night."

A sudden thought occurred to Lane. Taking out his check-book, he carefully counted the checks remaining and compared them with the number of stubs, and found, to his surprise and much to his dismay, that at least five or six checks were missing.

"Send for a cab at once. I must go down to the bank. You stay here, and when Lieutenant Noel comes, give him my compliments, and ask him to sit down and wait awhile and read the morning paper. I'll be back in a very short time."

Following the custom established by his predecessor, Captain Lane had always kept the recruiting-funds in the First National Bank. His own private funds he preferred to keep in an entirely different establishment,—the Merchants' Exchange.

The cab whirled him rapidly to the building indicated, and, although it lacked half an hour of the time of opening, he made his way into the office and asked to see the paying teller.

"Will you kindly tell me if any checks on the recruiting-fund have lately been presented for payment?" he eagerly asked.

The captain was referred to the book-keeper, and that official called him within the railing.

"No less than four checks were brought here yesterday for payment, and they came between half-past two and three o'clock in the afternoon," was the book-keeper's report. "There seemed to us something wrong in the simultaneous presentation of the four, and I was on the point of addressing a note to you this morning to ask you to come down to the bank. Everything about it appears in proper shape and form, except that three of the checks have been endorsed payable to your clerk, William Taintor, who came in person and drew the money."

"Let me see the checks, if you please," said the captain.

They were speedily produced. Lane took them to the window and closely examined them.

"I could not tell them," he said, "from my own handwriting; and yet those three checks are forgeries. I believe that the endorsements on the back are equally forgeries. Now, can I take these with me to the office of the Chief of Police? or do you desire that the detectives should be sent here? Taintor deserted last night, and all traces have been lost. What is the amount that he has drawn?"

"One check, payable to the order of William Hayden for board furnished to the recruiting-party, is to the amount of forty-five dollars and fifty cents. The second, payable to James Freeman, and endorsed by him to William Taintor, as was the first, is for rent of the building occupied by the recruiting rendezvous, precisely similar in form and amount to the previous checks, for the sum of sixty dollars. The third check is payable to William Taintor himself, marked 'for extra-duty pay as clerk at the recruiting office for the past six months.' The fourth is made payable to the order of Sergeant James Burns, 'extra-duty pay as non-commissioned officer in charge of the party for the six months beginning January 1 and ending June 30.'"

This check, too, had been endorsed payable to the order of William Taintor. All four checks, amounting in all to the sum of about one hundred and sixty dollars, had been paid to the deserting clerk during the afternoon of the previous day.

"Had you no suspicion of anything wrong?" said Lane.

"I knew nothing about it," said the book-keeper. "They were presented to the paying teller at the desk, and it was not until after bank was closed, when we came to balance up cash, that the matter excited comment and then suspicion. Taintor has frequently come here before with drafts and checks; and if you remember, sir, on one or two occasions he has been sent for new check-books when the old ones had run out."

"That's very true," said Lane. "He has been employed here in this rendezvous for the last ten years, and has borne, up to within my knowledge of him, an unimpeachable character. If any more checks come in, stop payment on them until you see me, and, if possible, detain the person who presents them."

Half an hour afterwards the captain was back in his office, and there true to his appointment, was Lieutenant Noel.

"I have had a strange and unpleasant experience, Noel," said Lane. "Most of my papers have been faultily made out. My clerk deserted last night and has turned out to be a most expert forger. He has stolen half a dozen checks from my book, made them out to the order of various parties, forged the endorsements himself, got the money yesterday afternoon, and cleared out, no one knows where."

"Great Scott, old man! that is hard luck! How much has he let you in for?" asked Noel, in the slang of the period.

"Only a hundred and sixty dollars, fortunately; and I have made that good this morning,—placed my own check to the credit of the recruiting-fund in the First National Bank, so that in turning over the funds to you there will be no loss. We have to make new papers for the clothing account; but as quickly as possible I will have them ready for your signature and mine."

"There is no hurry whatever, old fellow," answered Noel, cheerily. "I've come back from the regiment a little short of money, and I want to have a nest-egg in the bank to begin with. It's a good thing to have a fat cousin, isn't it? He has always been very liberal and kind to me, and, luckily, I've only drawn on him twice. So I'll hurry along."

Five minutes after Noel left, a district messenger entered with a note for Captain Lane. It was addressed to him in the handwriting of Mr. Vincent. He opened it with a trembling hand. It contained merely these words:

"I am obliged to leave for New York this afternoon. Can you come to my office at one o'clock? We can then talk without interruption; and I much desire to see you.
"T. L. V."

As the big bell on the city hall had struck one, Captain Lane appeared at the office of Vincent, Clark & Co., and was shown without delay into the private room of the senior partner. Mr. Vincent, looking even older and grayer in the wan light at the rear of the massive building, was seated at his desk and busily occupied with a book of memoranda and figures. He pushed back his chair and came forward at once at sight of Lane, and motioned to the clerk to retire. The cavalryman's heart was beating harder then he had any recollection of its ever doing before, except in her presence, and he felt that his knees were trembling. But the old gentleman's greeting gave him instant hope:

"I am glad you have come, my dear sir: I am glad to know a man who has been taught as I was taught. Young people nowadays seem to rush into matrimony without the faintest reference to their parents, and your letter was a surprise to me,—a surprise, that is, in the fact that you should have sought my permission at all.

"Take this chair, captain," he continued, as he returned to his desk. "I have much to say to you," he added, with a sigh. "Let me say at once that from what I know and have heard of you there is no man of my acquaintance to whom I could intrust my daughter's future with more implicit confidence. It is true that both her mother and I had at one time other hopes and views for her, and that we wish your profession was not that of arms. And now I beg you to be patient with me, and to pardon my alluding to matters which you yourself broach in this—this most manful letter. You tell me that you are not dependent on your pay alone, but that from investments in real estate in growing cities in the West and in mines in New Mexico your present income is some five thousand dollars. As I understand you, the property is steadily increasing in value?"

"It has steadily increased thus far, sir, and I think it will continue to do so for several years to come,—in the real estate investments at least."

"I am glad of this, on your account as well as hers, for Mabel has been reared in comparative luxury. She has never known what it was to want anything very much or very long. She has been educated on the supposition that her whole life would be one equally free from care or stint; and if I were to die to-morrow, sir, she would be a beggar."

And here, in great agitation, the old gentleman rose from his chair and began nervously pacing up and down the little room, wringing his white, tremulous hands, and turning his face away from the silent soldier, that he might not see the tears that hung to the lashes, or the piteous quivering of the sensitive lips. For a moment or two nothing more was said. Then, as though in surprise, Mr. Vincent stopped short.

"Did you understand me, Captain Lane? I do not exaggerate the situation in the least. I do not know how soon the axe will fall. We are safe for to-day, but know not what the morrow may bring forth. I may be met *en route* by telegrams saying that the journey is useless,—that we are ruined,—and the money I hope to get in New York to tide us over would come only too late. Next month at this time the house in which Mabel was born and reared may be sold over her head, with every scrap and atom of its furniture, and we be driven into exile. Do you realize this, sir? Do you understand that if you win her affection and she become your wife I have not a penny with which to bless her?"

"Mr. Vincent," answered Lane, "I would hold myself richer than any man in this world if I could know that your daughter cared for me and would be my wife. Do not think that I fail to sympathize and feel for you and all who are dear to you in your distress and anxiety, but I am almost glad to hear that she is not the heiress people said

B*

she was. It is Mabel I want,"—and here his voice trembled almost as much as the old man's, and his honest gray eyes filled up with tears he could not down,—"and with her for my own I could ask nothing of any man. I have your consent to see her, then, at once if need be? You know I am relieved from duty here and must rejoin my regiment within ten days."

"My full consent, and my best wishes, captain," said Mr. Vincent, grasping the outstretched hand in both his own. "You have not spoken to her at all?"

"Not a word, Mr. Vincent; and I can form no idea what her answer will be. Pardon me, sir, but has she or has Mrs. Vincent any knowledge of your business troubles?"

"My wife knows, of course, that everything is going wrong and that I am desperately harassed; Mabel, too, knows that I have lost much money—very much—in the last two years; but neither of them knows the real truth,—that even my life-insurance is gone. A year ago I strove to obtain additional amounts in the three companies in which I had taken out policies years ago. Of course a rigid examination had to be made by the medical advisers, and the result was the total rejection of my applications, and in two cases an offer to return with interest all the premiums hitherto paid. The physicians had all discovered serious trouble with my heart. Last winter our business was at its lowest ebb. I had been fortunate in some speculations on 'Change in the past, and I strove to restore our failing fortunes in that way. My margins were swept away like chaff, and I have been vainly striving to regain them for the last three months, until now the last cent that I could raise is waiting the result of this week's deal. Every man in all the great markets East and West knew three weeks ago that a powerful and wealthy syndicate had 'cornered,' as we say, all the wheat to be had, and was forcing the price up day by day; and I had started in on the wrong side. Even if the corner were to break to-morrow I could not recover half my losses. The offer the insurance companies made was eagerly accepted, sir: I took their money, and it dribbled away through my broker's fingers. If wheat goes up one cent, we cannot meet our obligations,—we are gone. We have been compelled to borrow at ruinous rates in order to meet our calls: I say we, for poor Clark is with me in the deal, and it means ruin for him too, though he, luckily, has neither wife nor child. Are you ready, sir, to ally your name with that of a ruined and broken man,—to wed a beggar's daughter?" And here poor old Vincent fairly broke down and sobbed aloud. Long watching, sleepless nights, suspense, wretched anxiety, the averted looks and whispered comments of the men he daily met on 'Change, the increasing brusqueness and insolence of his broker, Warden,—all had combined to humiliate and crush him. He threw himself upon the sofa, his worn old frame shaking and quivering with grief. The sight was too much for Lane. This was *her* father: it was her home that was threatened, her name that was in jeopardy.

"Mr. Vincent," he cried, almost imploringly, "I cannot tell you how utterly my sympathy is with you in your anxiety and distress. I beg you not to give way,—not to abandon hope. I—I think it may be in my power to help a little; only—it must be a secret between us. She—Mabel must never know."

VI.

In the three days that followed, the transfer of funds and property at the recruiting rendezvous took place, and Mr. Noel stepped in, *vice* Lane, relieved and ordered to join his regiment. The former was having a delightful time. A guest of the wealthy Witherses could not long be a stranger within their gates to the Queen citizens, and every afternoon and evening found him enjoying hospitalities of the most cordial character. At the club he had already become hail-fellow with all the younger element and had made himself decidedly popular among the elders, and every man who had not met that jolly Captain Noel was eager to be presented to him. He was ready for pool, billiards, bowling, or a drink the moment he got within the stately door-way; and, as he sang, whistled, laughed, chatted, and cracked innumerable jokes during the various games, was a capital mimic, and could personate Pat, Hans, or Crapaud with telling effect, his presence was pronounced by every one as better than a solid week of sunshine,—something the Queen City rarely, if ever, experienced.

Poor Lane, on the contrary, was nearly worrying his heart out. He had gone to the Vincents' the very evening on which he had seen the father of the family off for New York, and had nerved himself to put his fortune to the test,—to tell her of his deep and devoted love and to ask her to be his wife. That she well knew he loved her, without being told, he felt sure must be the case; but, beyond a belief that she liked and trusted him, the captain had not the faintest idea as to the nature of her feelings towards him. He was a modest fellow, as has been said. His glass told him that, despite a pair of clear gray eyes and a decidedly soldierly cut to his features, he was not what women called a handsome man; and, what was more, there were little strands of gray just beginning to show about his broad forehead and in the heavy moustache that shaded his mouth. Lane sighed as he remembered that he was in his thirty-sixth year. How *could* she care for him,—fifteen years her senior? Lane rang the door-bell that night and felt once more that his heart was beating even as it did at one o'clock when he was ushered into the awful presence of her father.

"Miss Vincent has not left her room to-day, and is not well enough to come down to-night, sir," said the servant who came to the door, "and Mrs. Vincent begged to be excused because of Miss Mabel's needing her."

"I—I am very, very sorry," stammered the captain. "Please say that Mr. Lane called" (they had known him so well for two months as *Mr.* Lane that he could not yet refer to himself by his new title), "and—and would call again to-morrow, hoping to hear Miss Vincent was much better."

And then, dejected and miserable, and yet with something akin to the feeling one experiences when going to a dentist's to have a tooth drawn and the dreaded wielder of the forceps proves to be away, Lane retreated down the broad stone steps until he reached the walk, gazed up at the dim light in the window which he thought might be hers, anathematized himself for his lack of self-possession in not having asked whether there wasn't something he could bring her,—something she would like,—for the simple-hearted fellow would have tramped all night all over town to find and fetch it,—and then a happy thought occurred to him: "Women always love flowers." He ran to the next street, boarded a west-bound car, and was soon far down town at his favorite florist's.

"Give me a big box of cut flowers,—the handsomest you have," he said; and while they were being prepared he wrote a few lines on a card, tore it up, tried again on another, and similarly reduced that to fragments, and finally, though far from content, limited the expression of his emotions to the simple words,—

"*Do* get well by Saturday at latest. I cannot go without seeing you. F. L."

"Where shall we send them, sir?" asked the florist, as he came forward with the box in his hand.

"Never mind: I'll take it myself," was the answer, as the captain popped in the little missive.

And when he got back to the house the light was still burning in the window in the second story, and the doctor had just left, said the sympathetic Abigail, and had said that it was nothing serious or alarming: Miss Mabel would have to keep quiet a day or two; that was all.

But what hard luck for poor Lane, when the days of his stay were so very few! All Thursday morning was spent at the rendezvous, counting over property and comparing papers with Noel. Then, while that gentleman went to the club for luncheon the captain hastened to the Vincents' door to renew inquiries, and was measurably comforted by the news that Miss Mabel was much better, though still confined to her room. Would he not come in? Mrs. Vincent was out, but she thought—did that most intelligent young woman, Mary Ann—that perhaps there was a message for him. Like Mr. Toots, poor Lane, in his anxiety to put no one to any trouble, came within an ace of stammering, "It's of no consequence," but checked himself in time, and stepped into the bright parlor in which he had spent so many delicious hours listening to her soft rich voice as she sang, or as she chatted blithely with him and her frequent guests. It was some time before Mary Ann returned. Evidently, there was a message, for the girl's face was dimpled with smiles as she handed him a little note. "Miss Mabel says please excuse pencil, sir; she had to write lying down. Miss Holton has just gone away, after spending most of the morning."

Excuse pencil! Lane could hardly wait to read the precious lines. How he longed to give the girl a five-dollar bill! but this wasn't England, and he did not know how Mary Ann would regard such a proffer. She promptly and discreetly retired, leaving the front door open for his exit, and the sweet June sunshine and the soft warm breath of early summer flowing in through the broad vestibule.

"How good you are to me!" she wrote. "The flowers were—and are still—exquisite. I shall be down-stairs a little while to-morrow afternoon, if the doctor is good to me as you are. Then I can thank you, can I not? M. L. V."

The hours dragged until Friday afternoon came. He had to go to the Witherses' to dinner on Thursday evening, and a dreary, ostentatious, ponderous feast it was. Noel, in his full-dress uniform, was the hero of the hour. He greeted Lane a trifle nervously.

"I meant to have telephoned and begged you to bear me out, old man," said he, "but this thing was sprung on me after I got home. Cousin Mattie simply ordered me to appear in my war-paint, and I had to do it. You are to go in to dinner with her, by the way; and I wish you were *en grande tenue* instead of civilian spike-tail. Here's Amos."

And Amos marched him around to one guest after another,—"self-made men, sir,"—heavy manufacturers and money-makers, with their overdressed wives. Lane strove hard to be entertaining to his hostess, but that lady's mind was totally engrossed in the progress of the feast and dread of possible catastrophe to style or service. Her eyes glanced nervously from her husband to the butler and his assistants, and her lips perpetually framed inaudible instructions or warnings, and so it happened that the captain was enabled to chat a good deal with a slight, dark-eyed, and decidedly intelligent girl who sat to his right and who was totally ignored by the young cub who took her in, —the eldest son of the house of Withers, a callow youth of twenty.

"You did not hear my name, I know," she had said to him. "I am Miss Marshall, a very distant connection of Mrs. Withers's, the teacher of her younger children, and the merest kind of an accident at this table. Miss Faulkner was compelled to send her excuses at the last moment, and so I was detailed—isn't that your soldier expression?— to fill the gap."

"And where did you learn our army expressions, may I ask?" said Lane, smilingly.

"I had a cousin in the artillery some years ago, and visited his wife when they were stationed at the old barracks across the river. There's no one there now, I believe. Listen to Captain Noel: he is telling about Indian campaigns."

Indeed, pretty much everybody was listening already, for Noel, with much animation, was recounting the experiences of the chase after the Chiricahua chieftain Geronimo. He was an excellent talker, and most diplomatic and skilful in the avoidance of any direct reference to himself as the hero of the series of dramatic incidents which he so graphically told, and yet the impression conveyed—and intended to be conveyed— was that no man had seen more, endured more, or ridden harder, faster, and farther, than the narrator. Flattered by the evident interest shown by those about him, and noting that conversation was brisk at Lane's end of the table, the lieutenant soon lost himself in the enthusiasm of his own descriptions, and was only suddenly recalled to earth by noting that now the whole table had ceased its dinner-chat, and that, with the possible exception of the hostess, who was telegraphing signals to the butler, every man and woman present was looking at him and listening. The color leaped to his face, and he turned towards Lane with a nervous laugh.

"I'd no idea I was monopolizing the talk," he said. "Fred, old man, wasn't it G Troop that tried to get across the range from your command to ours when we neared the Guadalupe? Amos and Mr. Hawks had been asking me about the chase after Geronimo."

"Yes; it was G Troop,—Captain Greene's," answered Lane.

"You know that Captain Lane and I are of the same regiment, and, though not actually together in the chase, we were in the same campaign," said Noel, apologetically, and then, quickly changing the subject, "By the way, Mr. Hawks, is Harry Hawks of the artillery a relative of yours?"

"A nephew, captain,—my brother Henry's son. Did you know him?"

"Know him? Why, he is one of the warmest friends I have in the whole army,—outside of my own regiment, that is. We were constantly together one winter when I was on staff duty in Washington, and whenever he could get leave to run up from the barracks he made my quarters his home. If you ever write to him just ask him if he knows Gordon Noel."

"Do you know, Captain Lane, that I have found your comrade captain a very interesting man?" observed Miss Marshall; and her eyes turned upon her next-door neighbor in calm but keen scrutiny.

"Noel is *very* entertaining," was the reply; and the dark-gray eyes looked unflinchingly into the challenge of the dark-brown.

"Yes, I have listened to his tales of the frontier, at breakfast, dinner, and during the evening hours, since Sunday last. They are full of vivacity and variety."

"One sees a good deal of strange country and many strange people in the course of ten or a dozen years' service in the cavalry."

"And must needs have a good memory to be able to tell of it all,— especially when one recounts the same incident more than once." And

Miss Marshall's lips were twitching at the corners in a manner suggestive of mischief and merriment combined.

Lane "paused for a reply." Here was evidently a most observant young woman.

"There! I did not mean to tax your loyalty to a regimental comrade, captain: so you need not answer. Captain Noel interests and entertains me principally because of his intense individuality and his entire conviction that he carries his listeners with him. 'Age cannot wither nor custom stale his infinite variety;' but there should not be quite so much variety in his descriptions of a single event. This is the fourth time I have heard him tell of the night-ride from Carrizo's Ranch to Cañon Diablo."

"You have the advantage of me, Miss Marshall," answered Lane, his eyes twinkling with appreciation of her demure but droll exposure of Noel's weak point. "It is the first time I ever heard his version of it."

"It is the last time he will mention it in your presence, if he saw the expression in your face, Captain Lane."

"Do those introspective eyes of yours look clear through and see out of the back of your head, Miss Marshall? Your face was turned towards him. You stopped short in telling me of your cousin in the artillery and your visit to the barracks, and bade me listen to something I did not care half as much to hear as your own impressions of garrison-life. Never mind the quadruplex account of the night-ride. Tell me what you thought of the army."

"Well, of course the first thing a girl wants to know is what the shoulder-straps mean; and I learned the very first day that the blank strap meant a second lieutenant, a single silver bar a first lieutenant, and two bars a captain,—that is, in the artillery. Now, why this provoking distinction in the cavalry? Here's a captain with only one bar, a captain whose letters from the War Department come addressed to *Lieutenant* Gordon Noel!"

"Noel never speaks of himself as captain, I'm sure," said Lane.

"Neither do you; and for a year past, ever since I have known you by sight,"—and here a quick blush mounted to her temples,—"you occasionally came to our church, you know," she hastened to explain,—"you have been referred to as Lieutenant Lane or Mr. Lane; but we know you are a captain now, for we saw the promotion recorded in the Washington despatches a fortnight ago. What was the date of Captain

Noel's elevation to that grade? I confess I took him for your junior in the service and in years too."

"Yes, Noel holds well on to his youth," answered Lane, smilingly.

"And about the captaincy?"

"Well, he is so very near it, and it is so apt to come any day, that perhaps he thinks it just as well to let people get accustomed to calling him *that*. Then he won't have to break them all in when the commission *does* come."

"Then he is your junior, of course?"

"Only by a file or so. He entered service very soon after me."

"But was not in your class at West Point?"

"No: he was not in my class."

"In the next one, then, I presume?"

"Miss Marshall, is your first name Portia? I should hate to be a witness whom you had the privilege of cross-examining. There are ladies 'learned in the law,' and I expect to read of you as called to the bar within a year or two."

"Never mind, Captain Lane. I will ask you nothing more about him."

"No, Miss Marshall, I presume that my clumsiness has rendered it totally unnecessary."

That night, as the guests were dispersing, Lane did what most of them entirely omitted: he went over to the piano and bade Miss Marshall good-night.

"Captain Lane," she said, "I beg your pardon if I have been too inquisitive and too critical, as I know I have been; but you have taught me that you know how to guard a comrade's failings from the world. Will you not forgive a woman's weakness?"

"There is nothing to forgive, Miss Marshall. I hope sincerely that we may meet again before I go back to the regiment."

And later, as Lane was walking homeward from a final peep at the dim light in a certain window, he had time to think how intolerable that dinner would have seemed had it not been for the accident which placed that dark-eyed governess by his side.

VII.

Lane was awake with the sun on Friday morning, and lay for a few moments listening to the twittering of the sparrows about his window-sills, and watching the slanting, rosy-red shafts of light that streamed through the intervals in the Venetian blinds. "Does it augur bright fortune? Does it mean victory? Is it like the 'sun of Austerlitz'?" were the questions that crowded through his brain. To-day— to-day she was to "be down for a little while in the afternoon," and then she "hoped to be able to thank him. Could she?" Ten thousand times over and over again she could, if she would but whisper one little word—Yes—in answer to his eager question. It lacked hours yet until that longed-for afternoon could come. It was not five o'clock; but more sleep was out of the question, and lying there in bed intolerable. Much to the surprise of his darky valet, Lane had had his bath, dressed, and disappeared by the time the former came to rouse him.

Noel was late in reaching the rendezvous. It was after ten when he appeared, explaining that Mrs. Withers was far from well, and therefore Cousin Amos would not leave the house until the doctor had seen her and made his report. Lane received his explanation somewhat coldly, and suggested that they go right to work with their papers, as he had important engagements. It was high noon when they finished the matters in hand, and then the captain hastened to the club, and was handed a telegram with the information that it had only just come. It was evidently expected. Lane quickly read it and carefully stowed it away in an inside pocket. In another moment he was speeding down town, and by half-past twelve was closeted with the junior partner of the tottering house of Vincent, Clark & Co. Mr. Clark was pale and nervous; every click of the "ticker" seemed to make him start. A clerk stood at the instrument, watching the rapidly-dotted quotations.

"Have you heard from Mr. Vincent?" was the first question; and, without a word, a telegram was handed him. It was in cipher, as he saw at once, and Clark supplied the transcription:

"Rossiter refuses. Watch market closely. See Warden instant touches half. Break predicted here."

"Twenty minutes more!" groaned Clark, as he buried his face in his hands. "Twenty minutes more of this awful suspense!"

"What was the last report?" asked Lane, in a low voice.

"Ninety-eight and a quarter. My God! Think of it! Three-quarters of a cent between us and beggary! I could bear it, but not Vincent: 'twould kill him. Even his home is mortgaged."

There came a quick, sharp tap at the glazed door: the clerk's head was thrust in:

"Three-eighths, sir."

"It's time to move, then," said Lane. "I cannot follow you to the floor,—I have no ticket; but I will be awaiting your call at the Merchants' Exchange. Mr. Vincent has told you—— Better have it in Treasury notes,—one hundred each,—had you not?"

"I'll see Warden at once. D—n him! he would sell us out with no more compunctions than he would shoot a hawk."

"You infer that Mr. Vincent has had no success in raising money in New York?" asked Lane, as they hurried from the office.

"Not an atom! He made old Rossiter what he is,—hauled him out of the depths, set him on his feet, took him in here with him for ten years, sent him East with a fortune that he has trebled since in Wall Street, and now, by heaven! the cold-blooded brute will not lend him a pitiful twenty thousand."

At the bank Lane found an unusual number of men, and there was an air of suppressed excitement. Telegraph-boys would rush in every now and then with despatches for various parties, and these were eagerly opened and read. Scraps of low, earnest conversation reached him as he stood, a silent watcher. "They cannot stand it another day." "They've been raining wheat on them from every corner of the North and West. No gang can stand up under it." "It's bound to break," etc. To an official of the bank who knew him well he showed the telegram he had received at the club, and the gentleman looked up in surprise:

"Do you want this *now*, captain? Surely you are not——"

"No, I'm *not*, most emphatically," replied Lane, with a quiet laugh. "Yet I may have sudden use for that sum. I telegraphed to my agents at Cheyenne yesterday. You, perhaps, ought to wire at once and verify it."

"Those are our bank rules, and I presume it will be done; though of course we know——"

"Never mind. I much prefer you should, and at once." And, leaving the man of business to attend to the necessary formality, Lane strolled to a window and looked down the crowded street towards the massive building in which the desperate grapple 'twixt bull and bear was at its height. The day was hot; men rushed by, mopping their fevered brows; a throng of people had gathered near the broad entrance to the Chamber, and all its windows were lowered to secure free and fresh currents of air. Lane fancied he could hear the shouts of the combatants in the pit even above the ceaseless roar and rattle of wheels upon the stone pavement. Little by little the minute-hand was stealing to the vertical, and still no sign from Clark. "Has she touched a half yet?" he heard one man eagerly ask another as they dived into the broker's office underneath.

"Not yet; but I'm betting she does inside of five minutes and reaches ninety-nine first thing to-morrow."

At last, boom went the great bell,—a single, solemn stroke. There was a rush of men for the street, a general scurry towards the great Board of Trade building, a rapidly-increasing crowd along the curb-stones as the members came pouring out, and brokers and their customers hurried away towards numberless little offices all over the neighborhood. Dozens of them passed along under his post of observation, some flushed, some deathly pale, and finally Clark himself appeared, and Lane hastened forth to meet him.

"Saved by a mere squeak so far," was the almost breathless whisper as Clark removed his hat and wiped his clammy forehead. "But we know not what a day may bring forth. It's a mere respite."

"Can the syndicate carry any more weight, think you? Prices jumped up two and three weeks ago. Now they only climb a hair's-breadth at a time. I hear they are loaded down,—that it *must* break; but I'm no expert in these matters."

"If you were, you'd be wise to keep out of it. Who can say whether they will break or not? It is what everybody confidently predicted when eighty-nine was touched twelve days ago; and look at it!"

"Do you go back to the office from here? Good! I'll join you there in ten minutes," said Lane, "for I shall not come down town this afternoon, and may not be able to in the morning."

And when Captain Lane appeared at the office of Vincent, Clark & Co. he brought with him a stout little packet, which, after the exchange of a few words and a scrap or two of paper, Mr. Clark carefully stowed in the innermost compartment of the big safe. Then he grasped Lane's hand in both of his, as the captain said good-by.

That afternoon, quite late, the captain rang at the Vincents' door, and it was almost instantly opened by the smiling Abigail whom he so longed to reward for her evident sympathy the day before, yet lacked the courage to proffer a greenback. Lane was indeed little versed in the ways of the world, howsoever well he might be informed in his profession.

"Miss Vincent is in the library, sir, if you will please to walk that way," was her brief communication; and the captain, trembling despite his best efforts to control himself, stepped past her into the broad hall, and there, hurrying down the stairway, came Mrs. Vincent, evidently to meet him. Silently she held forth her hand and led him into the parlor, and then he saw that her face was very sad and pale and that her eyes were red with weeping.

"I will only detain you a moment, captain," she murmured, "but I felt that I must see you. Mr. Vincent wrote to me on the train as he left here, and he tells me you know—the worst."

"Mr. Vincent has honored me with his confidence, dear lady; and I—saw Mr. Clark to-day."

She looked up eagerly: "What news had he from New York? Did he tell you?—about Mr. Rossiter, that is? I knew perfectly well what Mr. Vincent's hopes and expectations were in going."

"There was a telegram. I fear that he was disappointed in Mr. Rossiter; but the money was not needed up to the closing of the board at one o'clock."

"I am not disappointed. I thank God that the Rossiters refused him money. It will open his eyes to their real characters,—father and son. I would rather go and live in a hovel than be under obligations to either of them." And now the tears were raining down her cheeks.

"Do not grieve so, Mrs. Vincent," said Lane. "I cannot believe the danger is so great. I have listened to the opinions of the strongest men on 'Change this afternoon. A 'break' in this corner was predicted in New York at eleven this morning, and that is the universal opinion among the best men now."

"Yes, but it may be days away yet, and Mr. Vincent has confessed to me that his whole fortune hangs by a single hair,—that this wretched speculation has swallowed everything,—that a rise of a single penny means beggary to us, for he can no longer answer his broker's calls."

"That may have been so when he wrote; but Mr. Clark seems to have had a little better luck locally. I infer from what he told me that they were safe for to-day and could meet the raise of that critical cent or two: so that, despite the great loss they have sustained, there is not the certainty of ruin that so overwhelmed Mr. Vincent on Wednesday."

"You give me hope and courage," cried the poor, anxious-hearted woman, as she seized and pressed his hand. "And—and you come to us in the midst of our troubles! Mr. Vincent was so touched by your writing first to him: it brought back old days, old times, old fashions, that he loved to recall,—days when he, too, was young and brave and full of hope and cheer."

"And I have your good wishes, too, Mrs. Vincent?—even though I am only a soldier and have so little to offer her beyond—beyond——"

But he could not finish. He had looked into her face with such eager hope and delight when he began, yet broke down helplessly when he tried to speak of his great love for her sweet daughter.

"I know what you would say," she answered, with quick and ready sympathy. "I have seen how dear my child has been to you almost from the very first. Indeed I *do* wish you happiness, Mr. Lane; but Mr. Vincent told you that—we once had other views for Mabel. It is only fair and right that you should know."

"How could it have been otherwise, Mrs. Vincent? Is there any man quite worthy of her? Is there any station in life too high for one like her? I never dared hope that your consent could have been so freely given. I do not dare hope that she can possibly care for me —yet."

"I will not keep you longer, then," said she, smiling through her tears. "I shall see you after a while, perhaps. Mabel is in the library. Now I'll leave you."

With tumultuously-throbbing heart, he softly entered and quickly glanced around. The tiers of almost priceless volumes, the antique furniture, the costly Persian rugs and portières, the pictures, bronzes, bric-à-brac,—all were valueless in his eager eyes. They sought one object alone, and found it in a deep bay-window across the room. There, leaning back in a great easy reading-chair, with a magazine in her lap, her fair head pillowed on a silken cushion, reclined the lady of his heart, smiling a sweet welcome to him, while the rosy color mounted to her brows as he came quickly forward and took her soft, white hand. How he was trembling! How his kind gray eyes were glowing! She could not meet them: she had to look away. She had begun some pleasant little welcoming speech, some half-laughing allusion to the flowers, but she stopped short in the midst of it. A knot of half-faded roses—his roses—nestled in her bosom, contrasting with the pure white of her dainty gown; and now those treasured, envied flowers began to rise and fall, as though rocked on the billows of some clear lake stirred by sudden breeze. What he said, he did not know: she hardly heard, though her ears drank in every word. She only realized that both his hands were tightly clasping hers, and that, scorning to seek a chair and draw it to her side,—perhaps, too, because he could not bear to release even for an instant that slender little hand,—perhaps still more because of the old-time chivalry in his nature that had prompted him to ask parental sanction before telling her of his deep and tender love,—Captain Lane had dropped on one knee close beside, and, bending over her, was pouring forth in broken, incoherent words the old, old story of a lover's hopes and fears and longings,—the sweet old song that, day after day, year after year, ay, though sung since God's creation of the beautiful world we live in, never, never can be heard or sung except in rapture. Even though she be cold to him as stone, no true woman ever listened to the tale of a man's true love without a thrill at heart. Once, once only, in the lifetime of men like Lane—yes, and of men not half his peers in depth of character, in intensity of feeling—there comes a moment like this, and, whether it be in the glow and fervor and enthusiasm of youth or the intensity and strength of maturer years, it is the climax of a lifetime; it is the date from which all others, all scenes, trials, triumphs, take their due apportionment; it is the memory of all others that lingers to the very last, when all, all but this are banished from the dying brain. Rome, in her pride of place, made the building of her Capitol the climax of mundane history: everything in her calendar was "*ante urbem conditam*" or the reverse. The old world measured from the Flood; the new world —our world—measures from the birth of Him who died upon the cross; and the lifetime of the man who has once deeply and devotedly loved has found its climax in the thrilling moment of the avowal.

"Have you no word to say to me, Mabel?—not one word of hope?—not one?" he pleaded.

Then she turned her lovely face, looking into his deep eyes through a mist of tears.

"I do like you," she murmured; "I do honor you so, Captain Lane; but that is not what you deserve. There is no one, believe me, whom I so regard and esteem; but—I do not know——I am not certain of myself."

"Let me try to win your love, Mabel. Give me just that right. Indeed, indeed I have not dared to hope that so soon I could win even your trust and esteem. You make me so happy when you admit even that."

"It is so little to give, in return for what you have given me," she answered, softly, while her hand still lay firmly held in the clasp of his.

"Yet it is so much to me. Think, Mabel, in four days at most I must go back to my regiment. I ask no pledge or promise. Only let me write to you. Only write to me and let me strive to arouse at least a little love in your true heart. Then by and by—six months, perhaps,—I'll come again and try my fate. I know that an old dragoon like me, with gray hairs sprouting in his moustache——"

But here she laid her fingers on his lips, and then, seizing both her hands, he bowed his head over them and kissed them passionately.

The day of parting came, all too soon. Duty—the mistress to whom he had never hitherto given undivided allegiance—called him to the distant West, and the last night of his stay found him bending over her in the same old window. He was to take a late train for St. Louis, and had said farewell to all but her. And now the moment had arrived. A glance at his watch had told him that he had but twenty minutes in which to reach the station.

She had risen, and was standing, a lovely picture of graceful womanhood, her eyes brimming with tears. Both her hands were now clasped in his; she could not deny him *that* at such a time; but—but was there not something throbbing in her heart that she longed to tell?

"It is good-by now," he murmured, his whole soul in his glowing eyes, his infinite love betrayed in those lips quivering under the heavy moustache.

She glanced up into his face.

"Fred,"—and then, as though abashed at her own boldness, the lovely head was bowed again almost on his breast.

"What is it, darling? Tell me," he whispered, eagerly, a wild, wild hope thrilling through his heart.

"Would it make you happier if—if I—told you that I knew myself a little better?"

"*Mabel!* Do you mean—do you care for me?"

And then she was suddenly clasped in his strong, yearning arms and strained to his breast. Long, long afterwards he used to lift that travelling-coat of gray tweeds from the trunk in which it was carefully stowed away, and wonder if—if it were indeed true that her throbbing heart had thrilled through that senseless fabric, stirring wild joy and rapture to the very depths of his own.

"Would I be sobbing my heart out," at last she murmured, "if I did not love you and could not bear to have you go?"

VIII.

"What an awfully pretty girl that Miss Vincent is, Amos!" said Mr. Noel one morning, as the cousins were quietly breakfasting together before going down town.

"Pretty? yes," said Amos, doubtfully. "But look here, my boy: recollect that you want to think of something more than 'pretty' in selecting a wife while you are in here on this detail. Now, Mrs. Withers and I have been keeping our eyes open, and our ears too, for that matter: the fact is, I always have both eyes and ears open,—travel with them that way, sleep with them that way. I would not be the man I am in the business world, Noel, if that weren't the case. And, pretty though Miss Vincent may be, she's not the girl for you to waste your time on."

"But why not?" asked Noel. "They have a magnificent home, and everything about it indicates wealth and refinement and culture; and there is no denying that she is one of the most attractive girls in society in this city: certainly I have seen none whom I have admired more."

"That is all very true, perhaps," was the reply; "but her father was very badly bitten during that wheat corner last month, and in fact he has been losing heavily for the last two years. Warden, who is his broker on 'Change, let it leak out in more ways than one; and that wife of Warden's is a regular scandal-monger,—she can't help talking, and everything she manages to extract from him in the way of information goes broadcast over the entire city. Of course, when the corner broke, as it did, old Vincent managed to pull out of it without absolute loss of his homestead and his entire business. But the rally came only in the nick of time. I am told that Warden has said that if wheat had gone up one cent higher it would have knocked Vincent out of time; he never could have come to again. Gordon Noel, we have another plan for you. Wait until Ned Terry's sister gets back from the East; between her and her brother they have just about as much money invested in the best-paying business in this town as any people that I can possibly name. She's a belle; she's just as pretty as Miss Vincent. She isn't as smart, perhaps, but she is a woman worth cultivating. Now, hold your horses. Where did you meet her, by the way?"

"I first met her at the Thorntons' dinner-party. She was there with Captain Lane, and some other young people whom I had not previously met."

"Oh, yes; that reminds me. It seems to me I have heard once or twice that your friend Lane was very much smitten in that quarter. Now, you'd much better let him carry off Miss Vincent, if he can. She would suit his modest views of life very well. But I don't believe the girl has a penny to her fortune; at least she certainly won't if Vincent has no more luck in the future than he has had in the last year."

"I took her down to dinner," said Noel, thoughtfully, "and I remember that she talked a good deal about the army, and asked a great many questions about the cavalry. Now that you speak of it, I noticed that Lane, who sat on the opposite side of the table, didn't seem to be particularly interested in the lady whom he was escorting, although of course he had to be civil and tried to keep up a conversation, but every now and then I would catch him looking at us, and particularly at her. But she looked so pretty that I didn't wonder at it."

"When did you next see her?" said Withers.

"Only last night. You know, I was called away almost immediately after the Thornton affair, and had to go on to New York on the court-martial, where I was summoned as a witness, then only got back in time for the party last night. That was my second meeting with her, and by this time Lane had gone out to join the regiment. I didn't even have a chance to say good-by to him. Do you think, really, that he was smitten in that quarter?"

"That's what I certainly heard," said Withers; "and as soon as you get to know young people in society, I venture to say that you can readily find out all about it. These girls all know one another's secrets, and are generally pretty ready to tell them. That's the result of my experience."

It was evident that Amos Withers's cousin was not to be neglected in the Queen City. Two parties at private houses, a reception at the club, and three dinners were the invitations which he found awaiting him at his office. Half an hour was occupied in acknowledging and accepting or declining, as happened to be the case, these evidences of hospitality; then, having no especial interest in the morning paper, his thoughts again reverted to what Mr. Withers had been telling him about Miss Vincent, and the possible relation between her and his regimental comrade. He had been very much impressed with her the night before. Her beauty was of such a rare and radiant character, she was so genial and unaffected in her manner, so bright and winning, with such an evident liking for his society, that Mr. Noel had come away flattering himself that he had made in this quarter a most favorable impression. He had thought of her very much as he went home from the party,—of her interested face, as he talked or danced with her; and she danced delightfully, and was so good as to say that his step perfectly suited hers. He remembered now, too, her remark that it was so delightful to dance with army officers, and graduates of the Point, they all seemed to feel so thoroughly at home on the floor.

Noel was not a graduate of the Point by any means; but he saw no reason for disenchanting her on that score. He was quite as good as any of the West-Pointers, in his own opinion, and in society was very much more at home than many of their number. As a dancer he was looked upon in his regiment and throughout the cavalry as one of the most accomplished in the whole service. And all this interest and all this cordiality he had accepted without hesitation as a tribute to his own superior qualifications and attractiveness. It was therefore with a feeling akin to pique that he heard of this possible engagement existing between her and Captain Lane.

In all the Eleventh Cavalry there was no man whom Gordon Noel feared and possibly hated more than he did Captain Lane. This arose from the fact that Lane as adjutant of the regiment had seen all the communications that passed from time to time relative to Noel's absence from his command when his services were most needed and when any man of spirit would have taken every possible precaution to be with it. He knew how silent Lane had always been, and how thorough a custodian of regimental secrets he was considered. But all the same the mere fact that Lane knew all these circumstances so much to his disadvantage, and had seen all his lame and impotent excuses, had made him fear him as a possible enemy and hate him simply because he stood in awe of him.

No one, to watch Noel in society or in the presence of his brother officers, would suppose for a moment that he looked upon Lane with other than feelings of the warmest regard and comradeship. It was only in his secret thoughts, which he admitted to no soul on earth, that Noel realized what his real feelings were towards a man who had never done him a wrong, but who had treated him on all occasions, public and private, with courtesy and consideration.

For some reason or other the lieutenant felt restless and dissatisfied this morning. The atmosphere of the office was decidedly uncongenial. He was a man who rarely read anything, and to whom letter-writing was a bore. To be sure, he had little of it to do, for no man in the regiment had expressed a desire to hear from him. It was a hot, sultry day; the stylish white flannel suit in which he had arrayed his handsome self was wasting its elegance on the desert air of a bare and empty room, instead of being seen in the boudoirs of beauty or the billiard-rooms at the club. Business was slack: no recruits were coming in, and Mr. Noel could stand it no longer. A ring from his bell summoned the sergeant to the room.

"There doesn't seem to be any likelihood of recruits coming in such a day as this, sergeant," said Mr. Noel. "I'm going up to the club for a while; if anybody should come in, send one of the men up there for me; I'll return at once." And with that he took his straw hat and light cane and strolled leisurely up the street. His was a figure that many a man—and more women—would turn to look at more than once. Tall, slim, elegant in build, always dressed in excellent taste, Gordon Noel in any community would have been pronounced a remarkably presentable man. His face, as has been said, was very fine; his eyes dark and handsome, shaded by deep, thick lashes; his hair dark and waving; his moustache, dark and drooping, served only to enhance the brilliancy of the even white teeth that flashed underneath it in his frequent smiles and joyous laughter. One would say, in looking at Noel, that he was a man of singularly sunny disposition; and so he was, and so they found him at the club; and so the loungers there hailed him with jovial shouts as he entered; for, though only a fortnight had elapsed since his arrival, and four days of that time he had been absent, giving his testimony before the court-martial in New York harbor, he had nevertheless won his way into the hearts of all the young fellows around the club, and no more popular man than Gordon Noel had ever come within the doors of "The Queen City."

"What are you going to have, old man?" was the first question asked, and Noel laughingly ordered a sherry-cobbler, saying the day was far too hot for anything stronger.

"Who's that I just saw going into the billiard-room?" he asked.

"That? that's Regy Vincent. Haven't you met him yet?"

"Regy Vincent," said Noel. "Is he the brother of the Miss Vincent whom I met at the party last night?"

"The very same," was the reply. "Mighty bright fellow, too, and a very jolly one; though he has been in hard luck of late."

"How in hard luck?" asked a quiet-looking man seated in a big arm-chair, lowering for a moment the newspaper which he had been reading.

"Well, through his father's ill luck on 'Change. You all know, of course, that Vincent was nearly busted before that corner went under last week."

"I know this," was the calm reply, "that while he did stand for a few days on the 'ragged edge,' and while it may be that had that corner not broken when it did he would have been in sore straits, in some way he or his partner, Clark, came to taw with additional funds, and had the consummate pluck to put up more at the very moment when it was believed that that syndicate was going to have everything their own way. So far from being badly bitten by that deal, it's my belief that Vincent, Clark & Co. came out of it with a very pretty penny to the good."

"Well, of course, Harris, you must know more about it than I do. But you cannot be gladder than I am to hear that Vincent's status is so much better than we supposed. I'm glad on his account, I'm glad on Regy's account, and I'm particularly glad on Miss Mabel's account. And now I'm particularly chuckling over Billy Rossiter's frame of mind when he hears the real truth of this matter. When he went after her to Rome last year, and everybody supposed that Vincent was worth a million, there's no doubt in the world that he did his best to win her, and that was what he was sent abroad by his father to do. But he didn't win her then, for she strenuously denied any engagement when she came back here; yet it was supposed that if he persevered his chances would be good. Why, he's not half a bad fellow, only he can't marry so long as he is in his father's employ and dependent on him, unless he marries according to his father's wishes; and the old man called him off just as soon as he found out that Vincent was on the verge of failure. Billy Rossiter has lost any chance that he might have had in that quarter; for she'll never look at him again."

"Served him right, if that be the case. Any man who hasn't sense enough to stick to a girl who is bright and pretty as Mabel Vincent, rich or poor, deserves no luck at all in this world. But that reminds me, Captain Noel, according to rumor and what the girls say in society,—and you know they generally know pretty much everything that is going on,—there is something more than a mere understanding between her and your predecessor here, the recruiting officer, Lieutenant Lane. Did he say anything about it to you?"

"No, not a word. I think, though, that had there been anything in the story Lane would have let me know something about it, for we are very old and intimate friends. Did you say that that was Mr. Reginald Vincent who has just gone into the billiard-room?"

"Yes," answered Mr. Morris, "that's he. Would you like to know him?"

"Very much indeed; and if you've nothing better to do, come in and present me. Perhaps he will want to play a game of billiards, and if so I'm his man."

And so it happened that, that very morning, Gordon Noel was presented to Reginald Vincent, and when Regy went home to luncheon he spoke enthusiastically of his new-found acquaintance, whom he pronounced to be one of the most delightful fellows he had ever met anywhere, and who was such a warm and devoted friend of Captain Lane. "I want, if I meet him this afternoon, as I probably shall, to bring him back to dinner with me. What say you, mother?—just informally."

"Don't you think it would be better to wait a day or two, and have a little dinner, and invite a few friends to meet him?" asked Mrs. Vincent. "Your father, perhaps, would like to be consulted in the matter. I've no doubt that he would like to do something to show attention to any friend of Captain Lane's. What do you think, Mabel?"

"I vote for both," replied that young woman, with much alacrity. "I have met Mr. Noel twice."

"Captain Noel, dear," said Regy; "Captain Noel."

"He is not a captain yet, Reginald: I happen to know from the regimental roster: I have a copy up-stairs, that Captain Lane very kindly left me." And here a decided blush stole up the fair cheeks of the young lady. "I learned a good deal about the officers of the regiment from Mr. Lane—Captain Lane—while he was here. Mr. Noel ranks second among the lieutenants of the regiment. As Captain Lane said, he is so very near his captaincy that perhaps he accepts the title that you all give him at the club as only a trifle premature."

"Well, captain or lieutenant, it doesn't make any difference," said Regy, impulsively: "he's a mighty good fellow, and a mighty good friend of your friend Captain Lane, and if you have no objection, mother, I'll bring him around to dinner to-night, and then perhaps we might go to the theatre afterwards. I'm very sure that Captain Noel will enjoy it. Fact is, he enjoys everything. Everybody in the club is perfectly delighted with him. You ought to hear him sing an Irish song or tell a French story! I'll try and get him started when he comes here. He's a wonderful mimic; and he's so full of information about their service on the frontier. Now, Lane so seldom spoke of anything of the kind; but Noel will talk for hours at a time about the wonderful country through which they have scouted and fought, and all that they have been through in their campaigns. By Jove! but that fellow has seen a lot of hard service, and has been through some hair-breadth escapes!"

"Who?" inquired Mrs. Vincent; "Captain Lane or Mr. Noel?"

"Noel, of course,—Noel I'm speaking of. Lane, no doubt, saw a great deal of service with the regiment; but Noel says that he was adjutant so much of the time, and on other staff-duty, while he (Noel) was almost incessantly scouting, hunting after various Indian parties, and being on the war-path, as he laughingly expresses it."

"Does he mean that Captain Lane didn't see much actual service there?" asked Miss Mabel, with heightened color.

"Oh, I don't know that he means that. Don't understand me as saying for a moment that Noel disparages Lane's services; on the contrary, he never speaks of him except with the most enthusiastic regard. Neither does he boast at all of his own service; only you can't help seeing, in the modest, off-hand way in which he speaks of his campaigning, what a deal of hardship and danger he has encountered for the simple reason that he was with the command that had to go through it all."

"Your father tells me," said Mrs. Vincent, "that he met him one day on 'Change when Mr. Withers brought him in; that was before the crash, and when he had no time to pay him any attention. Of course the cousin of Mr. Amos Withers was received with a great deal of bowing and scraping by Mr. Withers's friends in that honorable body. But all the same I know your father will be glad to meet Mr. Noel now; and by all means bring him, if you feel disposed, to-night. What manner of looking man is he?"

"A remarkably handsome man, mother," said Mabel, at once,—"one of the handsomest I ever saw; and he certainly made himself very entertaining and very jolly the night we sat together at dinner at the Thorntons'."

"There's a great contrast physically between him and Lane," put in Regy. "Noel is such an elegantly built fellow,—so tall and fine-looking. Lane would be almost undersized when standing beside him, and is very much at a disadvantage when they appear together, I should judge."

A very bright and joyous party it was, seated around the home-like table of the Vincents that evening, and, as Regy had predicted, Noel proved very entertaining and a most agreeable guest. While showing much deference to Mr. Vincent and attention to his good wife, he nevertheless managed to have a great deal to say about the regiment and its daring and perilous service on the frontier, and to throw in here and there many a pleasant word about Captain Lane and their long and intimate acquaintance, and before dinner was over had won a warm place in Mabel Vincent's heart by the way in which he so frequently spoke of the man to whom she had plighted her troth.

And that very evening, as Frederick Lane,—far out under the star-lit sky of Arizona,—with his heart full of longing and love for her, and thinking only of her as he rode over the desolate plain with the lights of old Fort Graham already in view, Mabel Vincent, seated by Gordon Noel's side, was looking up into his handsome face and listening to his animated voice between the acts of "Twelfth Night."

IX.

Only a short distance from the Arizona border, with the blue range of the Santa Catarina shutting out the sunset skies, with sand and cactus and Spanish bayonet on every side, the old post of Fort Graham stood in the desert like a mud-colored oasis. All the quarters, all the store-houses, stables, corrals, and barracks, were built of the native *adobe;* and though whitewash had been liberally applied, especially about the homes of the officers, and the long Venetian blinds at their front windows had been painted the coolest of deep greens, and clear running water sparkled through the *acequias* that bordered the parade, it could not be denied that at its best Graham was an arid and forbidding station, so far as one could judge by appearances. Trees, verdure, turf, were items almost unknown within a day's march of the flag-staff; but in the old times when the Navajoes were the terror of the wide Southwest and even the Comanches sometimes carried their raids across the Rio Bravo del Norte—the Rio Grande of to-day—the post had been "located" where it might afford protection to the " Forty-Niners" and to the pioneers of the prairies; the trans-continental trail led past its very gates, and many a time and oft the miner and the emigrant thanked God and the general government that the old fort was placed just where it was, for Indian pursuers drew rein when once in sight of its dingy walls; and so from year to year for more than thrice a decade the flag was raised at sunrise, the post was always garrisoned; and now, with the Southern Pacific piercing the range but a short distance below, and landing stores and forage at the quartermaster's dépôt within four miles of the corrals, it became easier to maintain a force of cavalry at Graham; and one of the troops there stationed was Lane's new command, the relict of the late lamented Curran, "the Devil's own D."

An easy-going old dragoon was Curran, and for years before his retirement it was an open secret that his first sergeant "ran the troop" to suit himself and that the captain never permitted his subalterns to interfere. A more independent, devil-may-care, and occasionally drunken lot of troopers were rarely gathered in one such organization, and, while steady and reliable men on getting their discharges at the end of their term of enlistment would refuse to "take on" again in D Troop, but would go over to Captain Breese or perhaps to a company at another station, all the scamps and rollicking characters in the regiment would drift over into "D" and be welcomed by the choice spirits therein assembled. And this was the gang that Captain Lane was now expected to bring up with a round turn and transform into dutiful soldiers. Obedient to the colonel's behest, he had stopped over a couple of days at head-quarters, had had a most cordial greeting from every officer at the post, had called on all the ladies,—not omitting his

C*

fair defamers,—and then had hastened on to Graham and his new and trying duties. Every day, as he was whirled farther away from the home of her whom he so devotedly loved, he wrote long letters to her, filled with—only lovers know what all. And his heart leaped with joy that topmost in the little packet of letters awaiting him at the adjutant's office when he reached his post was a dainty billet addressed to him in her beloved hand. Until he could get his quarters in habitable condition the new troop-commander was the guest of Captain and Mrs. Nash; and he could hardly wait for the close of that amiable woman's welcoming address to reach his room and devour every word of that most precious missive. She had written—bless her!—the very day after he left, and a sweet, womanly letter it was,—so shy and half timid, yet so full of faith and pride in him. Every one at Graham remarked on the wonderful change for the better that had come over Lane since he went East. Never had they seen him so joyous, so blithe in manner. He seemed to walk on air; his eyes beamed on every one; his face seemed "almost to have a halo round it," said Mrs. Nash, and neither she nor any woman in garrison had the faintest doubt as to the explanation of it all. Love had wrought the change, and being loved had intensified and prolonged it. Every man—every woman in garrison was his friend, and the happy fellow would gladly have taken dozens of them into his confidence and told them all about it, and talked by the hour of her.

But there were reasons, Mrs. Vincent had said, why it was most desirable that there should be no announcement of the engagement as yet. What these were she did not explain to Mabel herself, but assured her that it was her father's wish as well. Lane had rushed to the great jewelry-house of Van Loo & Laing, and the diamond solitaire that flashed among the leaves of the exquisite rose-bud he smilingly handed her that night was one to make any woman gasp with delight. Could anything on earth be rich enough, pure enough, fair enough, to lavish on her, his peerless queen?

She had held forth her soft white hand and let him slip it on the engagement finger and then bend the knee like knight of old and kiss it fervently. She revelled in it, rejoiced in it, but, heeding her mother's advice, stowed it away where none could see it, in the secret drawer of her desk, and Lane was perfectly satisfied. "I will tell you the reason some day," Mrs. Vincent had said to him, "but not just now, for I might be doing wrong;" and he had protested that she need never tell him. What cared he, so long as Mabel's love was his, and they understood each other as they did?

And so, while people at Graham plied him with questions and insinuations and side-remarks about the "girl he left behind him" in the East, he kept faithfully to the agreement, and though all the garrison knew he wrote to her every day and took long rides alone that he might think of her, doubtless, and though every one knew that those dainty missives that came so often for Captain Lane were written by Miss Mabel Vincent, never once did he admit the existence of an engagement,—never once until long afterwards.

The first real tidings that the Graham people had of her came in a letter from head-quarters. Mrs. Riggs had had such a long, charming letter from Mr. Noel that she called in several of her cronies and read it all to them; and that very evening one of the number, unable to bear the burden of so much information, shifted it from her mental shoulders by writing it all to Mrs. Nash. Perhaps the best plan will be to read the extract which referred to Lane exactly as Mr. Noel wrote it:

"By this time I presume Fred Lane is busily engaged with his new troop. I served with them in the Sioux campaign, and they never gave me any trouble at all. So, too, in the Geronimo chase a while ago, when Major Brace picked me out to go ahead by night from Carrizo's I asked for a detachment from D Troop, and the men seemed to appreciate it. I knew they would follow wherever I would lead, and would stand by me through thick and thin. If Lane starts in right I've no doubt they will do just as well for him; but I expect he is feeling mighty blue at having to rejoin just now. You know I've always been a warm friend of his, and it hurt me to see him so unwilling to go back. No one seemed to know him very well in society; and it's very queer, for this was his old home,—and I was never more delightfully welcomed anywhere; the people are charming. But Lane had held himself aloof a good deal, and fellows at the club say he didn't 'run with the right set.' Then, if all accounts be true, he had had hard luck in several ways. I'm told that he lost money in a big wheat speculation, and everybody says he totally lost his heart. I tell you this in confidence because I know you are a devoted friend of his,—as indeed you are of all in the dear old regiment,—but he was much embarrassed when it came to turning over the funds. There was quite a heavy shortage, which he had to make up at a time when it was probably most inconvenient. As to the other loss, it isn't to be wondered at. She is a beautiful and most charming girl, and many a man, I fancy, has laid his heart at her feet. It is said, however, that Lane's loss is the heavier in this case because—well, I fear it will come to nothing. A young lady told me yesterday that there was something back of it all,—that she, Miss Vincent, was deeply in love with a Mr. Rossiter, of New York, and had been for over a year, and they were to have been married this coming September, but that the gentleman (?) learned that her father had been nearly swamped in speculation and had not a penny to give her. My informant went to school with Miss Vincent, and knows her intimately, and she says that Mr. Rossiter simply threw her over a short time ago, and that it was pique and exasperation and to hide her heart-break from the world that Mabel Vincent began to show such pleasure in Lane's devotions. She led him on, so her lady friends say ; and now Mr. Rossiter has found out that old Vincent was sharper and shrewder than any one supposed and made instead of losing a pile, and now he is suing to be taken back, and they say that she is so much in love with the fellow that the chances are all in his favor. This is why I feel such sorrow and anxiety for Lane.

"Well, I led the german at a lovely party at the Prendergasts' last night. Miss Vincent was there, looking like a peach-blossom, and we danced together a great deal. When it came time to break up I believe half the people in the rooms came to say good-night to me and to tell me they had never seen so delightful a german,—'everything so depends on the leader.' I have invitations for something or other for every night for the next fortnight; and yet I so often long for the old regiment and the true friends I had to leave. It did me a world of good last night to meet old Colonel Gray, of the retired list, whose home is here, but he commanded the —th Infantry in the Sioux campaign, and when he saw me he threw his arms around my neck and hugged me before the whole throng of people. Give my love to our chief, always, and believe me, dear, true friend of mine,

"Yours most affectionately,
"GORDON NOEL."

Condensed, edited by feminine hands, and accented here and there as suited the writer's mood, this was the letter which formed the basis of the one received by Mrs. Nash. Lane by this time was cosily ensconced in his quarters, and was giving all his time to the improvement of affairs about his troop's barracks, kitchens, and stables, to drill- and target-practice, and to company duties generally. His days knew no relaxation from labor from reveille until "retreat" at sunset, and then came the delicious evenings in which he could write to her and read a chapter or two of some favorite work before going early to bed. After the first week he seldom left his house after eight o'clock, and the garrison had therefore ample opportunity to discuss his affairs. Some color was lent to the story of his having lost money in speculation by a letter received from Cheyenne written to the new major of the ——th Infantry, who had recently joined by promotion from Fort Russell, near that thriving town. The writer said that Lane of the Eleventh Cavalry had sold his property there for fifteen thousand dollars about the end of June, and he had bought it for twenty-five hundred only nine years before. He could have got eighteen thousand just as well by waiting a few days; but he wanted the money at once.

No one, of course, could ask the captain any direct questions about his affairs of either heart or pocket, but Lane was puzzled to account for some of the remarks that were made to him,—the interrogatories about the methods of speculation, the tentatives as to chances of "making a good thing" in that way, and the sharp and scrutinizing glances that accompanied the queries. The sweet, sympathetic, semi-confidential manner, the inviting way in which the ladies spoke to him of his present loneliness and their hopes that soon he would bring to them a charming wife to share their exile and bless his army home,—all this, too, seemed odd to him; but, as he had never been in love nor engaged before, he did not know but that it was "always the way with them," and so let it pass.

And then he was very happy in her letters. They were neither as frequent nor as long as his, but then she had such a round of social duties; she was in such constant demand; there were visitors or parties every night, and endless calls and shopping-tours with mother every day, and she was really getting a little run down. The weather was oppressively warm, and they longed to get away from the city and go to the mountains. It was only a day's ride to the lovely resorts in the Alleghanies, but papa was looking a little thin and worn again, and the doctors had said his heart was affected,—not alarmingly or seriously, but mamma could not bear to leave him, and he declared it utterly impossible to be away from his business a single day. He and Mr. Clark were very hopeful over a new venture they had made, the nature of which she did not thoroughly understand.

But let us take a peep at some of those early letters,—not at the answers to his eager questions, not at the shy words of maiden love that crept in here and there, but at those pages any one might read.

"Tuesday night.

". . . Such a delightful german as we had last night at the Prendergasts'! Captain Noel led—I have to call him captain, for every one does here, and if I say 'Mr.' they want to know why, and it is embarrassing to explain how I know. He leads remarkably well, and I was very proud of 'our regiment,' sir, when listening to all the nice things said about him. How I wished for a certain other cavalry captain, now so many cruel miles away! Mr. Noel took me out often,—and indeed I was a decided belle,—and he told me that he had to lead with Miss Prendergast, but would so much rather dance with me.

"It is almost settled that we go away in August for the entire month. Dr. Post says mother must go, and that father ought to go. Of course I go with mamma. Deer Park will doubtless be the favored spot. I wish August were here; I wish you were here; I wish—oh, so many things! Your letters are such a delight to me. I wonder if other girls have anything like them. Yes, you shall have the picture on my birthday; but mind, sir, you are to take the utmost care of it, or the original will feel neglected."

"Friday night.

". . . So many interruptions to-day, dear Fred! You see what an incoherent thing this is thus far, and now I'm tired out. We had a charming time at the Woodrows' dinner last evening. The day had been hot, but their table was set on the lawn under a canopy, and, the walls being raised, we had a delightful breeze from the river. Their place is one of the finest on the heights. I did so wish you could have seen it. Captain Noel took me in, and was so bright and jolly and full of anecdote. Everybody likes him, and I like him mainly because he is such a loyal friend of yours. He talks so much of you and of all the dangers you have shared in common; and you know how interesting all this must be to me. Sometimes I wonder that you had so little to say about him,—though you never *did* talk much about the regiment and never would talk much about yourself. Wednesday evening we had a little theatre-party. Regy got it up, and we just filled two adjoining loges. Captain Noel was Fanny Holton's escort, but he talked most of the time with me,—a thing that my escort, Mr. Forbes, did not seem to like; but, as he *couldn't* talk, and Mr. Noel would, what could I do?"

"Sunday evening.

"It is late, and I ought to be asleep, but the last caller has just gone, and to-morrow there may be no time to write at all, and you are such an exacting, tyrannical, dear old boy that—— Well, there, now, let me tell you of the day. You say anything and everything that I say or do is of interest. So, to begin with, yesterday I had a headache, due, I fear, to the late supper Regy gave us at the club after the theatre. Fanny Holton came to take me for a drive, but I did not feel like going, and begged off. Then she told me that Captain Noel was in the carriage waiting, and that he would be so disappointed. Mother came in and said the air would do me good; and so we went, and I came back feeling so much brighter. Mr. Noel was very amusing, and kept us laughing all the time. Coming home, Fanny got out at her house, as she had to dress for dinner, but told the coachman to drive me home and Mr. Noel to the club. He began talking of you the moment she disappeared, and said he so hoped you were going to write regularly to him. Are you? He seems so fond of you; but I do not wonder at that.

"This morning we went to church, and afterwards Mr. Noel joined and walked home with us, and papa begged him to come in to luncheon, which he did. You dear fellow! what have you done to my beloved old daddy, that he is so ardent an admirer of yours? He shook Mr. Noel's hand three times before he would let him go, and begged him to come often: he liked to know men, he said, who could so thoroughly appreciate—whom do you think, sir?—Captain Fred Lane. After he had gone, papa spoke of him delightedly on two or three occasions. Will they take him away too as soon as he is really a captain?"

"Wednesday.

"You dear, dear, extravagant fellow! Never have I had such exquisite flowers, or such profusion of them. You must have given your florist *carte blanche*. Nothing that came to me compared with them. My birthday was the cause of quite a little *fête* in the family, and I had some lovely presents. Mr. Noel, too, sent a beautiful basket of roses, and it pleased me very much. I want your comrades to like me, and yet I know he did this on your account. Though he is so thoughtful and delicate and never refers to our engagement, I feel that he knows it; and it seems better that way, somehow.

"You did not answer my questions about him, Fred. Didn't you read my letter?"

Among the letters that came from the Queen City was one which bore the tremulous superscription of the head of the firm of Vincent, Clark & Co. It was brief, but it gave Captain Lane a thrill of gladness:

"It was your timely and thoughtful aid that enabled us to recover so much of our losses. You alone came to our rescue, and I fully appreciate the risk you ran. It will never be forgotten.

"Clark will send draft for the entire am't, or deposit to your credit, as you may direct. I go to New York and Chicago in two or three days. Our prospects are flattering."

X.

August was close at hand. Queen City "society" had scattered in every direction. The mountains and the sea-shore were levying tribute on the plethoric pockets of the "big men" on 'Change and in business of every conceivable kind. Blinds and shutters were closed at scores of hospitable mansions in the narrow streets of the old city and even in the elegant villas that crowned the surrounding heights. The sun-glare at mid-day was so intense that no man was safe in venturing forth without a huge sunshade of some kind, and even within the sacred precincts of the club, where broad awnings hung on every side and palm-leaf fans were in constant motion, the men strolled in to luncheon in shirts of lightest flannel or pongee, with rolling collars and infinitesimal neckties. Every one who could leave town had long since gone; and yet the Vincents lingered. Each day seemed to add to the anxiety in the mother's eyes as she watched her husband's aging face. He had returned from a business-trip of ten days or so looking hopeful and buoyant, and had gone to the office the following morning with light step and cheery demeanor, but came home long after the dinner-hour listless and dispirited,—a severe headache, he said, but the wife knew that it was far more than head- or heartache. The family physician took occasion to warn Mr. Vincent that he was doing himself grievous wrong,—that his health imperatively demanded rest and change of scene. Vincent looked in the good old doctor's face with a world of dumb misery in his eyes, and only answered, "I will,—I will,—in a week or so. I cannot quit my post just now. Clark is taking his vacation. When he returns I'll go." And until he could accompany them Mrs. Vincent refused to budge; and yet she began to urge that Mabel should start now. What was to prevent her going at once and joining the Woodrows at Deer Park? Clarissa and Eleanor Woodrow were always such friends of hers. But Mabel begged that she might stay until both papa and mamma could go too; she could not be content there without them, or at least without mother; and Mrs. Vincent could not find the words in which to frame the cause of her greatest apprehension.

The one man whom the heat was powerless to subdue was Gordon Noel. In the most immaculate and becoming costumes of white or straw color, that genial officer would saunter into the club at noontide, looking provokingly cool and comfortable, and, as he expressed it, "without having turned a hair."

"Hot!" he would say. "Call this hot? Why, bless your hearts, fellows, you ought to live in Arizona awhile! Gad! I've come in sometimes from a scout through the Gila desert and rushed for cold cream to plaster on my nose and cheeks: it would be all melted, of course; but when I clapped it on it would sizzle just like so much lard in a frying-pan. And down at Fort Yuma our hens laid hard-boiled eggs from June to October." And then his eyes would twinkle with fun, and he would bury his dark moustache in the cracked ice of his julep with infinite relish.

"I say," queried Mr. Morris of his chum, Terry junior, one languid afternoon after Noel had jauntily strolled away, "don't you envy a feller who can enjoy life like that?"

"Never saw anything like it!" quoth the younger. "One would suppose that after being a slave all mawning in those beastly works I ought to enjoy a little recreation; but I can't, you know."

"Queer ducks, those army fellers. Gad! this love-making by proxy is what gets me,—this sort of Miles Standish courtship business. She's prettier, though, than the original Priscilla."

"How do you mean?" queried young Terry, vaguely. He had been brought up under the thumb of his elder brother, and, from the outset, had been given to understand that if he expected to share in the profits he must learn the business. There had been no college for him, and New England legends were sealed books.

"Why, I mean that 'twouldn't surprise me a bit if we had a modern version of the old 'Why don't you speak for yourself, John?' He's with her incessantly."

"Oh! Miss Vincent you're speaking of. Her name's Mabel, I thought, not—what'd you call her?"

"Never mind, Jimmy," said Morris, rising. "Come and have a cigarette."

And it was not only in the club, over their cigars, that men spoke significantly of Noel's attentions to the lovely daughter of the house of Vincent. It was not the men, indeed, who did the greater part of the talk. If *they* noticed and spoke of it, what must not the women have been saying! Noel, quitting the hospitable roof of Cousin Amos, had taken rooms down in town, midway between the club and the Vincent homestead, and those two points became the limits of his field of action. The Withers household had gone to the Maryland mountains, and the massive master of the establishment was treating himself to a month's vacation. Almost all the pretty girls were gone. What more natural than that Mr. Noel should so frequently seek the society of the prettiest of all, even if she were engaged to Frederick Lane, as people said she was before he went away? There was no monitorial Amos to call him off, no one to bid him turn his devotions elsewhere; and she herself could see no harm, for was not almost all his talk of Captain Lane? was he not his loyal and devoted friend? The captain's letters came every day, and he seemed pleased to know that Noel had such pleasant things to say of him, and was so attentive,—or rather kind, because it wasn't really on her account that he came so frequently. To be sure, Captain Lane did not say much about the matter one way or the other; and if he saw no harm, if he expressed no dissatisfaction, who else had any right to find fault?

Her mother, was the answer that conscience pricked into her heart quicker even than she could think. For days past the good lady's manner to Noel had been gaining in distance and coolness. "She is ill at ease,—worried about papa," was Mabel's attempt at a self-satisfying plea; but conscience again warned her that she knew better,—far better. Her father, engrossed in business cares that seemed only to increase with every day, had no eyes or ears for affairs domestic; and so it resulted that when Noel came sauntering in at evening with his jaunty, debonair, joyous manner, there was no one to receive him but Mabel, and he wanted no one more.

"Does Captain Lane know of this and approve it?" was the grave question her mother had at last propounded.

"I have written to him with the utmost frankness, mother," was Miss Vincent's reply, while a wave of color swept over her face and a rebellious light gleamed in her eyes, "and he has never hinted at such a thing as disapproval. He has more confidence in me than you have. If he had not——"

But the rest was left unsaid.

Poor Mrs. Vincent! She turned away, well knowing that argument or opposition in such matters was mistaken policy. The words that sprung to her lips were, "Alas! he does not know you as I do!" but she shut those lips firmly, rigorously denying herself the feminine luxury of the last word and the launching of a Parthian arrow that would have made, indeed, a telling shot. If heaven is what it is painted, there can be no more joy over the sinner that repenteth than over the woman who tramples down her fiercest temptation and "bridleth her tongue." Mrs. Vincent deserved to be canonized.

And meantime how went the world with Lane? Faithful, honest, simple-hearted man that he was, holding himself in such modest estimate, marvelling as he often did over the fact that he could have really won the love of a being so radiant, so exquisite, as Mabel, he lived in a dream that was all bliss and beauty, except for the incessant and all-pervading longing to see her,—to be near her. He loved her with an intensity that he had no means of expressing. Not a waking instant was she absent from his thoughts, and in his dreams she appeared to him, crowned with a halo such as never angel knew. He used to lie awake at times in the dead hours of the night, wondering if the very newsboys and workmen of the city realized their blessed privilege, that they could step upon the flagstones her little foot had pressed, that they could see her face, perhaps hear her voice, as she strolled in the cool of evening along the gravelled pathway of the little park that adjoined her home. Loving her as he did, his heart went out to any one who knew her or was even familiar with the city where she dwelt. He had felt for years a contempt for Gordon Noel that, at times, he had difficulty in disguising. Now he was tempted to write to him, to shut out the past, to open confidential relations and have him write long letters that should tell of her. There were three men in his troop in whom he felt a vague, mysterious interest simply because they had been enlisted at the old rendezvous on Sycamore Street, only three squares from her home. He was so full of hope and faith and love and gratitude that the whole garrison seemed to hold naught but cheer and friendliness. He never dreamed of the stories the men were telling or the confidences women were whispering about the post. Noel had written again to Mrs. Riggs, and Mrs. Riggs had not spared her information. It was now said in Queen City society that the engagement was of Mr. Vincent's making. He had been associated with Lane in some speculations that proved disastrous, but the captain had shown such command of money and had "put up" at such an opportune moment that they came out in good shape after all, and as soon as the old man found that Lane loved his daughter he insisted on her accepting him. The information about Lane's coming to the rescue with money he had heard from Mr. Vincent himself,—as indeed he had. One evening when they were for the moment alone, in a burst of confidence to the man whom he believed to be a devoted friend of his prospective son-in-law, Vincent had told the silent officer the story of that perilous crisis and of Lane's prompt and generous loan,—but not as Noel told it to Mrs. Riggs.

"Do not distress yourself, my darling one," wrote Lane to his *fiancée*, " because your letters are a little less frequent just now. I know how occupied you must be with preparation, and how anxious you are about the dear old father. Next week you will be in the mountains; and then, as you say, people will give you time to write, and then, too, I shall be happy in your regaining health and spirits. The papers tell me how intense has been the heat: it almost equals ours here in one way, and is much worse in being moist and muggy. There is a prospect of my going on a two weeks' scout with my whole troop early in the month ; but your letters will reach me safely."

Why was it that she should experience a feeling almost of relief in reading that he was going to be absent from the garrison awhile,— going out on a two weeks' scout?

She had sent him, as she promised, a lovely cabinet photograph of herself that had been taken expressly for him. It came to the old frontier fort just as the men were marching up from evening stables, and the messenger, distributing the mail about the post, handed the packet to the captain as he stood with a little knot of comrades on the walk. There was instant demand that he should open it and show the picture to them, but, blushing like a girl, he broke away and hid himself in his room; and then, when sure of being uninterrupted, he took it to the window and feasted his eyes upon the exquisite face and form there portrayed. He kept it from that time in a silken case, which he locked in a bureau drawer whenever he left the house, but in the evenings, or when writing at his desk, he brought it forth to light again and set it where every moment he could look upon and almost worship it.

And then came her letters announcing their safe arrival at Deer Park:

"Our journey was most trying, for the heat was intolerable until we got well up among the mountains. Papa came; but I know he is simply fretting his heart out with anxiety to get back to the office. Mr. Clark only returned from his vacation the day we started. Gordon Noel came down to the train to see us off, and brought mother a basket of such luscious fruit. He says that he has no home to go to, now that we are gone. Indeed, he has been very thoughtful and kind, and I don't think he is quite happy, despite his efforts to be always gay and cheerful. . . .

"Do you really mean that you will be gone a fortnight? How I shall miss your dear letters, Fred! And now indeed I will try to write regularly. There's no one here I care anything about, though the hotel seems very full, and there is much dancing and gayety. You say my letters will reach you; but I wonder how."

Lane read this with a sigh of relief. He had persuaded himself that it was because he dreaded the effect of the long-continued hot weather upon her that he so desired her to get to the mountains. Any other thought would have been disloyalty to his queen. He wished—just a little bit—that she had not written of him as Gordon Noel: he much preferred that she should call him Captain. She would not write so fully and frankly of him if he were anything but friendly, he argued, and she would not tolerate his visits on any other grounds. Yet she did not tell him that they had walked up and down the platform together for ten minutes before the train started, and that when it was time to part he had bent down and said, almost in a whisper,—

"Do you want to send a message for me to Fred Lane in your next letter?"

"I will do so, if you wish," she murmured; but her eyes fell before the gaze in his, and the hot blood rushed to her face.

"Tell him there's no man in all the regiment I so long to see, and no man in all the world—I so envy."

Probably conscience smote her, for during the week that followed five letters came,—five letters in seven days! His heart went wild with delight over their tenderness. The last was written Saturday, and then none came for three days; and when the fourth day came and brought the longed-for missive it was a disappointment, somehow.

"Papa left us to go back to the office last night," she wrote. "He could stand it no longer. I fear it did him little good here. The Witherses came on Saturday, and that strange girl, Miss Marshall, is with them. She always impresses me with the idea that she is striving to read my thoughts. She speaks so admiringly of you, and says you were 'so courteous' to her the night you dined at the Witherses'; and I do not remember your ever saying anything about her to me. You see, sir, I am much more communicative about my friends.

"We had such a delightful surprise Saturday night. Who should appear in the hop-room but Gordon Noel? He stayed until the midnight train Sunday; and I really was very glad to see him."

And here Lane stopped reading for a while.

XI.

For some reason or other, the scout which Lane's company had been ordered to hold itself in readiness to make was postponed, no further orders coming from Department head-quarters which required sending any troops into the mountains west of Fort Graham. The captain, far from being disappointed, seemed strangely relieved that he was not required to take his troop into the field at that particular moment. "Something had happened," said Mrs. Breese, who was a keen observer, "to change the spirit of his dream within the last few days." His face lacked the radiant and joyous look that it had had ever since he came back from the East. "Is he getting an inkling of the stories that are in circulation?" was the natural inquiry. "Is he beginning to learn that others were before him in that fair charmer's regard?" Still, no one could question him. There was something about him, with all his frankness and kindliness, that held people aloof from anything like confidence. He never had a confidant of either sex; and this was something that rendered him at one time somewhat unpopular among the women. Younger officers almost always, as a rule, had chosen some one of the married ladies of the regiment as a repositary of their cares and anxieties, their hopes and fears; but Lane had never indulged in any such luxury, and all the better for him was it. Now it was noticed with what eagerness and anxiety he watched for the coming of the mail. It was also observed that during the two weeks that followed only four letters were received in her, by this time, well-known superscription. Lane, of course, reading the contents, could readily account for the scarcity. Her letters were full of descriptions of dances and picnics and riding-parties to the neighboring mountains. They had met scores of pleasant people, and had become acquainted with a large circle from all parts of the country. They danced every evening regularly in the hop-room, and were so thoroughly acquainted, and so accustomed to one another's moods and fancies, that hardly an hour passed in which they were not occupied in some pleasant recreation. Lawn-tennis had always been a favorite game of hers, and her mother was glad, she said, to see her picking it up again with such alacrity. The open air was doing her good: her color was returning; the languor and weakness which had oppressed her when she first arrived after the long hot spell at home had disappeared entirely. But with returning health came all the longing for out-door active occupation, and, instead of having, as she had planned, hours in which to write to him, almost all her time now was taken up in joyous sports, in horseback-rides, in long drives over the mountain-roads and through the beautiful scenery by which they were surrounded. "And so," she said, "Fred, dear, in regaining health and color, I fear, your Mabel has very sadly neglected you."

His reply to her letter telling him of Mr. Noel's unexpected appearance at the Park was rather a difficult one for him to write. It was dawning upon him that the attentions of his regimental comrade to his *fiancée* were not as entirely platonic as they might be. Desire to show all courtesy and kindliness to the lady-love of another officer was all very well in its way, but it did not necessitate daily calls when at home, and far less did it warrant his leaving his station without permission—running the risk of a reprimand, or even possible court-martial—and taking a long journey, being absent from his post all Saturday and certainly not returning there before the afternoon of Monday.

If this were known at the head-quarters of the recruiting service, Lieutenant Noel in all probability would be rapped severely over the knuckles, if nothing worse. Lane could not, and would not, for an instant blame his *fiancée*, but he gently pointed out to her that Mr. Noel ran great risks in making such a journey, and that it would be well on that account to discourage similar expeditions in the future. To this she made no direct reply; but that she observed his caution is quite possible. At all events, no further mention of visits on the part of Mr. Noel appeared in any of the letters which reached him before the orders for the scout actually did arrive; but that was not until near the very end of the month. It was just about the 28th of August when rumors came of turbulence and threatened outbreak among the Indians at the Chiricahua Reservation. Troops were already marching thither from the stations in Arizona, and Captain Lane was ordered to cross the range and scout on the east side of the reservation, in order to drive back any renegades who might be tempted to "make a break." Just one day before the start he was surprised at receiving a letter from Mrs. Vincent. She spoke gladly of Mabel's improved health and appearance; she spoke hopefully of Mr. Vincent, whose letters, she said, were more cheerful than they had been, and who had been able to come up and spend two Sundays with them. Mabel had doubtless told him of Mr. Noel's visit, and how glad they were just then to see any face so pleasant and familiar. And now she wished to remind him of their contract before his leaving for the frontier. He doubtless remembered that she had promised that in the near future she would give him the reasons why it seemed best to her that the engagement should not be announced. It would take a pretty long letter to tell all the reasons why, so she would not venture upon that at the moment; but the necessity no longer existed, and if he so desired she would gladly have it now made known to his relatives, as she would now proceed to announce it to Mabel's.

Lane was greatly rejoiced at this. He had been a trifle uneasy and despondent of late, yet scarcely knew why. Her letters were not all he had hoped they would be by this time; but then he did not know but that it was all natural and right; he had never had love-letters before,—had never seen them,—and his ideas of what a woman's letters to her betrothed should be were somewhat vague and undefined. However, there was no one in the garrison to whom he specially cared to formally announce his engagement. People had ceased of late making remarks or inquiries, as nothing had been successful in extracting information from him in the past. Giving directions that his mail should be forwarded once a week, or twice a week if possible, to the railway-station nearest the Chiricahua Mountains, where he could get it by sending couriers once in a while, provided there was no danger in doing so, Lane marched away one evening on what proved to be an absence of an entire month. He never again saw Fort Graham until the end of September, and then only long enough to enable him to change from his scouting-rig into travelling costume, to throw a few clothes into a trunk, and to drive to the railway-station as fast as the ambulance could carry him, in order to catch the first express-train going East.

Nothing of very great importance had occurred on the scout. A few renegades managed to escape eastward from the reservation and to take to the mountains, through which Lane's command was then scouting; and to him and to his troop was intrusted the duty of capturing and bringing them back to the reservation. This took him many a long mile south of the railway. It was three weeks and more before he made his way to the reservation with his prisoners. There he found a small package of letters which had been forwarded direct from Graham, where they evidently knew that he would go into the Agency before reaching the railway, where his other letters were probably awaiting him. Among those which he received was one from Mr. Vincent. Briefly, it said to him, "If a possible thing, come to us as soon as you can obtain leave of absence. There are matters which excite my greatest apprehension, and I feel that I must see you. My health, I regret to say, is failing me rapidly. Come, if you can." Another was from Mrs. Vincent: she spoke with great anxiety of Mr. Vincent's waning health; said very little of Mabel, nothing whatever of Mr. Noel. She told him that the engagement had been formally announced to all their relatives, and that letters of congratulation had been showered on Mabel from all sides,—although there was some little surprise expressed that she should marry an army officer. "She, herself, has not been well at all, and I really believe that a visit from you would do much to restore her health and spirits. She has been unlike herself ever since we came back from the mountains."

In this same package of letters were two from Mabel. These he read with infinite yearning in his heart, and they only served to increase the wordless anxiety and the intolerable sense of something lacking which he had first felt after the letter that announced Gordon Noel's visit to Deer Park. One more letter there was: this he opened, saw that it was type-written and had no signature, indignantly tore it into fragments, and tossed them to the wind.

The commanding general of the Department—an old and kind friend of Lane's—was then looking over affairs for himself, at the reservation. Lane obtained a few moments' conversation with him, briefly stated his needs, and showed him Mr. Vincent's letter. The instant the general saw the signature he looked up, startled, and then arose from his seat, put his hand on the captain's shoulder, and drew him to one side.

"My dear boy," he said, "there is later news than this. It is dated September 14, you see. Have you heard nothing more?"

"Nothing, general. What has happened?" answered Lane, his voice trembling and his bronzed face rapidly paling. "Am I—am I too late?"

"I fear so, Lane. Had Mr. Vincent a partner named Clark?"

"Yes, sir,—his junior partner."

"Clark defaulted, embezzled, hypothecated securities and heaven knows what all, blew out his brains in his private office, and Mr. Vincent stumbled over the body an hour afterwards, was prostrated by the shock, and died of heart-failure three days later. The papers were full of the tragedy for nearly a week; but there are none to be had here, I'm afraid. Now you will want to start at once. Never mind your troop. Just tell your lieutenant to report here to Captain Bright for orders, and I'll have them sent back to Graham by easy marches."

Late at night Lane reached the railway, only to find his train five hours behind. He telegraphed to Mabel that he would come to her as fast as train could bring him,—that the sad news had only just reached him. He strode for hours up and down the little platform under the glittering stars, yearning to reach her, to comfort and console her in this bitter sorrow. Time and again he turned over in mind the few particulars which he had obtained from the Department commander. They were all too brief, but pointed conclusively to one fact,—that Clark had been encouraged by the success of June to plunge still more deeply, in the hope of retrieving the losses of the past two years. Luckily for Vincent, he had used his June winnings in lifting the mortgage from his homestead and in taking up any of his outstanding paper, and so had little wherewith to supply his confident partner; but Lane wondered if the kindly old man had any idea that up to the end of August, at least, Clark had not sent to him, as directed, "the draft for the entire amount" to which referred the first letter Mr. Vincent had ever written him.

It was daybreak when the train came. It was noon when he sprang from the cars at Graham Station and into the ambulance sent to meet him in response to his telegraphic request. Were there any letters? he eagerly asked. None now. A small package had been forwarded to the reservation last night, and must have passed him on the way. Others had been waiting for him at the mountain-station until he was reported by wire as arriving with his prisoners at the Agency. Everything then had been sent thither, and there would be no getting them before starting. At Graham the telegraph operator showed him the duplicates of the telegrams that had come for him in his absence,—only two. One announced Mr. Clark's suicide and Vincent's prostration and danger; the other, two days later, briefly read, "Mr. Vincent died this morning. Mrs. Vincent and Mabel fairly well."

Both were signed "Gordon Noel," and a jealous pang shot through the poor fellow's heart as he realized that in all their bereavement and grief it was Noel's privilege to be with them and to be of use to them, while he, her affianced husband, was far beyond hail. He was ashamed of his own thoughts an instant after, and bitterly upbraided himself that he was not thankful that they could have had so attentive and thoughtful an aid as Noel well knew how to be. Yet—why was not Reginald sufficient?

He had torn into fragments the anonymous sheet that had met him at the reservation, and yet its words were gnawing at his heartstrings now, and he could not crush them down:

"Why was your engagement denied? Because she still cared for Will Rossiter and hoped he might come back to her after all.

"Why did Gordon Noel stay at the other hotel the second and third times he spent Sunday at Deer Park? Because she wished to hide from her mother, as she did from you, that he came at all.

"Why does she meet him on the street instead of at home? Because her father interposed in your behalf; but all the same you are being betrayed."

These words—or others exactly of their import, were what met his startled eyes at Chiricahua, but the instant he noted that these carefully type-written sentences were followed by no signature at all,—not even the oft-abused "A Friend,"—indignation and wrath followed close on the heels of his amaze, and in utter contempt he had destroyed the cowardly sheet; but he could not so easily conquer the poison thus injected in his veins. All the long, long journey to the East they haunted him, dancing before his eyes, sleeping or waking, and it was with haggard face and wearied frame that he reached the Queen City, and, taking a cab, drove at once to her home.

It was a lovely evening in early October. The sun had been shining brilliantly all day long, and almost everywhere doors and windows were open to woo the cool air now gently stirring. The cab stopped before the well-remembered steps, and Lane hastened to the broad door-way. No need to ring: the portals stood invitingly open. The gas burned brightly in the hall and in the sitting-room to the left. He entered unhesitatingly, and stood all alone in the room where he had spent so many happy hours listening to the music of her voice, watching the play and animation in her lovely face. He caught a glimpse of his own, gaunt, haggard, hollow-eyed, in the mirror over the old-fashioned mantel. What was he, that he should have won a creature so radiant, so exquisite, as the girl who had made these silent rooms a heaven to him? There was the heavy portière that shut off the little passage to the library. His foot-fall made no sound in the deep, rich carpeting. It was there she welcomed him that wonderful Friday afternoon,—that day that was the turning-point, the climax, of his life. Hark! was that her voice, low, sweet, tremulous, in there now? Hush! Was that a sob?—a woman's suppressed weeping? Quickly he stepped forward, and in an instant had thrust aside the second portière; but he halted short at the threshold, petrified by the scene before him.

Mabel Vincent, clasped in Gordon Noel's embrace, her arms about his neck, gazing up into his face with almost worship in her weeping eyes, raised her lips to meet the passionate kiss of his. "My darling," he murmured, "what can you fear? Have you not given *me* the right to protect you?" And the handsome head was tossed proudly back and for one little minute was indeed heroic. Then, with instantaneous change, every drop of blood fled from his face, leaving it ashen, death-like.

"*Gordon!*" she cried, "what is it? Are you ill?"

Then, following the glance of his staring eyes, she turned, and saw, and swooned away.

XII.

A dreary winter was that of 188- at old Fort Graham. Captain Breese became major of the —th, and his troop was ordered to exchange with K, which had been so long at head-quarters, and this brought old Jim Rawlins up to take command of the little cavalry battalion at "the oasis." There were many of the officers—Rawlins among them—who thought that after his success with "the Devil's Own," as D Troop had been called, Lane was entitled to enjoy the position of battalion commander; but Mrs. Riggs had promptly asserted her belief that he was not in position to enjoy anything. He had come back to the post late in the fall, looking some years older and graver; he had been very ill at Jefferson Barracks, said letters from that point, while waiting to take out a party of recruits to the regiment; he had resumed duty without a word to anybody of the matters that had so suddenly called him East, but there was no need of telling: they knew all about it; at least they said and thought they did. Mrs. Riggs had had such complete accounts from Noel, and had received such a sweet letter from Miss Vincent in reply to the one she had written congratulating her upon her engagement to *her* (Mrs. Riggs's) "*favorite among all the officers*,—and the colonel's, too." "She was so sorry—so painfully distressed—about Captain Lane," said Mrs. Riggs. "She never really cared for him. It was gratitude and propinquity, and pleasure in his attentions, that she mistook for love; but she never knew what love was until she met Gordon. They were to be married early in the spring, and would take only a brief tour, for he had to be at his station. She dreaded coming to the regiment, though she would follow Gordon to the end of the world if he said so, for she knew there were people who would blame her for breaking with Captain Lane as she had to; but she knew long before she did so that they could never be happy together. She had written to him, telling him all, long before he came East and they had that dreadful scene in which Mr. Noel had behaved with such perfect self-command and such excessive consideration for Captain Lane's feelings. Of course, as Gordon said, all possibility of reconciliation or future friendship between them was at an end unless Captain Lane humbly apologized. She had been mercifully spared hearing it; for the fearful expression of his face when they discovered him listening at the portière had caused her to faint away, and she only came to, Gordon said, in time to prevent his pitching him out of the window, so utterly was he tried. She was so thankful to have in Mrs. Riggs a friend who would not see Gordon wronged, and who could be counted on to deny any stories that poor Captain Lane in his disappointment might put in circulation."

But Lane never mentioned the subject. As for the letters to which she referred, they all followed him East in one bundle and were sent to her unopened; and she knew when she wrote to Mrs. Riggs that, though she might have "told him all," as she said, he never knew a word of it until his eyes and ears revealed the truth that wretched night in the library where his brief, sweet love-dream began and ended.

There were other matters wherein Mr. Noel himself was consulting Mrs. Riggs. He was now senior first lieutenant. Any accident of service might make him a captain, and then, if precedent were followed, "he might be ordered to join at once. Ordinarily, as she well knew, nothing would give him greater joy; but now—solely on Mabel's account—he hesitated. A friend at the War Department had said that, if Colonel Riggs would approve, a six months' leave to visit Europe, for the purpose of prosecuting his professional studies, might be obtained. Would she kindly, etc., etc."

There was no one to write or speak for Lane: only one side of the story was being told, and, though the men had had little else than contempt for Noel, they were of small account in moulding garrison opinions as compared with two or three determined women.

But no one saw the sorrowful, almost heart-broken, letter written by Mrs. Vincent to Lane. She had no words in which to speak of Mabel's conduct. They had both been deceived; and yet she implored him for forgiveness for her child. The world was all changed now. Their home remained to them, and her own little fortune, together with the wreck of Mr. Vincent's, but Regy had to go out into the world and seek to earn what he could. He had no idea of business. There was no one to step in and build up the old firm, and the executors had advised that everything be closed out. Mr. Clark's affairs had been left in lamentable confusion, but luckily he had nothing else to leave,— nothing, that is, but confusion and creditors. People were constantly importuning her for payment of his liabilities, claiming that they were contracted by the firm. Her lawyers absolutely forbade her listening to such demands. If she paid one-fourth of them she would have nothing left. Lane thought of his sacrificed Cheyenne property and the little fortune he had so freely offered up to save to the girl he loved the home in which she had been reared. The very roof under which the girl had plighted her troth to him and then dishonored it for Noel—under which, day after day, she was now receiving, welcoming, caressing him—was practically rescued for her and her mother by the money of the man she had cast aside.

The wedding-cards came in April. It was to be a quiet affair, because of the death of Mr. Vincent within the year. Lane read the announcement in the *Army and Navy Journal,* and sat for a while, the paper dropping to the floor and his head upon his hands. Elsewhere in its columns he found a full account, written evidently by some one thoroughly well acquainted with all the parties, except perhaps the gallant groom.

When Lane's servant tiptoed in at reveille the next morning to prepare the bath and black the boots, he was surprised to find that officer sitting at his desk with his head pillowed in his arms. He had not been to bed, and did not know that reveille had sounded. Was he ill? Did he need the doctor? No. He had to sit up late over some letters and papers, and had finally fallen asleep there. All the same Dr. Gowen, happening into the hospital while Lane was visiting one of his men after sick-call, stopped, and keenly examined his face.

"I want you to go right to your quarters and stay there, Lane, for you've got a fever, and, I believe, mountain fever," were his immediate orders. "I'll be with you in a moment." It was only the beginning of what proved to be a trying illness of several weeks' duration. When Lane was able to sit up again, it was the recommendation of the post-surgeon and of his regimental commander that he be sent East on sick-leave for at least three months. And the first week of June found him at West Point: he had many old and warm friends there, and their companionship and cordiality cheered him greatly. One night, strolling back from parade to the broad piazza of the hotel, he saw the stage drive up from the landing and a number of visitors scurry up the steps in haste to escape the prying eyes of the older arrivals, who invariably thronged the south piazza at such times and curiously inspected the travel-stained and cinder-spotted faces of those whose ill luck it was to have to run that social gauntlet. There was something familiar in the face of a young lady following a portly matron into the hall, and when a moment later he came upon the massive frame of Mr. Amos

Withers, registering himself, his wife, daughters, and Miss Marshall, of the Queen City, Lane knew at once that it was his friend of the dismal dinner of nearly a year ago. Later that evening he met her in the hall, and was surprised at the prompt and pleasant recognition which she gave him. It was not long before they were on the north piazza, watching that peerless view up the Hudson, and, finding that she had never been there before and was enthusiastic in her admiration of the scenery, Lane took pleasure in pointing out to her the various objects of interest that could be seen through the brilliant sheen of moonlight. And so, having made himself at once useful and entertaining, he finally went to his bed with a sensation of having passed rather a brighter evening than he had known in a long, long time.

On the following day Miss Marshall was in the hall, reading, when he came out from breakfast. She was waiting, she said, for Mrs. Withers to come down. The nurse was dressing the children.

"I want to ask you something, Captain Lane. I saw Mrs. Vincent just before I left home, and had a little talk with her. She has always been very kind to me. Did you ever receive a letter she wrote to you three or four weeks ago?"

"I never did," said Lane. "Do you think that she did write to me?"

"I know she did. She told me so, and expressed great surprise that you had accorded her no answer. She felt very sure of your friendship, and she was at a loss to understand your silence. Although I had only met you once or twice before, I felt that I knew you so well that you could not refuse to answer a letter from so lovable a woman as she, and I deemed it my duty to let you know what she had told me. I am very glad now that I did so."

"Is she at home?" asked Lane, eagerly.

"She was when I left, but they were expecting to go to the mountains. Mrs. Noel seems to be drooping a little. The weather is very warm there already, as you know, and the doctor has advised that both ladies go up to Deer Park. Mrs. Noel doesn't wish to go, as it takes her so far from her husband; but, as he was able to get there quite frequently when they were there before, I see no reason why he should not be able to join them every week now."

"Was he there frequently when they were there before?" asked Lane, an old, dull pain gnawing at his heart.

"He was there three or four times to my knowledge during our stay, but of course his visits were very brief: he came generally Saturday and went away at midnight Sunday."

"I will go and telegraph to Mrs. Vincent. If need be, I will go and see her; and I thank you very much, Miss Marshall."

That evening he received a despatch from Mrs. Vincent in response to the one sent almost immediately after this conversation. "If possible, come here. I greatly desire to see you. Wire answer." What could it mean?

By the first train on the following morning he left for New York, and was far on his way to the Queen City when sunset came. Arriving there, he went first to the old hotel, and, after changing his dress and removing the stains of travel, for the first time since his memorable visit of October he mounted the broad stone steps and asked to see Mrs. Vincent. She came down almost instantly, and Lane was shocked to see how she had failed since their last meeting. Years seemed to have been added to her age; her hair was gray; the lines in her gentle, patient face had deepened. She entered, holding forth both hands, but when she looked into his eyes her lips quivered and she burst into tears. Lane half led, half supported her to a chair, and, drawing one to her side, spoke soothingly to her. For a few moments she could not speak, and when she did he checked her.

"Oh, you too have aged and suffered! and it is all our doing,—all our doing!" she moaned, as her tears burst forth anew.

"Never mind my crow's-feet and gray hairs, dear lady," he said. "It is high time I began to show signs of advancing age. Then, too, I am just up from a siege of mountain fever."

"Was that the reason you did not answer?" she presently asked.

"I never got your letter, Mrs. Vincent. When was it mailed?"

"About the 10th of May. I remember it well, because—it was just after Mabel and Captain Noel got back from their tour."

"Pardon me, but did you post it yourself?"

"No. The postman always takes my letters. I leave them on the little table in the vestibule."

"Where any one can see them?"

"Yes; but who would touch my letters?"

Lane did not know, of course. He was only certain that nothing from Mrs. Vincent had reached him during the past six months.

"Captain Lane," she said, at last, "I want you to tell me the truth. Just after Mabel's marriage I heard that a story was in circulation to

D*

the effect that it was your money that enabled Mr. Vincent to tide over the crisis in his affairs a year ago. It was even said that you had sold property at a loss to supply him with means; and some people in society are so cruel as to say that Mabel's trousseau was actually purchased with your money, because it had never been repaid. I know that Mr. Vincent often spoke of his obligation and gratitude to you. Tell me truly and frankly, Captain Lane: did you give my husband money? Is this story true?"

"I never gave Mr. Vincent a cent."

"Oh, I am so thankful! We have been the means of bringing such sorrow to you——"

"I beg you, make no reference to that, Mrs. Vincent. Neither your honored husband nor you have I ever thought in the least responsible. And as for this other matter, you have been misinformed."

"What cruel, reckless stories people tell! It hurt me terribly; and then when no answer came to my letter I felt that probably there was something in it, and that you were hiding the truth from me. Mabel heard it too; but she said that Captain Noel investigated it at once and found that it was utterly false. I could not be satisfied until I had your own assurance."

"And now you have it," he said, with a smile that shone on his worn face and beamed about his deep-set eyes like sunshine after April showers. "You are going to be advised now, are you not, and seek change and rest in the mountains?"

"We meant to go this week; but Mrs. Paterson, of Philadelphia, is urging us to spend the summer with her at the sea-shore, where she has a roomy cottage. She is a cousin of Captain Noel's, and was an intimate friend of Mabel's at school. That was where my daughter first heard of him. Oh, I wish—I wish——"

And here once more Mrs. Vincent's tears poured forth, and it was some time before she could control herself.

At last the captain felt that he must go. It was now his purpose to leave town as soon as he could attend to one or two matters of business:

"Shall I not see you again?" she asked, as he rose to take his leave.

"I fear not," he answered. "There is nothing to require more than an hour or two of attention here, and then I shall seek a cooler spot for a few weeks' rest, then back to the regiment."

"But we—that is, I heard you had three months' sick-leave."

"Very true; but I only need one, and I am best with my troop."

"Tell me," she asked: "is it true that there is trouble brewing again among the Indians,—at San Carlos, isn't it?"

"There seems to be bad blood among them, and no doubt disaffection; but if sufficient troops are sent to the Agency and to scout around the reservation they can be held in check."

"But I have been told that you have too small a force to watch them. I wish you were not going back; but it is like you, Captain Lane."

And so they parted. He saw and heard and asked nothing of his whilom *fiancée*. He did not wish to see her husband. He meant to have left town that very evening, after brief consultation with a real-estate agent whom he had had occasion to employ in his service; but even as he was stowing his travelling-"kit" in a roomy leather bag there came a knock at his door and there entered a man in plain civilian dress, who motioned the bell-boy to clear out, and then held forth a photograph:

"Captain Lane, is that your man Taintor?"

"That is certainly like the man," was Lane's answer, after careful inspection. "Have you got him?"

"No, sir. We had him, and took Captain Noel to see him, and the captain said there was some mistake. He wears his hair and beard different now; but we know where he is,—at least, where he was up to yesterday. He left his lodgings at noon, and took a bag with him, as though he meant to be away a few days. He does copying and type-writing, and manages to get along and support a good-looking young woman who passes as his wife. *That's* what we think brought him back here last winter."

"Why didn't you take some of the recruiting-party to see him? They could identify him."

"All the old men that were with you are gone, sir. It's a new lot entirely. They said the sergeant couldn't get along with the captain at all, and they were all sent away."

"Where's the woman who kept the lodging-house for the party?"

"She's gone too, sir. They moved away last winter because Captain Noel gave the contract to another party in a different part of the town. We let the thing slide for quite a while; but when the Chief heard that you had arrived in town he thought he'd shadow the fellow until you could see him, but he had skipped. Was there any way he could have heard you were coming?"

"No. I telegraphed from West Point to Mrs. Vincent. She was the only one who knew."

"Beg pardon, sir, but isn't that Captain Noel's mother-in-law? The captain lives there, I think."

Lane turned sharply and studied the man's face. A question was at his very tongue's end,—"You do not suppose *he* could have given warning?"—but he stifled it, his lips compressing tight.

"If you think he has gone because of my coming, I will leave on the late train, as I purposed, and you can wire to me when he returns. Then keep him shadowed until I get here."

And with this understanding they parted, Lane going at once to a cool resort on one of the great lakes. Four days later came the despatch he looked for, and, accompanied by two detectives, Lane knocked at the indicated door-way one bright, sunshiny afternoon within forty-eight hours thereafter.

A comely young woman opened the door just a few inches and inquired what was wanted. "Mr. Graves was not at home." He certainly would not have been in a minute more, for a man swung out of the third-story window, and, going hand by hand down the convenient lightning-rod, dropped into the arms of a waiting officer, and that night the forger and deserter spent behind the bars in the Central Station. The identification was complete.

Lane was to appear and make formal charge against him the following morning. Going down to an early breakfast, he picked up one of the great dailies at the news-stand, and, after taking his seat at table and ordering a light repast, he opened the still moist sheet. The first glance at the head-lines was enough to start him to his feet. "Indian Outbreak." "The Apaches on the War-Path." "Murder of Agent Curtis at San Carlos." "Massacre of a Stage-Load of Passengers." "Captain Rawlins, Eleventh Cavalry, a victim." "Horrible Atrocities." "Troops in Pursuit."

It was the old, old story briefly told. Warnings disregarded; official reports of the neighboring troop-commanders pooh-poohed and pigeon-holed by functionaries of the Indian Bureau; a sudden, startling rush of one body upon the agent and his helpless family; a simultaneous dash from the other end of the reservation upon the scattered ranches in the valley; a stage-coach ambushed; a valued old soldier butchered in cold blood. There was no more thought of breakfast for Lane. He hurried to the telegraph-office, thence to the police-station, thence to an attorney whom he was advised to employ, and by noon he was whirling westward. "No laggard he" when the war-cry rang along the blazing border.

XIII.

The *Morning Chronicle,* a most valuable sheet in its way, in its Sunday edition contained the following interesting item:

" No event in social circles has eclipsed of late the banquet given at the club last night in honor of Captain Gordon Noel, of the Eleventh Cavalry, on the eve of his departure to take command of his troop, now hastening to the scene of Indian hostilities in Arizona. As is well known to our citizens, the news of the murderous outbreak at the reservation was no sooner received than this gallant officer applied instantly to be relieved from his present duties in our midst and ordered to join his comrades in the field, that he might share with them the perils of this savage warfare.

" Covers were laid for forty. The table was decorated with flowers and glistened with plate and crystal. The most conspicuous device was the crossed sabres of the cavalry, with the number 11 and the letter K, that being the designation of the captain's company. His honor Mayor Jenness presided, and the Hon. Amos Withers faced him at the other end of the banquet-board. The speech of the evening was made by Mayor Jenness in toasting 'our gallant guest,' which was drunk standing and with all honors. We have room only for a brief summary of his remarks. Alluding to the previous distinguished services of the captain, he said that 'In every Territory of our broad West his sabre has flashed in the defence of the weak against the strong, the poor settler against the powerful and numerous savage tribes too often backed by official influence at Washington. And now, while cheeks were blanching and hearts were still stricken by the dread news of the butcheries and rapine which marked the Indians' flight, when others shrank from such perilous work, where was the man who could suppress the fervent admiration with which he heard that there was one soldier who lost no time in demanding relief from duty here, that he might speed to the head of the gallant fellows already in the field, who had followed him in many a stirring charge and through all "the current of many a heady fight;" whose hearts would leap for joy at sight of their beloved leader's face,—the man who never yet had failed them, the man who never yet had faltered in his duty, the man whose sword was never drawn without reason, never sheathed without honor,—our soldier guest, Captain Gordon Noel?'

"Much affected, it was some minutes before the captain could respond. The modesty of the true soldier restrained his eloquence. 'He knew not how to thank them for this most flattering testimony of their confidence and regard; he far from deserved the lavish praise of their honored chairman. If in the past he had succeeded in winning their esteem, all the more would he try to merit it now. No soldier could remain in security when such desperate deeds called his comrades to the fray; and as he had ever shared their dangers in the old days, so must he share them now. His heart, his home, his bride, to part from whom was bitter trial, he left with them to guard and cherish. Duty called him to the front, and with to-morrow's sun he would be on his way. But, if it pleased God to bear him safely through, he would return to them, to greet and grasp each friendly hand again, and meantime to prove himself worthy the high honor they had done him.'

"There was hardly a dry eye at the table when the gallant soldier finished his few remarks and then took his seat.

"Besides winning the heart and hand of one of the loveliest of the Queen City's daughters, the captain has made hosts of friends in our midst, and we predict that when the records of the campaign are written no name will shine with brighter lustre than that of Gordon Noel."

This doubtless was delightful reading to Noel and to Noel's relatives. Doubtless, too, it was some comfort to poor Mabel as she lay pale, anxious, sore at heart on the following day, while her husband and lover—as he undoubtedly was—sped westward with the fast express. But there was a great deal about the *Chronicle's* account that would have elicited something more than a broad grin from officers who knew Noel well.

An entire week had elapsed from the time that the first tidings were received to the moment when he finally and most reluctantly left the Queen City. The first intimation was enough to start Captain Lane, despite the fact that his health was far from restored and that he was yet by no means strong. He felt confident that the Indians would be joined by some of the Chiricahuas, and that the campaign would be fierce and stubborn. Telegraphing to the regimental adjutant and the general commanding the department that he intended to start at once, and asking to be notified *en route* where he could most speedily join the troop, he was on his way within six hours.

That very night, although no mention was made of this in the *Chronicle* account, Captain Noel received a despatch from the Adjutant-General's Office at Washington briefly to this effect: "You become Captain of K Company, *vice* Rawlins, murdered by Apaches. Hold yourself in readiness to turn over the rendezvous and join your regiment without delay." No news could have been more unwelcome. Despite his many faults, there was no question that Gordon Noel was very much in love with his wife; but he never had been in love with the active part of his profession. That night he telegraphed to relatives who had stood by him in the past, and wrote urgent and pleading letters informing them that his wife's health was in so delicate a state that if he were compelled at this moment to leave her and to go upon perilous duty in the Apache country there was no telling what might be the effect upon her. If a possible thing, he urged that there should be a delay of a fortnight. He calculated that by that time the Indians would either be safe across the Mexican border or whipped back to the reservation; then he could go out and join with a flourish of trumpets and no possible danger. But a new king reigned in the War Department, who knew Joseph rather than knew him not. In some way the honorable Secretary had become acquainted with the previous history of Captain Noel's campaign services, and, though the influential gentlemen referred to made prompt and eloquent appeal, they were met by courteous but positive denial. "Every man who was worth his salt," said the Secretary, "should be with his regiment now." An officer was designated to proceed at once to the Queen City and take over Noel's rendezvous and property, and peremptory orders were sent to him to start without delay and to notify the department by telegraph of the date of his departure,—a most unusual and stringent proceeding. This correspondence Noel never mentioned to anybody at the time, and it was known only to the official records for some time afterwards. As soon as he found that go he must, he dictated to his clerk a letter in which, gallant soldier that he was, he informed the Adjutant-General that the news from Arizona had now convinced him that an outbreak of alarming dimensions had taken place, and he begged that he might be relieved as at his own request and permitted to join his comrades in the field. To this no reply was sent, as the order directing him to proceed had already been issued. Perhaps a grim smile played about the moustached lips of that functionary when he read this spirited epistle.

Noel left the Queen City a hero in the eyes of the populace. He was just six days behind Lane, of whose movements the Queen City had no information whatever.

And now came an odd piece of luck,—a slip in the fortunes of war. The cavalry stationed in Arizona were so far from the reservation at the time that they had long and difficult marches to make. Only two or three troops that happened to be along the line of the railway reached the mountains neighboring San Carlos in time to quickly take the trail of the hostiles. Except the one little troop of cavalry on duty at the reservation, none of the horsemen in Arizona had as yet come in actual conflict with the renegades, and, oddly enough, it was the Eleventh that first met and struck them. Old Riggs himself had not taken the field, but the battalion from head-quarters had been whirled westward along the railway and actually reached the pass through the Chiricahua Range before the Indians. Expecting just such a possibility, these wary campaigners had their scouts far in advance of the main body, and prompt warning was given, so that only the rear-guard of the Indians was reached by the eager cavalrymen; the bulk of the Apaches turned eastward and swept down like ravening wolves upon the defenceless settlers in the San Simon Valley, burning, murdering, pillaging as they went, full fifty miles a day, while their pursuers trailed helplessly behind. When they had succeeded in crossing the railway most of their number were mounted on fresh horses, and the section-hands, who saw them from afar off, telegraphed from the nearest station that they had with them six or eight women and children whose husbands and fathers doubtless lay weltering in their blood along the route. Full seven days now had they been dodging through the mountains and swooping down upon the ranchmen, and so skilfully had they eluded their pursuers and defeated their combinations that now they had a commanding lead and actually nothing between them and the Mexican frontier,—nothing in Arizona, that is to say. But look just across the border. There, spurring steadily southwestward until halted for the night in San Simon Pass, comes a little troop of cavalry, not more than thirty-five in number. All day long since earliest dawn had they ridden across the burning sands of a desert region; lips, nostrils, eyelids smarting with alkali-dust, throats parched with thirst, temples throbbing with the intense heat; several men and horses used up and left behind were now slowly plodding back towards the railway. Look

at the letter one of those leaders wears upon his worn old scouting-hat,
—D. Yes, it is the "Devil's own D's," and Lane is at their head.

At the moment of the outbreak, both companies from Graham, K and D, or strong detachments from both, were scouting through the country,—one through the northern Peloncillo Range, the other far up among the head-waters of the Gila. Not a word did they hear of the trouble until it was several days old; then D Troop was amazed by the sudden appearance of their captain in their midst,—Lane, whom they supposed to be on sick-leave far in the distant East. It was then for the first time they learned how their comrades of K Troop had lost their popular old commander, and that the great outbreak had occurred at San Carlos. Stopping only long enough to cram their pouches with ammunition and to draw more rations, the troop hastened away towards the railroad by way of Graham, and at the station, just at dawn, Lane sent a brief despatch to the commanding general saying that he was pushing with all speed to head the Indians off *via* San Simon Pass. He had then forty-five men and horses, in fair condition. K Troop would reach Graham that evening, and he urged that they be sent at once to reinforce him. This despatch "the Chief" received with an emphatic slap of his thigh and an expression of delight: "Bless that fellow Lane! he is always in the nick of time. I had not hoped for an instant that either D or K would be available, and now look," he said to his aide-de-camp, "he has started for San Simon Pass, and will probably throw himself across their front. Only I wish he had more men."

"Shall I wire to Graham to have K rush after him, sir?"

"Yes. Order them to start the instant they can refit, and not to take more than an hour in doing that. They have been having easy work on their scout,—probably taking it leisurely all the time; they ought to be in first-rate trim. D, on the contrary, has been making long and rapid marches to get down from the Upper Gila. Where was K at last accounts?"

"Couriers had gone to the Upper Peloncillo for them several days ago, and, as Lane says, they are expected at Graham this evening. Lane, himself, rode after his own men two hours after he got to the post from the East, and Noel, who is K's new captain, is due at Graham Station to-night."

"Then send him orders to lead his troop instantly, follow and support Lane. Tell him not to lose a moment on the way. Everything may depend upon his promptness and zeal."

And so it happened that when Captain Noel stepped from the train that afternoon at the old station the telegraph messenger came forward to meet him, touching his cap and saying, "This despatch has been awaiting you, sir, since eleven o'clock this morning. I have just had a despatch from the post, and K Troop got in two hours ago and is already starting. Lieutenant Mason says an orderly is coming ahead with a horse and the captain's field-kit. Shall I wire for anything else?"

Noel opened the despatch which had been handed him, and read it with an expression that plainly indicated perturbation, if not dismay. He had not been in saddle for an entire year.

"Why, I must go out to the post!" he said to the operator. "I am not at all ready to take the field. Let them know that I have arrived, and will come out there without delay. Better have the troop unsaddled and wait for my coming."

"Will the captain pardon me?" said the operator; "the orders from the Department commander that went through this morning were that the troop should not take more than an hour in refitting at the post and should start at once. I thought I could see them coming over the divide just as the whistle blew."

The captain's face gave no sign of enthusiasm as he received this news. He was still pondering over the contents of his despatch from the commanding general,—its tone was so like that of his order from the War Department,—so utterly unlike what his admiring circle of relatives and friends would have expected. Stepping into the telegraph-office, he took some blanks and strove to compose a despatch that would convince the general that he was wild with eagerness to ride all night to the support of Lane, and yet that would explain how absolutely necessary it was that he should first go out to the post. But the Fates were against him. Even as he was gnawing the pencil and cudgelling his brains, the operator called out,—

"Here come some of 'em now, sir."

And, looking nervously from the window, Noel saw three horsemen galloping in to the station. Foremost came a lieutenant of infantry, who sprang to the ground and tossed the reins to his orderly the instant he neared the platform. One of the men had a led horse, completely equipped for the field, with blankets, saddle-bags, carbine canteen, and haversack; and Noel's quick intuition left him no room to believe that the steed was intended for any one but him.

The infantryman came bounding in: "Is this Captain Noel? I am Mr. Renshaw, post-adjutant, sir, and I had hoped to get here in time to meet you on your arrival, but we were all busy getting the troop ready. You've got your orders, sir, haven't you? My God! captain, *can't* you wire to the fort and beg the major to let me go with you? I'll be your slave for a lifetime. I've never had a chance to do a bit of real campaigning yet, and no man could ask a bullier chance than this. Excuse me, sir, I know you want to get right into scouting rig, —Mr. Mason said his 'extras' would fit you exactly,—but if you could take me along—you're bound to get there just in time for the thick of it." And the gallant little fellow looked, all eagerness, into Noel's unresponsive face. What wouldn't the hero of the Queen City Club have given to turn the whole thing over to this ambitious young soldier and let him take his chances of "glory or the grave"!

"Very thoughtful of you all, I'm sure, to think of sending horse and kit here for me, but I really ought to go out to the post. There are things I must attend to. You see, I left the instant I could induce them to relieve me, and there was no time to make preparations."

"But—you can't have heard, captain: your troop will be here in ten minutes. Captain Lane by this time is past Pyramid Mountain, and will strike them early in the morning. There won't be any time to go out to the post: you've got to ride at trot or gallop most of the night as it is——"

"Captain Noel, pardon me, sir," interposed the operator. "The general is in the office at Wilcox Station. He wants to know if you have started from here."

"Tell him the troop isn't here yet. I—I'm waiting for it."

"Yonder comes the troop, sir," called out Mr. Renshaw, who had run to the door. "Now let me help you off with your 'cits.' Bring that canvas bag in here, orderly."

Three minutes brought a message from "the Chief:" "Lose not a moment on the way. Report here by wire the arrival of your troop and the moment you start. Behind time now."

Poor Noel! There was no surgeon to certify that his pallid cheeks were due to impaired heart-action, no senatorial cousin to beg for staff duty, no Mrs. Riggs to interpose. He had just time to send a despatch to Mabel announcing that he took the field at the head of his troop at once, another (collect) to Amos Withers, Esq., of similar import, and one to the general, saying that at 4.45 they were just on the point of starting, when the troop, fifty strong and in splendid trim, came trotting in, and Mr. Mason grimly saluted his new captain and fell back to the command of the first platoon.

"Noel to the Front!" was the *Chronicle*'s head-line on the following morning far away in the Queen City.

XIV.

Not an instant too soon, although he has ridden hard since earliest dawn, has Lane reached the rocky pass. North and south the Peloncillos are shrouded in the gloom of coming night, and all over the arid plain to the eastward darkness has settled down. In previous scouts he has learned the country well, and he knows just where to turn for "tanks" of cool water for horses, mules, and men,—the cavalry order of precedence when creature comforts are to be doled out. He knows just where to conceal his little force in the recesses of the rocks and let them build tiny fires and make their coffee and then get such rest as is possible before the coming day; but there is no rest for him. Taking two veteran soldiers with him, and leaving the troop to the command of his lieutenant, an enthusiastic young soldier only a year out of the cadet gray, the captain rides westward through the gloaming. He must determine at once whether the Indians are coming towards the pass by which the San Simon makes its burst through the range, or whether, having made wide *détour* around the little post at Bowie among the Chiricahua Mountains, they are now heading southward again and taking the shortest line to the border before seeking to regain once more their old trail along the San Bernardino. How often have their war-parties gone to and fro along those rocky banks, unmolested, unpursued!

And now, secure in the belief that they have thrown all the cavalry far to the rear in the "stern-chase" which no Apache dreads, well knowing how easily he can distance his hampered pursuers, the renegades, joined by a gang of the utterly "unreconstructed" Chiricahuas, are taking things easily and making raids on the helpless ranches that lie to the right or left of their line of march. Fortunately for the records, these are few in number; had there been dozens more they would only have served to swell the list of butchered men, of plundered ranches, of burning stacks and corrals, of women and children borne off to be the sport of their leisure hours when once secure in the fastnesses of the Sierra Madres far south of the line. Death could not too soon come to the relief of these poor creatures, and Lane and all his men had been spurred to the utmost effort by the story of the railway-hands that they had plainly seen several women and children bound to the spare animals the renegades drove along across the iron track.

Among the passengers in the pillaged stage-coach were the wife and daughter of an Indian agent, who had only recently come to this arid Territory and knew little of the ways of its indigenous people. Nothing had since been seen or heard of them. Captain Rawlins and two soldiers going up as witnesses before a court-martial at Grant were found hacked almost beyond recognition, and the driver too, who seemed to have crawled out among the rocks to die. Verily the Apaches had good reason to revel in their success! They had hoodwinked the Bureau, dodged the cavalry, plundered right and left until they were rich with spoil, and now, well to the south of the railway, with a choice of either east or west side of the range, their main body and prisoners are halted to rest the animals, while miles to the rear their faithful vedettes keep watch against pursuers, and miles out to the west the most active young warriors are crying havoc at the ranch of Tres Hermanos. It is the red glare of the flame towards the sunset horizon that tells Lane the Apaches cannot be far away. The instant he and his comrades issue from the gorge and peer cautiously to the right and left, not only do they see the blaze across the wide valley, but northward, not more than half a mile away, there rises upon the night-wind a sound that they cannot mistake,—the war-chant of the Chiricahuas.

"Thank God," cries Lane, " we are here ahead of them !"

Half an hour's reconnoissance reveals to him their position. Far up among the boulders of the range, where pursuing horsemen cannot rush upon them in the night, they have made their bivouac, and are having a revel and feast while awaiting the return of the raiders or news from the rear that they must be moving. The range is rugged and precipitous north of the gorge; cavalry cannot penetrate it; but Lane's plan is quickly laid. He will let his men sleep until two o'clock, keeping only three sentries on the lookout, one of them mounted and west of the gorge to give warning should the Indians move during the night.

Then, leaving the horses concealed among the rocks south of the stream, with two men to guard them, he will lead his company up the heights and as close as possible to the Apache camp, lie in hiding until it is light enough to distinguish objects, then dash down into their midst, rescue the prisoners in the panic and confusion that he knows will result from the sudden attack, send them back as rapidly as possible, guided by three or four men, to where his horses are corralled, while he and his little band interpose between them and any rally the Apaches may make.

Knowing well that they are armed with magazine rifles and supplied by a paternal Bureau with abundant ammunition, knowing that they outnumber him three to one, knowing that by sunrise the whole tribe will have reassembled and must infallibly detect the pitiful weakness of his own force, it is a desperate chance to take; but it is the only one —absolutely the only one—to save those tortured, agonized women, those terror-stricken little ones, from a fate more awful than words can portray.

By eight or nine in the morning, he argues, K Troop must certainly reach him; he knows them to be fresh and strong, he knows that they have had only short and easy marches and therefore can easily come ahead all night long and be rounding the Pyramid Spur by daybreak. He knows Mason well, and can count on that young officer's doing his "level best" to support him. Alas! he does not know that Mason is compelled by this time to fall back to second place, and that the last man on whom he can possibly count "in a pinch" is now in command of the looked-for troop.

The night wears on without alarm. Well-nigh exhausted, Lane has thrown himself at the foot of a tree to catch what sleep he may, and he feels as though he had not closed his eyes when Corporal Shea bends over him to say it is two o'clock. Noiselessly the men are aroused; silently they roll out of their blankets, and, obedient to the low-toned "fall in" of the first sergeant, seize their arms and take their place in line. There Lane briefly explains the situation; tells them of the position of the Apache bivouac; details Corporal Riley and four men to search for, secure, and hie away with the prisoners, and orders all the rest to fight like the devil to drive the Apaches helter-skelter into the rocks. "Let not one word be said nor a trigger pulled until we are right among them. Wait for my command, unless we are detected and fired on. If we are, blaze away at once; but never stop your rush: get right in among them. Let Riley and his men make instant search, be sure they leave neither woman nor child behind, and start them back here. The rest of us will fall back slowly, keeping between them and the Apaches all the time. Never let them get near those prisoners. That is the main object of our attack. Once back here with the horses, we can pick out places in the rocks from which we can stand the Apaches off until K Troop comes. Rest assured Lieutenant Mason and his men will be along by eight or nine; and it cannot be that the cavalry now pursuing the Apaches from the north will be more than a few hours behind. Now, do you understand? for there will be no chance of orders up there. Leave your canteens; leave anything that will hinder or rattle. Those of you who have on spurs, take them off. Those of you who have Tonto or Apache moccasins, take off your top boots and put them on; they are all the better for going up these hill-sides. Now get your coffee, men; make no noise, light no additional fires, and be ready to move in twenty minutes."

Then he pencils this brief note:

"Commanding Officer Troop K, Eleventh Cavalry:

"We have headed the Apaches, and will attack their camp the instant it is light enough to see, rescue their captives, then fall back here to the gorge of the San Simon. They far outnumber us, and you cannot reach us too soon. I count upon your being here by eight in the morning, and hope with your aid to hold the enemy until Greene's command arrives. Then we ought to capture the whole band. Do not fail me.

"FREDERICK LANE,
"*Captain Eleventh Cavalry.*"

This he gives to Sergeant Luce with orders to ride back on the trail until he meets K Troop and deliver it to Lieutenant Mason or whoever is in command; and in half an hour Luce is away.

And now, just as the dawn is breaking and a faint pallid light is stealing through the tree-tops along the rocky range, there come creeping slowly, noiselessly along the slope a score of shadowy forms, crouching from boulder to boulder, from tree to tree. Not a word is spoken, save now and then a whispered caution. Foremost, carbine in hand, is the captain, now halting a moment to give some signal to those nearest him, now peering ahead over the rocks that bar the way. At last he reaches a point where, looking down the dark and rugged hill-side before him, he sees something which causes him to unsling the case in which his field-glasses are carried, to gaze thither long and fixedly. With all eyes upon their leader, the men wait and listen: some cautiously try the hammers of their carbines and loosen a few cartridges in the loops of their prairie-belts. A signal from Lane brings Mr. Royce, the young second lieutenant, to his side. It is the boy's first experience of the kind, and his heart is thumping, but he means to be one of the foremost in the charge when the time comes. Watching closely, the nearest men can see that the captain is pointing out some object nearer at hand than they supposed, and the first sergeant, crouching to a neighboring rock, looks cautiously over, and then eagerly motions to others to join him.

The Apache hiding-place is not three hundred yards away.

Down the mountain-side to the west and up the range to the north their sentries keep vigilant guard against surprise; but what man of their number dreams for an instant that on the south, between them and the Mexican line, there is now closing in to the attack a little troop of veteran campaigners, led by a man whom they have learned to dread before now? Invisible from the valley below or the heights up the range, their smouldering fires can be plainly seen from where Lane and his men are now concealed. But nothing else can be distinguished.

Far over to the western side of the valley the faint red glow tells where lie the ruins of the ranch their young warriors have destroyed, and any moment now their exultant yells may be heard as they come scampering back to camp after a night of deviltry, and then everybody will be up and moving off and well on the way southward before the sun gets over the crest. Lane knows he must make his dash before they can return. There would be little hope of rescue for the poor souls lying there bound and helpless, with all those fierce young fighters close at hand.

The word is passed among the men: "Follow closely, but look well to your footing. Dislodge no stones." Then, slowly and stealthily as before, on they go,—this time down the hill towards the faint lights of the Indian bivouac. A hundred yards more, and Lane holds up his hand, a signal to halt; and here he gives Mr. Royce a few instructions in a low tone. The youngster nods his head and mutters to several of the men as he passes, "Follow me." They disappear among the rocks and trees to the right, and it is evident that they mean to work around to the east of the bivouac, so as to partially encircle them. Little by little the wan light grows brighter, and, close at hand, objects far more distinct. An Indian is just passing in front of the nearest blaze, and is lost in the gloom among the stunted trees. One or two forms are moving about, but they can only dimly be distinguished. Lane argues, however, that they are getting ready to move, and no time is to be lost.

"Spread out now," is the order, "well to the right and left, and move forward. Be very careful." And once more they resume their cat-like advance. Nearer and nearer they creep upon the unsuspecting foe, and soon many a form of sleeping Apache can be made out, lying around in the grassy basin in which they are hiding for the night. Lane motions to Corporal Riley to come close to his side: "I can see nothing that looks like prisoners: they must be among the trees there, where that farthest fire is burning. Keep close to me with your men. Pass the word to the right, there. All ready."

And now they are so near the Indians that the voices of one or two squaws can be heard chatting in low tones; then the feeble wail of an infant is for a moment brought to their straining ears; then far out over the level valley to the west there is a sound that causes Lane's blood to tingle,—faint, distant, but unmistakable,—a chorus of Apache yells. The raiders are coming back: it is time to strike the blow. Now or never, seems to be the word as the men glance at their leader and then into each other's faces.

"Forward! no shot, no sound, till they see us; then cheer like mad as you charge! Come on, men!"

Quickly now following his lead, they go leaping down the hill-side. Thirty—fifty yards without mishap or discovery. Sixty, and still no sound from the defence; then a sudden stumble, the rattle of a carbine sliding down the rocks, a muttered execration; then a shrill, piercing scream from the midst of the bivouac; then——

"Charge!"

In they go!—the "Devil's own D's." The still air rings with their wild hurrahs and the crash of their carbines. The flame-jets light up the savage scene and show squaws and screaming children rushing for shelter among the rocks; Apache warriors springing from the ground, some manfully facing the rush of the foe, others fleeing like women down the hill-side. Never halting an instant, the soldiers dash through the camp, driving the dusky occupants helter-skelter. Lane finds himself confronted one instant by a savage warrior whose eyes gleam like tiger's under the thatch of coarse black hair, and whose teeth gnash in fury as he tries to force a fresh cartridge into his breech-loader. No time for Lane to reload. He clubs his carbine, and the hammer comes crashing down on the Indian's skull just as Corporal Riley drives a bullet through his heart.

"Look to the captives, man!" shouts Lane. "Don't follow me! Drive them! drive them, Royce!" are his ringing orders, as he himself dashes on past the fires and into the feeble morning light beyond.

Bang! bang! the carbines are ringing through the rocks and trees; cheer upon cheer goes up from the little command, mingled with Indian yells and the screams of the terrified children.

"Riley's got 'em, sir," he hears his boy-trumpeter call. "Some of 'em, anyhow. There's two white women."

"Never mind, lad," he answers. "Don't sound the recall till I tell you."

And again his ringing voice is heard among the tumult: "Forward! forward! drive them! keep them on the run, men!"

And so for five minutes longer, firing whenever a savage head appears, inflicting and receiving many a savage blow, but still victoriously forcing their way onward, the little band follow their leader down the rocks until apparently not an Apache is left in the immediate neighborhood of the old camp. Then at last the trumpet peals out its signal-recall.

And slowly and steadily, watchfully guarding against the possibility of leaving some wounded comrade among the rocks, the little command finally gathers once more around the fires in the camp.

Riley and his men have disappeared. A shout from up the rocks in the well-known Irish voice gives the glad intelligence that he has brought with him all the prisoners he could find in camp.

"There are three women, sir, and two little children,—two girls; they're so frightened that I can hardly find out much from them, but they say there was no more left."

"Very well, then. Now, men, open out right and left, and fall back very slowly. Sergeant, take six of the men and move up so as to be close to Riley in case they attack from the flank. Are we all here? Are any wounded or hurt?" He asks the question with a little stream of blood trickling down from his left temple, but of which he seems perfectly unaware: either an arrow or a bullet has torn the skin and made quite a furrow through the hair.

"Murphy, sir," says one of the men, "is shot through the arm, and Lathrop has got a bullet in the leg; but they're only flesh-wounds: they're lying here just back of us."

Lane turns about, and finds two of his men looking a little pale, but perfectly plucky and self-possessed. "We'll get you along all right, men," he says; "don't worry.—Now, lads, turn about every ten or fifteen steps, and see that they don't get close upon you. Look well to the left."

Then slowly they fall back towards the pass. Every now and then a shot comes whizzing by, as the Apaches regain courage and creep up to their abandoned camp. But not until they are well back over the ridge, and Riley and his little party, fairly carrying their rescued captives, are nearly out of harm's way, do the scattered warriors begin to realize how few in number their assailants must be. Rallying shouts can be heard among the rocks, and then there come the thunder of hoofs out on the plain below and the answering yells of the returning raiders.

"Run to Corporal Riley and tell him to make all the haste he can," Lane orders his trumpeter. "Tell him to get back to the horses, and then, as soon as he has left his women in a safe place there, to throw up stone shelters wherever it is possible.—Royce, you look out for this front. I will go to the left. If any of your men are hit, have them picked up and moved rapidly to the rear; of course we can't leave any wounded to fall into their hands; but, where possible, keep your men under cover; and keep under yourself, sir: don't let me see you exposing yourself unnecessarily, as I did a while ago."

And once again the retreat is resumed. Lane looks anxiously among the rocks down the hill to his left, every instant expecting to see the young braves hurrying to the assault. But now, as though in obedience to the signals of some leader, the Apaches cease their pursuit. Lane well knows that the matter is not yet concluded, but is thankful for the respite. Still warily his little force continues the withdrawal, and, without further molestation, reaches the gorge of the San Simon, and soon comes in sight of the dip among the rocks where the horses are still hidden. Here, too, Corporal Riley and his men are busily at work heaping up little breastworks of rock, and Lane directs that while the wounded—there are three now—are carried down to where the rescued women and children are lying, the other men fall to and help. In five minutes there are over a score of them at work, and not one instant too soon. Corporal Donnelly, who has been posted, mounted at the western entrance to the defile, comes clattering in to say that at least a hundred Indians are swarming down the ridge.

And now the fight that opens is one in which the odds are greatly against the defenders. Lane has just time to climb to the height on the east and take one long look with his glasses over the flats beyond the pass, praying for a sight of a dust-cloud towards the Pyramid Spur, when with simultaneous crash of musketry and chorus of yells the Apaches come sweeping down to the attack.

XV.

Meantime, where are the looked-for supports? Lane, with wearied horses, had made the march from the railway-station to the pass in a little over fourteen hours. It was 5.30 when he started and 8.15 when he unsaddled among the rocks. He had come through the blazing sunshine of the long June day; sometimes at the trot, sometimes at the lope, ofttimes dismounting and leading when crossing ridges or ravines. He was still pale and weak from his long illness, and suffering from a sorrow that had robbed him of all the buoyancy he had ever possessed. But the sense of duty was as strong as ever, and the soldier-spirit triumphed over the ills of the flesh.

Noel, starting at 4.45 P.M., with horses and men fresh and eager, with a guide who knew every inch of the way, and the bright starlight to cheer his comrades, could reasonably be expected to cover the same ground in the same time; every old cavalryman knows that horses travel better by night than by day. By good rights he and his men should be at the pass at least an hour before the time set by Lane. It was only a week before that the captain had declared at the "Queen City" that he had never felt so "fit" in his life and a campaign would just suit him. Things seemed to have a different color, however, as he watched the going down of the sun behind the distant Peloncillos. The words of the young infantry adjutant kept recurring to him, and he knew of old that when Lane started after Indians he was "dead sure to get 'em," as Mr. Mason was good enough to remind him.

Twice before sunset the guide had ventured to suggest a quicker gait, but Noel refused, saying that he did not mean to get his horses to the scene worn out and unfit for pursuit. Mr. Mason, who heard this, begged to remind the captain that pursuit was not the object:

they were expected to get there in time to help Lane head off the attempt at further flight, and to hold the Apaches, wherever met, until the pursuing force could reach them from the north and hem them in. Noel ranked Mason only a few files and knew well that all the regiment would side with his subaltern: so he was forced to a show of cordiality and consideration. He rode by the lieutenant's side, assuring him of the sense of strength it gave him to have with him a man of such experience. "For your sake, Mason, I wish I had been twelve hours later, so that you could have had the glory of this thing to yourself; but you know I couldn't stand it. I had to pull wires like sin to get relieved, as it was. Old Hudson, the head of the recruiting-service, just swore he wouldn't let me go, because I had had good luck in the class and number of the recruits I sent him. Personally, too, I'm in no shape to ride. See how fat I've grown?"

Mason saw, but said a fifty-mile ride ought not to stagger any cavalryman, hard or soft, and made no reply whatever to the captain's account of how he succeeded in getting relieved. He didn't believe a word of it.

Night came on and found them still marching at steady walk. Halts for rest, too, had been frequently ordered, and at last Mason could stand it no longer. After repeated looks at his watch, he had burst out with an earnest appeal:

"Captain Noel, we'll never get there in time at this rate. Surely, sir, the orders you got from the general must be different from those that came to the post. *They* said, make all speed, lose not a moment. Did not yours say so too?"

"The general knew very well that I had marched cavalry too often not to understand just how to get there in time," was Noel's stately reply; and, though chafing inwardly, Mason was compelled to silence. Ten o'clock came, and still it was no better. Then both the lieutenant and the guide, after a moment's consultation during a rest, approached the captain and begged him to increase the gait; and when they mounted, the command did, for a while, move on at a jog, which Mason would fain have increased to the lope, but Noel interposed. Midnight, and more rests, found them fully ten miles behind the point where the guide and the lieutenant had planned to be. Even the men had begun to murmur among themselves, and to contrast the captain's spiritless advance with Mr. Mason's lively methods. Two o'clock, and the Pyramid Range was still far away. Daybreak came, and Mason was nearly mad with misery, the guide sullen and disgusted. Broad daylight,—six o'clock,—and here at last were the Pyramid Buttes at their right front, and, coming towards them on the trail, a single horseman. "It is Sergeant Luce," said some of the foremost troopers.

And Luce had a note, which he handed to Lieutenant Mason; but that gentleman shook his head and indicated Noel. The captain took it in silence, opened it, glanced over the contents, changed color, as all could see, and then inquired,—

"How far is it, sergeant?"

"It must be fifteen miles from here, sir. I came slowly, because my horse was worn out, and because Captain Lane thought that I would meet the troop very much nearer the pass. It's more than fifteen miles, I reckon."

"Had the attack begun before you left?"

"Yes, sir; and I could hear the shots as I came out of the pass,—hear them distinctly."

"May I inquire what the news is, captain?" said Mr. Mason, riding up to his side.

"Well," was the reply, "Lane writes that he has headed the Apaches, and that he is just moving in to the attack."

"Will you permit me to see the note, sir?" said Mason, trembling with exasperation at the indifferent manner in which it was received.

Noel hesitated: "Presently,—presently, Mr. Mason. We'll move forward at a trot, now."

Sergeant Luce reined about, and, riding beside the first sergeant of K Troop, told him in low tones of the adventures of the previous day and night, and the fact that the Apaches were there just north of the pass and in complete force. The result seemed to be, as the word was passed among the men, to increase the gait to such an extent that they crowded upon the leaders, and Noel, time and again, threw up his hand and warned the men not to ride over the heels of his horse.

Seven o'clock came, and still they had not got beyond the Pyramids. Eight o'clock, and they were not in sight of the pass. Nine o'clock, and still the gorge was not in view. It was not until nearly ten that the massive gate-way seemed to open before them, and then, far to the front, their eager ears could catch the sound of sharp and rapid firing.

"My God!" said Mason, with irrepressible excitement, "there's no question about it, captain, Lane's surrounded there! For heaven's sake, sir, let's get ahead to his support."

"Ride forward, sergeant," said Noel to Luce, "and show us the shortest way you know to where Captain Lane has corralled his horses. —I don't like the idea of entering that pass in column, Mr. Mason. The only safe way to do it will be to dismount and throw a line of skirmishers ahead. If Lane is surrounded, the Apaches undoubtedly will open fire on us as we pass through."

"Suppose they do, sir: we've got men enough to drive them back. What we want is to get through there as quickly as possible."

But Noel shook his head, and, forming line to the front at a trot, moved forward a few hundred yards, and then, to the intense disgust of Mr. Mason, ordered the first platoon dismounted and pushed ahead as skirmishers. Compelled to leave their horses with number four of each set, the other troopers, sullenly, but in disciplined silence, advanced afoot up the gentle slope which led to the heights on the right of the gorge.

Not a shot impeded their advance; not a sound told them that they were even watched. But far up through the pass itself the sound of sharp firing continued, and every now and then a shrill yell indicated that the Apaches were evidently having the best of it.

Again Mason rode to his captain. "I beg you, sir," he said, "to let me take my platoon, or the other one, and charge through there. It isn't possible that they can knock more than one or two of us out of the saddle; and if you follow with the rest of the men they can easily be taken care of." But Noel this time rebuked him.

"Mr. Mason, I have had too much of your interference," he said, "and I will tolerate no more. I am in command of this troop, sir, and I am responsible for its proper conduct."

And Mason, rebuffed, fell back without further word.

The pass was reached, and still not a shot had been fired. Over the low ridge the dismounted troopers went, and not an Apache was in sight. Then at last it became evident that to cross the stream they would have to ford; and then the "recall" was sounded, the horses were run rapidly forward to the skirmish-line, the men swung into saddle, the rear platoon closed on the one in front, and cautiously, with Mason leading and Noel hanging back a little as though to direct the march of his column, the troop passed through the river and came out on the other side. The moment they reached the bank, Mason struck a trot without any orders, and the men followed him.

Noel hastened forward, shouting out, "Walk, walk." But, finding that they either did not or would not hear him, he galloped in front of the troop, and sternly ordered the leaders to decrease their gait and not again to take the trot unless he gave the command.

Just at this minute, from the heights to the right and left, half a dozen shots were fired in quick succession; a trooper riding beside the first sergeant threw up his arms, with the sudden cry, "My God! I've got it!" and fell back from the saddle. Noel at the same instant felt a twinge along his left arm, and, wheeling his horse about, shouted, "To the rear! to the rear! We're ambushed!" And, despite the rallying cry of Mason and the entreaties of the guide, the men, taking the cue from their leader, reined to the right and left about and went clattering out of the pass.

More shots came from the Apaches, some aimed at the fleeing troop and others at the little group of men that remained behind; for the poor fellow who had been shot through the breast lay insensible by the side of the stream, and would have been abandoned to his fate but for the courage and devotion of Mason and two of the leading men. Promptly jumping from their horses, they raised him between them, and, laying him across the pommel of one of the saddles, supported by the troopers, the wounded man was carried back to the ford, and from there out of harm's way.

By this time Noel, at full gallop, had gone four or five hundred yards to the rear, and there the first sergeant—not he—rallied the troop, reformed it, counted fours, and faced it to the front.

When Mason returned to them, leading the two troopers and the dying man, his face was as black as a thunder-cloud. He rode up to his captain, who was stanching with a handkerchief a little stream of blood that seemed to be coming down his left arm, and addressed to him these words:

"Captain Noel, there were not more than six or eight Apaches guarding those heights. There was no excuse in God's world, sir, for a retreat. I can take my platoon and go through there now without difficulty, and once again, sir, I implore you to let me do it."

Noel's reply was, "I have already heard too much from you to-day, Mr. Mason. If I hear one more word, you go to the rear in arrest. I am wounded, sir, but I will not turn over this command to you."

"Wounded be hanged! Captain Noel, you've got a scratch of which a child ought to be ashamed," was the furious reply, upon which Noel, considering that he must at all hazards preserve the dignity of his position, ordered Lieutenant Mason to consider himself in arrest.

And, dismounting, and calling to one or two of the men to assist him, the captain got out of his blouse and had the sleeve of his under-shirt cut off, and then, in full hearing of the combat up the pass, proceeded to have a scratch, as Mason had truly designated it, stanched and dressed.

Meantime, the troop, shamefaced and disgusted, dismounted and awaited further developments. For fifteen minutes they remained there, listening to the battle a mile away, and then there came a sound that thrilled every man with excitement,—with mad longing to dash to the front: there came crashes of musketry that told of the arrival of strong reinforcements for one party or another,—which party was soon developed by the glorious, ringing cheers that they well recognized to be those of their comrades of Greene's battalion.

"By heavens!" said Mason, with a groan, "after all, we have lost our chance! It's Greene, not old K Troop, that got there in time to save them."

The looks that were cast towards their new captain by the men, standing in sullen silence at their horses' heads, were not those that any soldier would have envied.

Directing the first sergeant to take half a dozen troopers and feel their way cautiously to the front and ascertain what that new sound meant, the rest of the men meanwhile to remain at ease, Noel still sat there on the ground, as though faint from loss of blood. The bleeding, however, had been too trifling to admit of any such supposition on the part of those who had been looking on. The cheering up the pass increased. The firing rapidly died away. Soon it was seen that the first sergeant was signalling, and presently a man came riding back. The sergeant and the others disappeared, going fearlessly into the pass, and evidently indicating by their movements that they anticipated no further resistance. The arriving horseman dismounted, saluted the captain, and reported substantially that the pass was now in possession of Major Greene's men, and that the Apaches were in full flight towards the south, some of the troops pursuing.

Then at last it was that the "mount" was sounded by the trumpeter, and half an hour afterwards—full three hours after they should have been there—Captain Noel with K Troop arrived at the scene. Lane, faint from loss of blood, was lying under a tree; four of his men were killed; one of the helpless recaptured women had been shot by an Indian bullet; five more of the "Devil's own D's" were lying wounded

E*

around among the rocks. Desperate had been the defence; sore had been their need; safe, thoroughly safe, they would have been had Noel got there in time; but it was Greene's battalion that finally reached them only at the last moment. And yet this was the thrilling announcement that appeared in the Queen City *Chronicle* in its morning edition, two days afterwards:

"Gallant Noel! Rescue of the Indian Captives! Stirring Pursuit and Fierce Battle with the Apaches!

"A despatch received last night by the Hon. Amos Withers announces the return from the front of Captain Noel, who so recently left our midst, with a portion of his troop, bringing with him the women and children who had been run off by the Apaches on their raid among the ranches south of their reservation. The captain reports a severe fight, in which many of the regiment were killed and wounded, he himself, though making light of the matter, receiving a bullet through the left arm.

"While the rest of the command had gone on in pursuit of the Apaches, the captain was sent by the battalion commander to escort the captives back to the railway.

"This despatch, though of a private character, is fully substantiated by the official report of the general commanding the department to the Adjutant-General of the army. It reads as follows:

"'Captain Noel, of the Eleventh Cavalry, has just reached the railway, bringing with him all but one of the women and children whom the Apaches had carried off into captivity. The other was shot by a bullet in the desperate fight which occurred in San Simon Pass between the commands of Captains Lane and Noel and the Apaches, whose retreat they were endeavoring to head off. Greene's battalion of the Eleventh arrived in time to take part; but on their appearance the Apaches fled through the mountains in the wildest confusion, leaving much of their plunder behind them.

"'It is impossible as yet to give accurate accounts of the killed and wounded, but our losses are reported to have been heavy.'

"How thoroughly have the predictions of the *Chronicle* with regard to this gallant officer been fulfilled! To his relatives and his many friends in our midst the *Chronicle* extends its most hearty congratulations. We predict that the welcome which Captain Noel will receive will be all that his fondest dreams could possibly have cherished."

XVI.

For a week the story of Gordon Noel's heroism was the talk of Queen City society. He had led the charge upon the Indians after a pursuit of over a hundred miles through the desert. He had fought his way to the cave in which those poor captive women were guarded, and had himself cut the thongs that bound them. He was painfully wounded, but never quit the fight till the last savage was driven from the field. For daring and brilliant conduct he was to be promoted over the heads of all the captains in his regiment. His name was already before the President for a vacancy in the Adjutant-General's Department, and the appointment would be announced at once. He was coming East just as soon as the surgeon said he was well enough to travel. Mrs. Noel wanted to join him, but he had telegraphed saying no, that he would soon be with her.

So rang the chorus for several days. At the club the men shook hands over the news, and sent telegrams of praise and congratulation to Noel, and drank his health in bumpers; and two or three "old soreheads," who ventured to point out that the official reports were not yet in, were pooh-poohed and put down.

Amos Withers had left for Washington on a midnight train immediately after furnishing the *Chronicle* with the contents of his despatch, making no allusion to that part of it which said, "Now push for that vacancy. Not an instant must be lost." Nobody could say nay to the man who had subscribed the heaviest sum to the campaign fund in his own State, and therefore both its Senators and half its representatives in the House went with him to the President to urge the immediate nomination of Captain Noel to the majority in the Adjutant-General's Department made vacant by the promotion consequent upon the retirement of one of its oldest members. Already the War Department had furnished the Executive with the names and records of the four men whom it considered most deserving, and Gordon Noel's name was not one of the four. But what was that in comparison with the eminent pecuniary and political services of Mr. Withers, when the nephew had just behaved so superbly in action?

Meantime, the Apaches had scattered through the mountains and escaped across the border, the remnant of Lane's troop taking part in the pursuit, and they, with their commander, only slowly returning to the railway. For three or four days Noel had the wires and the correspondents pretty much to himself; but then some of those enterprising news-gatherers had been getting particulars from the men, and there were two or three of K Troop in the detachment who could not conceal their derision and contempt when the newspaper-men spoke of the bravery of their captain. This set the correspondents to ferreting, and then the despatches began to take a different color. The very day that Mabel received her first letter from her husband, and was reading extracts from it to envious friends who had come in to swell the chorus of jubilee and congratulation, an evening paper intimated that recent despatches received from the seat of war revealed a different state of affairs than was popularly supposed.

But by this time interest was waning. It is the first impression that is always the strongest, the first story that is longest remembered, and no man who has believed one version will accept the truth without vigorous resistance. In his letter to his wife, Noel had spoken modestly of himself and slightingly of his wounds. This only made her worship him—her hero, her gallant Gordon—the more insanely. He intimated that he had been compelled to place in arrest one of the prominent officers of the regiment for misconduct in the face of the enemy; and this *and previous matters*, he said, would surely make of this officer an unrelenting foe. She need not be surprised, therefore, if this gentleman should strive to do him grievous harm. Mabel blushed becomingly as she read these lines to some of her friends, and that night at the club it was hinted that Lane had been placed in close arrest for failing to support Noel in his desperate assault. Just at this time, too, Mr. Withers came back from Washington, looking mysterious.

The next published despatches were from the general himself. He was incensed over the escape of the Apaches. Measures for the capture were complete, and it was broadly hinted that a certain officer would be brought to trial for his failure to carry out positive orders.

"It is believed," said the *Chronicle*, "that the officer referred to is well known in our community, as he had, oddly enough, been a predecessor in the recruiting-service of the actual hero of the campaign."

Two weeks went by. There was no announcement of Noel's name as promoted. Other matters occupied the attention of the club and the coteries, and no one knew just what it all meant when it was announced that Mrs. Noel had suddenly left for the frontier to join her husband. Perhaps his wounds were more severe than at first reported. Then it was noticed that Mr. Withers was in a very nervous and irritable frame of mind, that constant despatches were passing between him and Captain Noel in the West, and that suddenly he departed again on some mysterious errand for Washington. And then it was announced that Captain Noel would not be able to visit the East as had been expected.

All the same it came as a shock which completely devastated the social circles of the Queen City when it was announced in the New York and Chicago papers that a general court-martial had been ordered to assemble at Fort Gregg, New Mexico, for the trial of Captain Gordon Noel, Eleventh Cavalry, on charges of misbehavior in the face of the enemy, and conduct unbecoming an officer and a gentleman.

The *Chronicle* made no allusion to the matter until after it was heralded over the city by the other journals. Then it announced that it was in possession of information showing conclusively that Captain Noel was the victim of the envy of certain officers in his regiment, and that the charges had been trumped up from the false and prejudiced statement of the man whom he had been compelled to place in arrest for misconduct in action. "Captain Noel had demanded a court-martial," said the *Chronicle*, "that he might be triumphantly vindicated, as he undoubtedly would be."

At the club several men surrounded Lieutenant Bowen with eager inquiry as to the facts in the case. Bowen, who was now in charge of the rendezvous as Noel's successor, was very reticent when interrogated. He said that while an officer might demand a court of inquiry, he could not demand a court-martial; they were entirely different things; and it was certainly the latter that had been ordered.

"Was there not some likelihood of malice and envy being at the bottom of the charges?" he was asked. "And was it not unfair to let him be tried by officers prejudiced against him?"

Bowen said he did not belong to the Eleventh, but he knew it well enough to say no to the first part of the question. As to the other, there were only two officers from that regiment on the court, and one was Noel's old friend and colonel,—Riggs.

It was in the midst of this talk that Mr. Amos Withers had suddenly appeared and begged a few words in private with Mr. Bowen.

Withers was in a state of nervous excitement, as any one could see. He talked eagerly, even pleadingly, with the silent lieutenant, and at last suddenly arose and, with the look of a defeated and discomfited man, left the club-house, entered his carriage, and was driven rapidly away.

That night an officer from the War Department arrived in the Queen City, and was closeted for a while with Lieutenant Bowen, after which the two went to the Chief of Police, and, in company with him, visited the cell where Taintor, deserter and forger, was confined, took his statement and that of the Chief, and with these documents the officer went on to division head-quarters.

Meantime, the campaign had come to an end. Captain Noel had reported, in arrest, to the commanding officer at Fort Gregg, and Mrs. Riggs had tearfully greeted him: "She would so love to have him under her roof, that she might show her sympathy and friendship; but so many officers of high rank were coming on the court that the colonel was compelled to give every bit of room he had to them." Noel thanked her nervously, and said he could be comfortable anywhere, but his wife was coming: she had telegraphed that she could not be separated from him when he was suffering wrong and outrage. Captain and Mrs. Lowndes, moved to instant sympathy, begged that he would make their quarters his home, and placed their best room at his disposal.

Two evenings afterwards he was permitted to go himself to the railway to meet poor Mabel, who threw herself into his arms and almost sobbed her heart out at sight of his now haggard and care-worn face. Mrs. Lowndes then came forward and strove to comfort her, while Noel rushed off to send some telegrams. Then they drove out to the post, and Mabel's spirits partially revived when she found that it was not a prison she had come to share with her husband. Everybody was so gentle and kind to her, she began to believe there was nothing very serious in the matter, after all.

It lacked yet five days to the meeting of the court, and in the intervening time there arrived at the post a prominent and distinguished lawyer from the East, sent to conduct the defence by Mr. Withers's orders; and many a long talk did he hold with his client and the officers who were gathering at Gregg.

The charges of misconduct in face of the enemy had been preferred by the Department commander, who cited as his witnesses Captain Lane, Lieutenant Mason, Lieutenant Royce, the guide, and two or three non-commissioned officers. To the charge of "conduct unbecoming an officer and a gentleman" there were specifications setting forth that he had caused to be circulated and published reports to the effect that it was his command that had been severely engaged, and his command that had rescued the captives and defeated the Indians, which statements he well knew to be false. Two or three correspondents and railway employees and the telegraph operator were witnesses. This would be a hard one to prove affirmatively, as the judge-advocate found when he examined his witnesses as they arrived, and the great lawyer assured the accused officer that he could secure him an acquittal on that charge. The real danger lay in the testimony of Captain Lane and Lieutenant Mason, who had not yet come.

And now, hour after hour, for two days, Mabel was reading in her husband's face the utter hopelessness that possessed him; nay, more, the truth was being revealed to her in all its damning details. It might be impossible for the prosecution to prove that he had actually caused the false and boastful stories to be given to the press and the public; but how about the telegrams and letters Mr. Withers had so proudly come to show her? How about the telegrams and letters she herself had received? What impression could she derive from them but that he was the hero of the whole affair, and that he was lying painfully wounded when he wrote? The gash through the beautiful white arm turned out to be a mere scratch upon the skin, that a pin might have made. It was Greene's command from Fort Graham that had rescued Lane, and Lane with his men who had rescued the captives, and then fought so hard, so desperately, against such fearful odds, and sustained their greatest losses, while her hero,—her Gordon,—with nearly fifty men, was held only a mile away by half a dozen ragamuffins in the rocks. She had almost adored him, believing him godlike in courage and magnanimity; but now on every side the real facts were coming to light, and she even wrung them from his reluctant lips. And yet—and yet—he was her husband, and she loved him.

Again and again did she question Mr. Falconer, the eminent counsel, as to the possibilities. This gentleman had fought all through the war of the rebellion, and had won high commendation for bravery. He had taken the case because he believed, on Withers's statement, that Noel was a wronged and injured man, and because, possibly, a fee of phenomenal proportion could be looked for. He met among the old captains of the Eleventh men whom he had known in Virginia in the war-days, and learned from them what Noel's real reputation was, and, beyond peradventure, how he had shirked and played the coward in the last campaign: so that he, who had known Mabel Vincent from her babyhood and loved her old father, now shrank from the sorrow of having to tell her the truth. Yet she demanded it, and he had to say that her husband's fate hinged on the evidence that might be given by Captain Lane and Mr. Mason.

That very night these two officers arrived, together with three members of the court. The following day at ten o'clock the court was to begin its session, and four of its members were still to come. That night Mr. Falconer and her husband were closeted with several men in succession, seeking evidence for the defence. That night there came a despatch from Withers saying he had done his best in Washington, but that it seemed improbable that the President would interfere and accept Noel's resignation from the service.

Noel showed this to Mabel and sank upon the sofa with a groan of despair.

"Oh, my darling!" she whispered, kneeling by his side and throwing her arms about his neck, "don't give way! There must be hope yet! They cannot prove such cruel charges! There must be a way of averting this trouble."

"There is one," said he, starting up. "There is one, if you will only do it to save me."

"What would I not do to save you, Gordon?" she asked, though her face was paling now with awful dread of what the demand might be.

"Mabel, my wife, it is to see—him at once. There is nothing that he will not do for you. I know it—for I know what he has done. See him. You know what to say. I cannot prompt you. But get him to tell as little as he possibly can in regard to this case."

"Gordon!" she cried, "you ask me to do this, after the great wrong I did him?"

"There is no other way," was the sullen answer. And he turned moodily from her side, leaving her stunned, speechless.

XVII.

Somewhere about ten o'clock that night the judge-advocate of the court dropped in at the "bachelor quarters," where both Lane and Mason had been made welcome, and asked to see those gentlemen. He was conversing with them over the affair at the San Simon, when Captain Lowndes was ushered into the room.

"Am I intruding?" asked the latter. "I merely wished to speak to Lane a moment."

"By no means, Lowndes. Come right in. We'll be through in one minute.—Then, as I understand you, Lane, you could distinctly see K Troop as it forded the stream, and could see the Apaches who fired upon them?"

"Yes,—distinctly. I was praying for their coming, as our ammunition was running low. The Indians seemed so encouraged by the ease with which they drove them back that the whole band swarmed out from cover and crowded on us at once. It was in the next fifteen minutes that my men were killed,—and that poor woman."

"And there were only six Indians who opened fire on Noel?"

"Only six, sir."

The judge-advocate was silent a moment. "There is, of course, a chance that our absentees may get here to-morrow morning in time. If they do, you will be the first witness called; if they do not, we adjourn to await their arrival. It promises to be a long case. A telegram has just reached me, saying that additional and grave charges are being sent by mail from division head-quarters."

Captain Lowndes listened to this brief conversation with an expression of deep perplexity on his kindly face, and as soon as the judge-advocate had gone and Mason had left the room he turned to Lane:

"You know they are staying with us. That poor girl has come all this weary journey to be with him, and there was absolutely no place where she could lay her head unless we opened our doors and took him in too."

Lane bowed assent: "I had heard, Lowndes. It was like you and that dear wife of yours."

"Lane," spoke the older man, impetuously, after a moment of embarrassed silence, "I want you to do something for my wife, and for me. Come home with me for a few minutes. You won't see him; but—it is that heart-broken girl. She begs that you will see her,—to-night. Here is a little note."

Lane's sad face had grown deathly pale. He looked wonderingly in his companion's eyes a moment, then slowly took the note and left the room, leaving Lowndes to pace the floor in much disquiet.

In five minutes the former reappeared in the door-way. "Come," he said, and himself led the way out into the starlit night. Not a word was spoken by either man as they slowly walked down the row.

Arriving at his quarters, Captain Lowndes ushered his friend into the little army parlor, and Mrs. Lowndes came forward, extending both her hands. "It is good of you to come," she said. "I will let her know, at once."

Two shaded lamps cast a soft, subdued light over the simply-furnished little room. What a contrast to the sumptuous surroundings of the home in which he had last met her! Lane stood by the little work-table a moment, striving to subdue the violent beating of his heart and the tremors that shook his frame. Not once had he seen her since that wretched night in the library,—in that man Noel's arms. Not once had he permitted the thought of seeing her to find a lodgement. But all was different now: she was well-nigh crushed, heartbroken; she had been deceived and tricked; she was here practically friendless. "I well know that at your hands I deserve no such mercy," she had written, "but a hopeless woman begs that you will come to her for a few moments,—for a very few words."

And now he heard her foot-fall on the stairs. She entered, slowly, and then stopped short almost at the threshold. Heavens! how he had aged and changed! How deep were the lines about the kind gray eyes! how sad and worn was the stern, soldierly face! Her eyes filled with tears on the very instant, and she hovered there, irresolute, not knowing what to do, how to address him. It was Lane that came to the rescue. For a moment he stood there appalled as his eyes fell upon the woman whom he had so utterly—so faithfully loved. Where was all the playful light that so thrilled and bewitched him as it flickered about the corners of her pretty mouth? Whither had fled the bright coloring, the radiance, the gladness, that lived in that exquisite face? Was this heavy-eyed, pallid, nerveless being, standing with hanging head before him, the peerless queen he had so loyally and devotedly served,—whose faintest wish was to him a royal mandate,—to kiss whose soft white hand was a joy unutterable? All this flashed through his mind in the instant of her irresolute pause. Then the great pity of a strong and manful heart, the tenderness that lives ever in the bravest, sent him forward to her side. All thought of self and suffering, of treachery and concealment and deception, vanished at once at the sight of her bitter woe. His own brave eyes filled up with tears he would gladly have hidden, but that she saw, and was comforted. He took her limp, nerveless hand and led her to a chair, saying only her name,—"Mrs. Noel."

For several minutes she could not speak, but wept unrestrainedly, he, poor fellow, walking the floor the while, longing to comfort her, yet powerless. What could he say? What could he do? At last she seemed to regain her self-control.

"Captain Lane," she said, "it is useless for me to tell you how much I have learned, since coming here, of which I was ignorant before. Every effort has been made to spare me; people have been so considerate and kind, that the truth, as I am beginning to see, has been kept from me. Mr. Falconer, Captain Noel's—our lawyer, has at last admitted that almost everything depends upon your evidence. Forgive me, if you can, that I believed for a while that you inspired the charges against him. I know now that you refused to press the matter, and that—that I am not to blame any one. In his deep misfortune my duty is with my husband, and he—consented that I should see you. Captain Lane," she said, rising as she spoke, "do not try to spare my feelings now. I am prepared for anything,—ready to share his downfall. If you are asked as to the contents of the note you sent him just before the fight, must you tell what they were? Do you recall them?"

"I must, Mrs. Noel. I remember almost the exact words," he replied, gently, sorrowfully.

"But that is all, is it not? You know nothing more about the delay in reaching you?" And her eyes, piteous in entreaty, in shame, in suffering, sought one instant his sad face, then fell before the sorrow and sympathy in his.

For a moment there was no answer; and at last she looked up, alarmed.

"Mrs. Noel," he said, "I could not help it. I was eagerly awaiting their coming. I saw them approach the ford and the pass. I saw that there were only six Apaches to resist them; and the next thing I saw was the retreat."

"Oh, Captain Lane!" she cried, "must you testify as to this?" And her trembling hands were clasped in misery. "Is there *no* way, —*no* way?"

"Even if there were," he answered, slowly and mournfully, "Mr. Mason's testimony and that of the men would be still more conclusive."

Throwing herself upon the sofa, the poor girl gave way to a fit of uncontrollable weeping; and Lane stood helplessly, miserably by. Once he strove to speak, but she could not listen. He brought her a glass of water presently and begged her to drink it: there was still something he had to suggest. She took the goblet from his hand and looked up eagerly through her tears. He was thinking only of her—for her—now. The man who had robbed him of happiness, of love, of wife and home and hope, and who had done the utmost that he dared to rob him of honor and his soldier reputation,—the man now wretchedly listening overhead to the murmur of voices below,—he forgot entirely except as the man she loved.

"Mrs. Noel, your friends—his friends—are most influential. Can they not be telegraphed to that his resignation will be tendered? Can they not stop the trial in that way?"

"It is hopeless. It *has* been tried, and refused. If he is found guilty there is nothing left,—nothing left," she moaned, "but to take him back to the East with me, and, with the little we have now, to buy some quiet home in the country, where our wretched past need not be known,—where we can be forgotten,—where my poor husband need not have to hang his head in shame. Oh, God! oh, God! what a ruined life!"

"Is there nothing I *can* do for you, Mrs. Noel? Listen: that court cannot begin the—the case to-morrow. Four members are still to come. It may be two days yet,—perhaps three. Perhaps Mr. Withers and his friends do not appreciate the danger and have not brought pressure to bear on the President, but—forgive me for the pain this must give you—there are other, new charges coming from division head-quarters, that I fear will harm him still more. I grieve to have to tell you this. Try and make Mr. Withers understand. Try and get the resignation through. If you will see Mr. Falconer and—and the captain now, I can get the telegraph operator."

"What charges—what new accusations do you mean?" she asked, her eyes dilating with dread. "Are we not crushed enough already? Oh, forgive me, Captain Lane! I ought not to speak bitterly, you—you have been so good, so gentle. You, the last man on earth from whom I should seek mercy," she broke forth impetuously,—"*you* are yet the one to whom I first appeal. Oh, if after this night I never see you again, believe that I suffer, that I realize the wrong I have done. I was never worthy the faintest atom of your regard; but there's one thing—one thing you must hear. I wrote you fully, frankly, imploringly, before—before you came—and saw. Indeed, indeed, I had waited days for your reply, refusing to see him until after papa died; and then I was weak and ill. You never read the letter. You sent them all back unopened. I cannot look in your face. It may have been hard, for a while, but the time will soon come when you will thank God—thank God—I proved faithless."

And then, leaving him to make his own way from the house, she rushed sobbing to her room. When next he saw her, Reginald, her brother, with Lowndes and his tearful wife, was lifting her into the ambulance that was to take them to the railway, and the doctor rode away beside them. But this was ten days after.

True to Lane's prediction, the court met and adjourned on the following day. Colonel Stannard and Major Turner telegraphed that they were delayed *en route* to the railway, and nothing was heard from the other missing members. Two days more found the court in readiness, but the trial did not begin. There arrived on the express from the East, the night before all seemed ready for the opening session, Lieutenant Bowen, of the cavalry recruiting-service, with two guards who escorted the ex-clerk Taintor.

Telegrams for Captain Noel had been coming in quick succession, but he himself was not seen. It was Lowndes who took the replies to the office. The first meeting of the court was to have occurred on Monday. Tuesday evening the judge-advocate sent to the accused officer a copy of the additional specifications to the charge of conduct unbecoming an officer and a gentleman, and notified him that the witnesses had just arrived by train.

At four o'clock Wednesday morning Mrs. Lowndes was aroused by a tapping at her door, and recognized the voice of Mrs. Noel calling her name. Hastily she arose and went to her, finding her trembling and terrified. Gordon, she said, had been in such misery that he would not undress and try to sleep, but had been restlessly pacing the floor until after midnight. Then he had gone down to make some memoranda, he said, at the desk in which he and Mr. Falconer had their papers, and, as she could not sleep, she soon followed; but he was not there. Occasionally he had gone out late at night and walked about the parade after every one but the guard had gone to bed, and she thought he must have done so this time, and so waited, and waited, and peered out on the parade and could see nothing of him. At last she could bear it no longer.

Lowndes had heard the sobbing voice and one or two words. He was up and dressed in no time, and speedily found the officer of the day. "Do you think he could have made away with himself?—suicide?"

"Suicide! no!" answered Lieutenant Tracy. "He's too big a coward even for that!"

No sentry had seen or heard anything of him. The whole post was searched at daybreak, and without success. A neighboring settlement, infested by miners, stock-men, gamblers, and fugitives from justice, was visited, but nothing was learned that would tend to dispel the mystery. One or two hard citizens—saloon-proprietors—poked their tongues in their cheeks and intimated that "if properly approached" they could give valuable information; but no one believed them. That night, deserted and well-nigh distracted, Mabel Noel lay moaning in her little room, suffering heaven only knows what tortures; far from the yearning mother arms, far from home and kindred, far even from the recreant husband for whose poor sake she had abandoned all to follow him, for better for worse, for richer for poorer, in sickness or in health,—only to be left to the pity and care of strangers.

But she was in an army home and among loving, loyal, simple hearts. The women, one and all, thronged to the little cottage, imploring that they might "help in some way." The men, when they were not damning the runaway, were full of suggestion as to the course to be pursued. Mabel would accept only one explanation of his disappearance: crazed by misfortunes, he had taken his own life; he had said he would. But the regiment could not believe it, and in forty-eight hours had traced him, on the saloon-keeper's horse, over to the Southern Pacific, and thence down to El Paso. More than one man gave a sigh of relief that the whole thing could be so easily settled without the scandal of all that evidence being published to the world. The court met and adjourned pending the receipt of orders from the convening authority. The telegraph speedily directed the return to their stations of the several members. Lieutenant Bowen went back to the East, leaving Taintor in the guard-house, and in a week Reginald Vincent came to take his sister home and to whisper that Gordon was safe in the city of Mexico,—Mr. Withers was sending him money there; and so from her bed of illness, suffering, and humiliation the poor girl was almost carried to her train, and all Fort Gregg could have wept at sight of her wan and hopeless face.

She shrank from seeing or meeting any of her old associates, yet was eager to reach her mother's roof, fondly believing that there she would find letters from her husband. It hurt her inexpressibly that he should have fled without one word to her of his intentions; but she could forgive it because of the suffering and misery that bore him down and unsettled his mind. It stung her that Mr. Withers, not she, should be the first to learn of his place of refuge; but perhaps he thought she had gone East at once, and so had written there. She attributed his desertion to the strain to which he had been subjected; but she had been spared the sight of those last "specifications." Her first inquiry, after one long, blessed clasping in her mother's arms, after the burst of tears that could not be restrained, was for letters from him; and she was amazed, incredulous, when told there were none. Mr. Withers was sent for at once: that eminent citizen would gladly have dodged the ordeal, but could not. He could only say that two telegrams and two drafts had reached him from Noel, and that he had honored the latter at sight and would see that he lacked for nothing.

She would have insisted on going to join him in his exile, but he had sent no word or line; he had ignored her entirely. He might be ill, was the first thought; but Mr. Withers assured her he was physically perfectly well. "Everything is being done now to quietly end the trouble," said Mr. Withers. "We will see to it at Washington that his resignation is now accepted; for they will never get him before a court, and might as well make up their minds to it. They cannot drop or dismiss him for a year, with all their red-tape methods and their prate about the 'honor of the service.' I've seen enough of the army in the last three months to convince me it's no place for a gentleman. No, my dear, you stay here,—or go up to the mountains. We'll have him there to join you in a month."

But the authorities proved obdurate. Even the millionaire failed to move the War Secretary. Unless Captain Noel came back and stood trial, he would be "dropped for desertion" ("and, if he came back and stood trial, would probably be kicked out as a coward and liar," thought to himself the official who sat a silent listener). This Noel would not do. Withers sent him to Vera Cruz on a pseudo business-visit, and Mabel, silent, sad-faced, but weeping no more, went to a little resort in the West Virginia mountains.

Meantime, another court had been convened, another deserter tried, convicted, and sentenced, and before being taken to prison he made full statement to Captain Lane and two officers called in as witnesses. This was Taintor. He had known Captain Noel ever since his entry into service. Taintor was an expert penman, a gambler, and at times a hard drinker. He had enlisted in the troop of which Noel was second lieutenant while they were in Tennessee, and had deserted, after forging the post-quartermaster's name to two checks and getting the money. The regiment went to the Plains: he was never apprehended, and long years afterwards drifted from a position in the quartermaster's dépôt at Jeffersonville to a re-enlistment and a billet as clerk in the recruiting rendezvous at the Queen City. Knowing that Noel would recognize him, he deserted there, as has been told, taking all the money he could secure by forged checks for small amounts which he trusted would not excite suspicion. But he had fallen in love with a young woman, and she was dependent on him. He came back to the neighborhood after he thought the hue and cry was over, was shadowed and arrested by the police, and had given himself up for lost when Captain Noel was brought to his cell to identify him. He could hardly believe his senses when the captain said it was all a mistake. Then he was released, and went to work again across the river, and one night Noel came,—told him he knew him perfectly and would keep his secret provided he would "make himself useful." It soon turned out that what was wanted was the imitation of Captain Lane's signature on one or two papers whose contents he did not see, and the type-writing of some letters, one of which, without signature of any kind, and referring to some young lady, her secret meetings with Captain Noel, and saying, "You are being betrayed," was sent to Captain Lane at Fort Graham. Very soon after this Captain Lane came back. Taintor again fled until he knew his old commander had gone away, and then, venturing home, was rearrested, as has also been told.

Lane knew the anonymous letter well enough, but now for the first time saw its object. It was to make him accuse Mabel Vincent of deceit and faithlessness and so bring about a rupture of the engagement which, at that time, Noel saw no other means of removing as the one obstacle that stood in the way of his hopes.

But what were the other papers?

August came, and with it the rumors of the appearance of the dreaded *vómito* at Vera Cruz; but in the remote and peaceful nook where mother and daughter—two silent and sorrowing women—were living in retirement, no tidings came. Vainly Mabel watched the mails for letters—if only one—from him. She had written under cover to Mr. Withers, but even that evoked no reply.

One sunshiny afternoon they were startled by the sudden arrival of Regy. He sought to avoid question and to draw his mother to one side, but Mabel was upon him.

"You have news!" she said, her white face set, her hands firmly seizing his arm. "What is it? Have they dismissed him?"

"They can never dismiss—never harm him more, Mabel," was the solemn answer.

*   *   *   *   *   *   *   *   *

Some months afterwards Mrs. Vincent received a packet of papers that belonged to the late Captain Noel. Mabel had been sent to Florida for the winter, and was spending her early widowhood with kind and loving friends. The consul at Vera Cruz had written to Mr. Withers full particulars of his cousin's death,—one of the first victims of the *vómito*,—and had sent these papers with the formal certificates of the Mexican officials. Mr. Woodrow, one of the executors of Mr. Vincent's estate, showed singular desire to examine these papers, but the widow thought they should be opened only by her daughter. It was not until then that, with much hesitancy, the gentleman explained that Mr. Vincent had given him to understand that he had intrusted some papers to Captain Noel which that officer had promised to send at once to his old friend Captain Lane. Mrs. Vincent could learn no more from him, but she lost no time in searching the packet.

Within twenty-four hours Mabel was summoned home by telegraph, and there for the first time learned that to her father's partner, for the use of the firm in their sore straits of nearly two years before, Captain Lane had given the sum of fifteen thousand dollars, and that among Captain Noel's papers was what purported to be a receipt in full for the return of the sum from Mr. Vincent, which receipt was signed apparently by Frederick Lane and dated July 2, 188–. But this, said Mr. Woodrow, must be a mistake: Mr. Vincent had assured him late in July that he had not repaid it, but that Clark had his instructions to repay it at once, and all Clark's books, papers, and receipts had been examined, and showed that no such payment had been made.

"It simply means that the very roof under which we are sheltered is not ours, but that noble fellow's," said Mrs. Vincent; and that night she wrote, and poured forth her heart to him, while Mabel locked herself in her room.

No answer came. Then Mr. Woodrow made inquiries of the officer at the rendezvous, and learned that Captain Lane had gone to

Europe with leave of absence for a year; and there her letter followed him. She demanded, as a right, to know the truth. She had given the executors to understand that the debt must be paid, if they had to sell the old homestead to do it. She would be glad to go and live in retirement anywhere.

Not only did she, but so did Mr. Woodrow, receive at last a letter from distant Athens. The widow sobbed and laughed and pressed her letter to her heart, while Woodrow read his with moistened eyes, a suspicious resort to his cambric handkerchief, and an impatient consignment of all such confounded quixotic, unbusinesslike cavalrymen to—to the deuce, by Jupiter; and then he went off to show it to his fellow-executors.

The long summer wore away. Autumn again found mother and daughter and Regy at the dear old home, but light and laughter had not been known within the massive walls since the father's death. The tragedy in Mabel's life, coming so quickly after that event, seemed to have left room for naught but mourning. "She has so aged, so changed," wrote Mrs. Vincent on one of the few occasions when she wrote of her at all to him, and she wrote every month. "I could even say that it has improved her. The old gayety and joyousness are gone, and with them the wilfulness. She thinks more—lives more—for others now."

Winter came again,—the second winter of Mabel's widowhood,—and she was urged to visit the Noels at their distant home; but she seemed reluctant until her mother bade her go. She was still wearing her widow's weeds, and her lovely face was never sweeter in her girlhood days than now in that frame of crape. Of the brief months of her married life they never spoke, but the Noels loved her because of her devotion to him when not a friend was left. In early March the news from home began to give her uneasiness: "mamma did not seem well," was the explanation, and it was decided that they would go on as far as Washington with her, and spend a day or two there, when Reginald would meet and escort her home.

And so, one bright morning in that most uncertain of months, Mabel Noel with her sister-in-law and that lady's husband stood at the elevator landing, waiting to be taken down to the hall-way of their hotel. Presently the lighted cage came sliding from aloft. Mrs. Lanier entered, followed by the others. Two gentlemen seated on one side removed their hats, and the next instant, before she could take her seat, the lady saw one of them rise, bow, and extend his hand to Mabel, saying, with no little embarrassment and much access of color, something to the effect that this was a great surprise,—a statement which her fair sister-in-law evidently could find no words to contradict, even had she desired so to do. Neither of the two seemed to think of any others who were present. Indeed, there was hardly time to ask or answer questions before they had to step out and give place to people desiring to ascend; and then the gentleman nearly tumbled over a chair in the awkwardness of his adieu. Mrs. Noel's face was averted as they left the hall, but all the more was Mrs. Lanier desirous of questioning:

"Who was your friend, Mabel?"

And Mabel had to turn or be ungracious. Her face was glowing as she answered, simply,—

"Captain Lane."

An hour later Mrs. Lanier said to her husband,—

"That was the man to whom she was said to be engaged before Gordon; and did you see her face?"

Once again they met,—this time at the entrance to the dining-room; and there Captain Lane bowed gravely to "my sister, Mrs. Lanier,—Mr. Lanier," when he was presented. The lady seemed distant and chilling. The man held out his hand and said, "I'm glad to know you, captain. I wish you could dine with us." But Lane had dined, and was going out.

The third day came, and no Reginald. Expecting him every moment, Mabel declined to go with her friends on a shopping-tour, and was seated in her room, thinking, when there came a tap at the door: a card for Mrs. Noel, and the gentleman begged to see her in the parlor. Her color heightened as she read the name. Her heart beat flutteringly as she descended the stairs. He was standing close by the door, but he took her hand and led her to the window at their right.

"You have news—from mamma!" she cried. "Tell me—instantly!"

"Mr. Woodrow thinks it best that you should come, Mrs. Noel; and she has sent for me. Reginald went directly West last night. Will you trust yourself to my care? and can you be ready for the next train?—in two hours?"

Ready! She could go instantly. Was there no train sooner? She implored him to tell if her mother's illness was fatal. He could only say that Mrs. Vincent had been quite suddenly seized; and yet they hoped she would rally. Mabel wept unrestrainedly, upbraiding herself bitterly for her dilatory journey; but she was ready, and had gained composure when it was time to start. Mrs. Lanier's farewell was somewhat strained, but the captain seemed to notice nothing.

Unobtrusively, yet carefully, he watched over her on the homeward way. Tenderly he lifted her to the pavement of the familiar old dépôt, where Regy met them. Mamma was better, but very feeble. She wanted to see them both.

Three days the gentle spirit lingered. Thrice did the loving woman send for Lane, and, holding his hand in hers, whisper blessing and prayerful charge as to the future. Regy wondered what it could all mean. Mabel, on her knees in her own little room, pleading for her devoted mother's life, knew well how to the very last that mother clung to him, but only vaguely did she reason why.

At last the solemn moment came, and the hush of twilight, the placid, painless close of a pure and gracious life, were broken only by the sobbing of her kneeling children and of the little knot of friends who, dearly loving, were with her at the gate into the new and radiant world beyond.

One soft spring evening a few weeks later Mabel stood by the window in the old library, an open letter in her hand. Twice had she looked at the clock upon the mantel, and it was late when Frederick Lane appeared. Mr. Woodrow had unexpectedly detained him, he explained, but now nothing remained but to say good-by to her. His leave was up. The old troop was waiting for him.

"Will you try to do as I asked you, and write to me once in a while?" he said.

"I will. It was mother's wish." But her head sank lower as she spoke.

"I know," he replied. "For almost a year past she had written regularly to me, and I shall miss it—more than I can say. And now —it is good-by. God bless you, Mabel!"

And still she stood, inert, passive, her eyes downcast, her bosom rapidly rising and falling under its mourning garb. He took her hand and held it lingeringly one minute, then turned slowly away.

At the portière he stopped for one last look. She was still standing there, drooping. The fair head seemed bowing lower and lower, the white hands were clasping nervously.

"Do you know you have not said good-by, Mabel?"

She is bending like the lily now, turning away to hide the rush of tears. Only faintly does he catch the whispered words,—

"Oh! *I cannot!*"

DUNRAVEN RANCH.

DUNRAVEN RANCH.

I.

IT was nearly midnight, and still the gay party lingered on the veranda. There had been a fortnight of "getting settled" at the new post, preceded by a month of marching that had brought the battalion from distant service to this strange, Texan station. The newcomers had been hospitably welcomed by the officers of the little garrison of infantry, and now, in recognition of their many courtesies, the field-officer commanding the arriving troops had been entertaining the resident officers and ladies at dinner. The colonel was a host in himself, but preferred not to draw too heavily on his reserves of anecdote and small-talk, so he had called in two of his subalterns to assist in the pleasant duty of being attentive to the infantry ladies, and just now, at 11.45 P.M., he was wondering if Lieutenant Perry had not too literally construed his instructions, for that young gentleman was devoting himself to Mrs. Belknap in a manner so marked as to make the captain, her lawful lord and master, manifestly uneasy.

Mrs. Belknap, however, seemed to enjoy the situation immensely. She was a pretty woman at most times, as even her rivals admitted. She was a beautiful woman at all times, was the verdict of the officers of the regiment when they happened to speak of the matter among themselves. She was dark, with lustrous eyes and sweeping lashes, with coral lips and much luxuriance of tress, and a way of glancing sideways from under her heavily-fringed eyelids that the younger and more impressionable men found quite irresistible when accorded the rare luxury of a *tête-à-tête*. Belknap was a big and boisterous man; Mrs. Belknap was small in stature, and soft—very soft—of voice. Belknap was either brusquely repellent or oppressively cordial in manner; Mrs. Belknap was either gently and exasperatingly indifferent to those whom she did not care to attract, or caressingly sweet to those whose attentions she desired. In their own regiment the young officers soon found that unless they wished to be involved in an unpleasantness with Belknap it was best to be only very moderately devoted to his pretty wife, and those to whom an unpleasantness with the big captain might have had no terrors of consequence were deterred by the fact that Mrs. Belknap's devotee among the "youngsters" had invariably become an object of coldness and aversion to the other dames and damsels of the garrison. Very short-lived, therefore, had been the little flirtations that sprang up from time to time in those frontier posts wherein Captain and Mrs. Belknap were among the chief ornaments of society; but now matters seemed to be taking other shape. From the very day that handsome Ned Perry dismounted in front of Belknap's quarters and with his soldierly salute reported to the then commanding officer that Colonel Brainard and his battalion of cavalry would arrive in the course of two or three hours, Mrs. Belknap had evinced a contentment in his society and assumed an air of quasi-proprietorship that served to annoy her garrison sisters more than a little. For the time being all the cavalrymen were bachelors, either by actual rank or "by brevet," as none of the ladies of the —th accompanied the battalion on its march, and none were expected until the stations of the regiment in its new department had been definitely settled. The post surgeon, too, was living a life of single blessedness as the early spring wore on, for his good wife had betaken herself, with the children, to the distant East as soon as the disappearance of the winter's snows rendered staging over the hard prairie roads a matter of no great danger or discomfort.

It was the doctor himself who, seated in an easy-chair at the end of the veranda, first called the colonel's attention to Perry's devotional attitude at Mrs. Belknap's side. She was reclining in a hammock, one little, slippered foot occasionally touching the floor and imparting a gentle, swinging motion to the affair, and making a soothing swish-swish of skirts along the matting underneath. Her jewelled hands looked very slender and fragile and white as they gleamed in the soft light that shone from the open windows of the parlor. They were busied in straightening out the kinks in the gold cord of his forage-cap and in rearranging a little silken braid and tassel that was fastened in clumsy, man-like fashion to one of the buttons at the side; he, seated in a camp-chair, was bending forward so that his handsome, shapely head was only a trifle higher than hers, and the two—hers so dark and rich in coloring, his so fair and massive and strong,—came rather too close together for the equanimity of Captain Belknap, who had essayed to take a hand at whist in the parlor. One or two of the ladies, also, were silent observers of the scene,—silent as to the scene because, being in conversation at the time with brother officers of Lieutenant Perry, they were uncertain as yet how comments on his growing flirtation might be received. That their eyes should occasionally wander towards the hammock and then glance with sympathetic significance at those of some fair ally and intimate was natural enough. But when it became presently apparent that Mrs. Belknap was actually unfastening the little silken braid that had hung on Ned Perry's cap ever since the day of his arrival,—all the while, too, looking shyly up in his eyes as her fingers worked; when it was seen that she presently detached it from the button and then, half hesitatingly, but evidently in compliance with his wishes, handed it to him; when he was seen to toss it carelessly—even contemptuously—away and then bend down lower, as though gazing into her shaded eyes,—Mrs. Lawrence could stand it no longer.

"Mr. Graham," said she, "isn't your friend Mr. Perry something of a flirt?"

"Who?—Ned?" asked Mr. Graham, in well-feigned amaze and with sudden glance towards the object of the inquiry. "How on earth should *I* know anything about it? Of course you do not seek expert testimony in asking me. He tries, I suppose, to adapt himself to circumstances. But why do you ask?"

"Because I see that he has been inducing Mrs. Belknap to take off that little tassel on the button of his cap. He has worn it when off duty ever since he came; and we supposed it was something he cherished; I know *she* did."

Graham broke forth in a peal of merry laughter, but gave no further reply, for just then the colonel and the doctor left their chairs, and, sauntering over to the hammock, brought mighty relief to Belknap at the whist-table and vexation of spirit to his pretty wife. The flirtation was broken up at a most interesting point, and Perry, rising suddenly, came over and joined Mrs. Lawrence.

If she expected to see him piqued or annoyed at the interruption and somewhat perturbed in manner, she was greatly mistaken. Nothing could have been more sunshiny and jovial than the greeting he gave her. A laughing apology to Graham for spoiling his *tête-à-tête* was accomplished in a moment, and then down by her side he sat and plunged into a merry description of his experiences at dinner, where he had been placed next to the chaplain's wife on the one hand, and she had been properly aggrieved at his attentions to Mrs. Belknap on the other.

"You must remember that Mrs. Wells is a very strict Presbyterian, Mr. Perry; and, for that matter, none of us have seen a dinner such as the colonel gave us this evening for ever and ever so long. We are quite unused to the ways of civilization; whereas you have just come from the East—and long leave. Perhaps it is the fashion to be all devotion to one's next-door neighbor at dinner."

"Not if she be as repellent and venerable as Mrs. Wells, I assure you. Why, I thought she would have been glad to leave the table when, after having refused sherry and Pontet-Canet for upwards of an hour, her glass was filled with champagne when she happened to be looking the other way."

"It is the first dinner of the kind she has ever seen here, Mr. Perry, and I don't suppose either Mr. or Mrs. Wells has been up so late before in years. He would have enjoyed staying and watching whist, but she carried him off almost as soon as we left the table. Our society has been very dull, you know,—only ourselves at the post all this last year, and nobody outside of it."

"One would suppose that with all this magnificent cattle-range there would be some congenial people ranching near you. Are there none at all?"

"Absolutely none! There are some ranches down in the Washita country, but only one fine one near us; and that might as well be on the other side of the Atlantic. No one from there ever comes here; and Dr. Quin is the only living soul in the garrison who ever got within the walls of that ranch. What he saw there he positively refuses to tell, despite all our entreaty."

"You don't tell me there's a ranch with a mystery here near Rossiter!" exclaimed Mr. Perry, with sudden interest.

"Why, I do, indeed! Is it possible you have been here two whole weeks and haven't heard of Dunraven Ranch?"

"I've heard there was such a thing; I saw it from a distance when out hunting the other day. But what's the mystery?—what's the matter with it?"

"That's what we all want to know,—and cannot find out. Now,

there is an exploit worthy your energy and best efforts, Mr. Perry. There is a big, wealthy, well-stocked ranch, the finest homestead buildings, we are told, in all this part of Texas. They say it is beautifully furnished,—that it has a fine library, a grand piano, all manner of things indicative of culture and refinement among its occupants,—but the owner only comes around once or twice a year, and is an iceberg of an Englishman. All the people about the ranch are English, too, and the most repellent, boorish, discourteous lot of men you ever saw. When the Eleventh were here they did everything they could to be civil to them, but not an invitation would they accept, not one would they extend; and so from that day to this none of the officers have had any intercourse with the people at the ranch, and the soldiers know very little more. Once or twice a year some very ordinary looking men arrive who are said to be very distinguished people—in England; but they remain only a little while, and go away as suddenly as they came."

"And you have never seen any of them?"

"Never, except at a distance. Nor has any one of the officers, except Dr. Quin."

"And you have never heard anything about the inmates and why they keep up this policy of exclusiveness?"

"We have heard all manner of things,—some of them wildly romantic, some mysteriously tragic, and all of them, probably, absurd. At all events, Captain Lawrence has told me he did not wish me to repeat what I had heard, or to be concerned in any way with the stories afloat: so you must ask somebody else. Try the doctor. To change the subject, Mr. Perry, I see you have lost that mysterious little silken braid and tassel you wore on your cap-button. I fancied there was some romance attached to it, and now it is gone."

Perry laughed, his blue eyes twinkling with fun: "If I will tell you how and where I got that tassel, will you tell me what you have heard about Dunraven Ranch?"

"I cannot, unless Captain Lawrence withdraws his prohibition. Perhaps he will, though; for I think it was only because he was tired of hearing all our conjectures and theories."

"Well, will you tell me if I can induce the captain to say he has no objection?" persisted Perry.

"I will to-morrow,—if you will tell me about the tassel to-night."

"Is it a positive promise?—You will tell me to-morrow all you have heard about Dunraven Ranch if I will tell you to-night all I know about the tassel?"

"Yes,—a promise."

"Very well, then. You are a witness to the compact, Graham. Now for my confession. I have worn that tassel ever since our parting ball at Fort Riley. That is to say, it has been fastened to that button ever since the ball until to-night; but I've been mighty careful not to wear that cap on any kind of duty."

"And yet you let Mrs. Belknap take it off to-night?"

"Why shouldn't I? There was no sentiment whatever attached to it. I haven't the faintest idea whose it was, and only tied it there for the fun of the thing and to make Graham, here, ask questions."

"Mr. Perry!" gasped Mrs. Lawrence. "And do you mean that Mrs. Belknap knows?—that you told her what you have just told me?"

"Well, no," laughed Perry. "I fancy Mrs. Belknap thinks as you thought,—that it was a *gage d'amour*. Halloo! look at that light away out there across the prairie. What can *that* be?"

Mrs. Lawrence rose suddenly to her feet and gazed southeastward in the direction in which the young officer pointed. It was a lovely, starlit night. A soft wind was blowing gently from the south and bearing with it the fragrance of spring blossoms and far-away flowerets. Others, too, had arisen, attracted by Perry's sudden exclamation. Mrs. Belknap turned languidly in her hammock and glanced over her pretty white shoulder. The colonel followed her eyes with his and gave a start of surprise. The doctor turned slowly and composedly and looked silently towards the glistening object, and then upon the officers of the cavalry there fell sudden astonishment.

"What on earth could that have been?" asked the colonel. "It gleamed like the head-light of a locomotive, away down there in the valley of the Monee, then suddenly went out."

"Be silent a moment, and watch," whispered Mrs. Lawrence to Perry. "You will see it again; and—watch the doctor."

Surely enough, even as they were all looking about and commenting on the strange apparition, it suddenly glared forth a second time, shining full and lustrous as an unclouded planet, yet miles away beyond and above the fringe of cottonwoods that wound southeastward with the little stream. Full half a minute it shone, and then, abruptly as before, was hidden from sight.

Perry was about starting forward to join the colonel, when a little hand was laid upon his arm.

"Wait: once more you'll see it," she whispered. "Then take me in to Captain Lawrence. Do you see that the doctor is leaving?"

Without saying a word to any one, the post surgeon had very quietly withdrawn from the group on the veranda. He could not well leave by the front gate without attracting attention; but he strolled leisurely into the hall, took up a book that lay on the table, and passed through the group of officers seated smoking and chatting there, entered the sitting-room on the south side of the hall,—the side opposite the parlor where the whist-game was in progress,—and there he was lost to sight.

A third time the bright light burst upon the view of the gazers. A third time, sharply and suddenly it disappeared. Then for a moment all was silence and watchfulness; but it came no more.

Perry looked questioningly in his companion's face. She had turned a little white, and he felt sure that she was shivering.

"Are you cold?" he asked her, gently.

"No,—not that; but I hate mysteries, after what I've heard, and we haven't seen that light in ever so long. Come here to the corner one moment." And she led him around to the other flank of the big wooden, barrack-like residence of the commanding officer.

"Look up there," she said, pointing to a dark window under the peaked dormer roof of the large cottage to the south. "That is the doctor's house."

In a few seconds a faint gleam seemed to creep through the slats. Then the slats themselves were thrown wide open, a white shade was lowered, and, with the rays behind it growing brighter every instant, a broad white light shone forth over the roof of the veranda. Another moment, and footsteps were heard along the doctor's porch,—footsteps that presently approached them along the grass.

"Come," she said, plucking at his sleeve,—"come away: it is the doctor."

"For what reason?" he answered. "That would seem like hiding. No, Mrs. Lawrence, let us stay until he comes."

But the doctor passed them with brief and courteous salutation,—

spoke of the beauty of the night and the balm of the summery air,—and went in again by the main door to the colonel's quarters.

Then Perry turned to his partner: "Well, Mrs. Lawrence, what does it all mean? Is this part of what you had to tell me?"

"Don't ask me now. I—I did not *want* to see what we have seen, but I had heard queer stories and could not believe them. Take me in to Captain Lawrence, please. And, Mr. Perry, you won't speak of this to any one, will you? Indeed, if I had known, I would not have come out here for the world; but I didn't believe it, even when she went away and took the children."

"*Who* went away?"

"Mrs. Quin,—the doctor's wife. And she was such a sweet woman, and so devoted to him."

"Well, pardon me, Mrs. Lawrence, I don't see through this thing at all. Do you mean that the doctor has anything to do with the mystery?"

She bowed her head as they turned back to the house: "I must not tell you any more to-night. You will be sure to hear something of it all, here. Everybody on the piazza saw the lights, and all who were here before you came knew what they meant."

"What were they?"

"Signals, of some kind, from Dunraven Ranch."

II.

Ned Perry hated reveille and morning stables about as vehemently as was possible to a young fellow who was in other respects thoroughly in love with his profession. A fairer type of the American cavalry officer, when once he got in saddle and settled down to business, one would hardly ask to find. Tall, athletic, slender of build, with frank, laughing blue eyes, curly, close-cropped, light-brown hair, and a twirling moustache that was a source of inexpressible delight to its owner and of some envy to his brother subalterns, Mr. Perry was probably the best-looking of the young officers who marched with the battalion to this far-away station on the borders of the Llano Estacado. He had been ten years in service, counting the four he spent as a cadet, had just won his silver bar as the junior first-lieutenant of the regiment, was full to the brim of health, energy, animal spirits, and fun, and, barring a few duns and debts in his earlier experiences, had never known a heavier care in the world than the transient and ephemeral anxiety as to whether he would be called up for recitation on a subject he had not so much as looked at, or "hived" absent from a roll-call he had lazily slept through. Any other man, his comrades said, would have been spoiled a dozen times over by the petting he had received from both men and women; but there was something essentially sweet and genial about his nature,—something "lacking in guile about his perceptions," said a cynical old captain of the regiment,—and a jovial, sunshiny way of looking upon the world as an Eden, all men and all women as friends, and the Army as the profession above all others, and these various attributes combined to make him popular with his kind and unusually attractive to the opposite sex. As a cadet he had been perpetually on the verge of dismissal because of the appalling array of demerits he could roll up against his name; and yet the very officers who jotted down the memoranda of his sins—omission and commission—against the regulations were men who openly said he "had the making of one of the finest soldiers in the class." As junior second-lieutenant—"plebe"—of the regiment, he had been welcomed by every man from the colonel down, and it was considered particularly rough that he should have to go to such a company as Captain Canker's, because Canker was a man who never got along with any of his juniors; but there was something so irrepressibly frank and contrite in Perry's boyish face when he would appear at his captain's door in the early morning and burst out with, "By Jove, captain! I slept through reveille again this morning, and never got down till stables were nearly over," that even that cross-grained but honest troop-commander was disarmed, and, though he threatened and reprimanded, he would never punish,—would never deny his subaltern the faintest privilege; and when promotion took the captain to another regiment he bade good-by to Perry with eyes that were suspiciously wet. "Why, blow it all, what do you fellows hate Canker so for?" the youngster often said. "He ought to put me in arrest time and again, but he won't. Blamed if I don't put myself in arrest, or confine myself to the limits of the post, or do something, to cut all this going to town and hops and such things. Then I can stick to the troop like wax and get up at reveille; but if I'm out dancing till two or three in the morning it's no use, I tell you: I just *can't* wake up." Indeed, it was part of the unwritten records of the —th that while at Riley and having very sociable times, Ned Perry actually declined invitations, cooped himself up in garrison, and wore metaphorical sackcloth and ashes, for a whole week, in penance for certain neglects of duty brought about by the presence of a bevy of pretty girls. It was not until Canker went to him in person and virtually ordered him out that Perry could be induced to appear at the party given in farewell to two of the prettiest, who were to leave for the East on the following day.

And yet he was a disappointment in a certain way. It was always predicted of Ned Perry that he would be " married and done for" within a year of his graduation. Every new face in the five years that followed revived the garrison prophecy, " Now he's gone, sure!" but, however devoted he might seem to the damsel in question, however restless and impatient he might be when compelled by his duties to absent himself from her side, however promising to casual observers—perchance to the damsel herself—might be all the surface-indications, the absolute frankness with which he proclaimed his admiration to every listener, and the fact that he "had been just so with half a dozen other girls," enabled the cooler heads of the regiment to decide that the time had not yet come,—or at least the woman.

"I do wish," said Mrs. Turner, "that Mr. Perry would settle on somebody, because, just so long as he doesn't, it is rather hard to tell whom he belongs to." And, as Mrs. Turner had long been a reigning belle among the married women of the —th, and one to whom the young officers were always expected to show much attention, her whimsical way of describing the situation was readily understood.

But here at the new station—at far-away Rossiter—matters were taking on a new look. To begin with, the wives of the officers of the cavalry battalion had not joined, none of the ladies of the —th were here, and none would be apt to come until the summer's scouting-work was over and done with. The ladies of the little battalion of infantry *were* here, and, though there were no maiden sisters or cousins yet at the post (rest assured that more than one was already summoned), they were sufficient in number to enliven the monotony of garrison life and sufficiently attractive to warrant all the attention they cared to receive. It was beginning to be garrison chat that if Ned Perry had not "settled on somebody" as the ultimate object of his entire devotion, somebody had settled on him, and that was pretty Mrs. Belknap.

And though Ned Perry hated reveille and morning stables, as has been said, and could rarely "take his week" without making one or more lapses, here he was this beautiful May morning out at daybreak when it was his junior's tour of duty, and wending his way with that youngster out to the line of cavalry stables, booted and spurred and equipped for a ride.

The colonel had listened with some surprise to his request, proffered just as the party was breaking up the night before, to be absent from garrison a few hours the following morning.

"But we have battalion drill at nine o'clock, Mr. Perry, and I need you there," he said.

"Oh, I'll be back in time for that, sir. I wanted to be off three hours or so before breakfast."

The colonel could not help laughing. "Of course you can go,—go wherever you like at those hours, when you are not on guard; but I never imagined you would want to get up so early."

"Neither I would, colonel, but I've been interested in something I heard about this ranch down the Monee, and thought I'd like to ride down and look at it."

"Go ahead, by all means, and see whether those lights came from there. It made me think of a play I once saw,—the 'Colleen Bawn,'—where a fellow's sweetheart signalled across the lake by showing a light in her cottage window just that way, three times, and he answered by turning out the lights in his room. Of course the distance wasn't anything like this; and there was no one here to turn down any light—— Eh! what did you say?"

"I beg pardon, colonel. I didn't mean to interrupt," put in a gentle voice at his elbow, while a little hand on Perry's arm gave it a sudden and vigorous squeeze, "but Captain Lawrence has called me twice,—he will not re-enter after lighting his cigar,—and I must say good-night."

"Oh! good-night, Mrs. Lawrence. I'm sorry you go so early. We are going to reform you all in that respect as soon as we get fairly settled. Here's Perry, now, would sit up and play whist with me an hour yet."

"Not this night, colonel. He has promised to walk home with us" (another squeeze), "and go he must, or be a faithless escort. Good-night. We've had such a lovely, *lovely* time."

And Ned Perry, dazed, went with her to the gate, where Captain Lawrence was awaiting them. She had barely time to murmur,—

"You were just on the point of telling him about the doctor's lights. I cannot forgive myself for being the means of your seeing it; but keep my confidence, and keep—this, until everybody is talking about it: it will come soon enough."

Naturally, Mr. Perry went home somewhat perturbed in spirit and all alive with conjecture as to what these things could mean. The first notes of "assembly of the trumpeters"—generally known as "first call"—roused him from his sleep, and by the time the men marched out to stables he had had his plunge-bath, a vigorous rub, and a chance to think over his plans before following in their tracks, dressed for his ride. The astonishment of Lieutenant Parke, the junior of the troop, was something almost too deep for words when Perry came bounding to his side.

"What on earth brings *you* out, Ned?" was his only effort.

"Going for a gallop,—down the Monee: that's all. I haven't had a freshener for a week."

"Gad! we get exercise enough at morning drill, one would think, and our horses too. Oh!——" And Mr. Parke stopped suddenly. It flashed across him that perhaps Perry was going riding with a lady friend and the hour was *her* selection. If so, 'twas no business of his, and remarks were uncalled for. Accepting this as the one possible explanation of Perry's abnormal early rising, he curbed his tongue, and Perry, absorbed in his own projects and thinking of anything but what was passing through his comrade's brain, strode blithely over the springy turf, saying nothing further of his plan.

When he mounted and rode away from the stable Mr. Parke was outside at the picket-rope, and busily occupied in his duties, supervising the fastening of the fresh, spirited horses at the line, for the troop-commander was a man intolerant of disorder of any kind, and nothing more offended his eye than the sight of two or three of his chargers loose and plunging and kicking up and down the stable-yard. On the other hand, there was no one exploit that seemed to give the younger animals keener delight,—nothing that made the perpetrator a bigger hero in his own eyes or the object of greater envy among his fellows,—and as a consequence every device of which equine ingenuity was master was called into play, regularly as the morning came around, to break loose either from the controlling hand of the trooper or from the taut and straining picket-rope. The first care of the officer in charge and the troop-sergeants was, therefore, to see that all the horses were securely lashed and knotted. Not until he had examined every "halter-shank" was Mr. Parke at leisure to look around; but when he did, his comrade had disappeared from view.

The valley of the Monee, shallow, and bare of trees except in scattered clumps along the stream, stretched away southeastward for many a mile until lost to sight in the general level at the horizon. Off to the north and east the prairie rose and fell in long, low undulations, so devoid of abrupt slope of any kind as to seem absolutely flat to the unpractised eye. Southward and to the west of the lonely post the surface was relieved of this monotony by occasional gentle rise and swell. Nowhere, however, over the broad expanse was there sign of other vegetation than the gray-green carpet of buffalo-grass, and this carpet itself was mapped in fantastic pattern, the effect of prairie-fires more or less recent in occurrence. Where within a fortnight the flames had swept over the surface, all the bosom of the earth was one black barren, a land shunned for the time being by every living thing. Where by sudden freak of wind or fall of rain the scourging fires had been checked in their course, there lay broad wastes of virgin turf, already bleaching under the fierce Texan sun to the conventional gray of the buffalo-grass. But contrasted with these wide mantles of black and gray—contrasting sharply, too, because never blending—every mile or so were sudden patches of bright and lively green; and this was the hue of the sturdy young grass peeping up through the wastes that the flames had desolated late in March.

And over this broad level, horizon-bounded, not a moving object could be seen. Far away, in little groups of three or four, black dots of grazing cattle marked the plain; and over in the "breaks" of the Monee, just beyond the fringing cottonwoods, two or three herds of Indian ponies were sleepily cropping their morning meal, watched by the little black imp of a boy whose dirty red blanket made the only patch of color against the southern landscape. Later in the day, when the sun mounted high in the heavens and the brisk westerly winds sent the clouds sailing swift across the skies, all the broad prairie seemed in motion, for then huge shadows swept its face with measured speed, and distant cattle and neighboring pony-herd appeared as though calmly and contentedly riding on a broad platform, Nature's own "observation-car," taking a leisurely journey towards the far-away Pacific.

But the sun was only just up as Mr. Parke came back from his inspection of the halter-fastenings and paused to look across the low valley. Far down to the southeast the rays seemed glinting on some bright objects clustered together within short range of the shadowy fringe, and the lieutenant shaded his eyes with his gauntlet and looked fixedly thitherward as he stood at the stable door.

"Some new tinning down at that English ranch they talk of, I suppose," was his explanation of the phenomenon, and then, "Wonder why Perry hasn't ridden to cultivate the acquaintance of those people before this. He was always the first man in the —th to find out who our neighbors were."

Pondering over this question, it occurred to Mr. Parke that Perry had said he was going down the Monee that morning; but nowhere was there a speck in sight that looked like loping horseman. To be sure, the trail bore close to the low bluffs that bounded the valley on the north by the time one had ridden a mile or so out from the post. He was probably hidden by this shoulder of the prairie, and would continue to be until he reached the bend, five miles below. No use watching for him then. Besides, he might not yet have started. Mr. Parke recalled the fact that he half suspected a while ago that Ned was going to ride—an early ante-breakfast ride—with a lady friend. Mrs. Belknap had her own horse, and was an accomplished *équestrienne;* Mrs. Lawrence rode fairly well, and was always glad to go, when somebody could give her a saddle and a reliable mount. There were others, too, among the ladies of the infantry garrison who were no novices *à cheval*. Mr. Parke had no intention whatever of prying into the matter. It was simply as something the officer in charge of stable-duty was entitled to know that he turned suddenly and called,—

"Sergeant Gwynne!"

He heard the name passed down the dark interior of the stable by the men sweeping out the stalls, and the prompt and cheery reply. The next instant a tall young trooper stepped forth into the blaze of early sunlight, his right hand raised in salute, and stood erect and motionless by the lieutenant's side.

"Did Mr. Perry take an extra horse, sergeant?"

"No, sir."

"I thought possibly he meant to take Roland. He's the best lady's-horse in the troop, is he not?"

"Yes, sir; but Roland is at the line now."

"Very well, then. That's all. I presume he has just ridden down to Dunraven." And Mr. Parke turned to look once more at the glinting objects down the distant valley. It was a moment or two before he was aware of the fact that the sergeant still stood there, instead of returning to his duties.

"I said that was all, sergeant: you can go back to your feeding." And then Mr. Parke turned in some surprise, for Sergeant Gwynne, by long odds the "smartest" and most soldierly of the non-commissioned officers of the cavalry battalion, for the first time in his history seemed to have forgotten himself. Though his attitude had not changed, his face had, and a strange look was in his bright blue eyes,—a look of incredulity and wonderment and trouble all combined. The lieutenant was fairly startled when, as though suddenly gathering himself together, the sergeant falteringly asked,—

"I beg pardon, sir, but—he had ridden—*where?*"

"Down to the ranch, sergeant,—that one you can just see, away down the valley."

"I know, sir; but—the name?"

"Dunraven Ranch."

For an instant the sergeant stood as though dazed, then, with sudden effort, saluted, faced about, and plunged into the dark recesses of the stable.

III.

Meantime, Lieutenant Perry was riding blithely down the winding trail, totally unconscious that his movements were of the faintest consequence to anybody but himself, and equally heedless of their being a source of speculation. His horse was one he rejoiced in, full of spirit and spring and intelligence; the morning was beautiful,—just cool enough to be exhilarating; his favorite hound, Bruce, went bounding over the turf under the slopes, or ranging off through the cottonwoods along the stream, or the shallow, sandy *arroyos*, where the grass and weeds grew rank and luxuriant. Every now and then with sudden rush and whir a drove of prairie-chickens would leap from their covert, and, after vigorous flapping of wings for a few rods, would go skimming restfully in long easy curve, and settle to earth again a hundred yards away, as though suddenly reminded of the fact that this was mating-time and no gentleman would be mean enough to shoot at such a season. Every little while, too, with prodigious kicking of dust and show of heels, with eyes fairly bulging out of his feather-brained head, and tall lop-ears laid flat on his back, a big jack-rabbit would bound off into space, and go tearing across the prairie in mad race for his threatened life, putting a mile between him and the Monee before he began to realize that the two quadrupeds ambling along the distant trail were obedient to the will of that single rider, who had no thought to spare for game so small. Some Indian ponies, grazing across his pathway, set back their stunted ears, and, cow-like, refused to budge at sight and hearing of the big American horse; whereat a little vagabond of a Cheyenne, not ten years old nor four feet high, set up a shrill chatter and screech and let drive a few well-directed clods of turf, and then showed his white teeth in a grin as Perry sung out a cheery "*How!* sonny," and spurred on through the opening thoroughfare, heedless of spiteful pony looks or threatening heels.

Perry's spirits rose with every rod. Youth, health, contentment, all were his, and his heart was warm towards his fellow-men. To the best of his reckoning, he had not an enemy or detractor in the world. He was all gladness of nature, all friendliness, frankness, and cordiality. The toughest cow-boy whom they had met on the long march down, the most crabbed of the frontiersmen they had ever encountered, was never proof against such sunshine as seemed to irradiate his face. He would go out of his way at any time to meet and hail a fellow-man upon the prairies, and rarely came back without knowing all about him,—where he was from, whither he was bound, and what were his hopes and prospects. And as for himself, no man was readier to answer question or to meet in friendliest and most jovial spirit the rough but well-meant greetings of "the Plains."

Being in this frame of mind to an extent even greater than his normal wont, Mr. Perry's eyes glistened, and he struck spur to hasten Nolan's stride, when, far ahead, and coming towards him on the trail, he saw a horseman like himself. Being in this mood of sociability, he was something more than surprised to see that all of a sudden that horseman had reined in—a mere black dot a mile away—and was presumably examining him as he advanced. Hostile Indians there had been none for many a long month, "road-agents" would have starved in a region where there practically were no roads, cow-boys might—and did—get on frolics and have wild "tears" at times, but who ever heard of their being hostile, man to man? Yet Perry was plainsman enough to tell, even at the mile of distance, that the stranger had halted solely to scrutinize *him*, and, next, to his vast astonishment, that something in his appearance had proved either alarming or suspicious, for the horseman had turned abruptly, plunged through the timber and across the stream, and in another moment, veering that way himself to see, Perry marked him fairly racing into the mouth of a shallow ravine, or "break," that entered the valley from the south, and there he was lost to sight.

"What an ill-mannered galoot!" was his muttered comment, as he gave Nolan brief chance to crop the juicy grass, while his perturbed rider sat gazing across the stream in the direction taken by the shy horseman. "I've half a mind to drop the ranch and put out after that fellow. That ravine can't go in so very far but what he must soon show up on the level prairie; and I'll bet Nolan could run him down." After a moment's reflection, however, Mr. Perry concluded that, as he had come so far and was now nearly within rifle-shot of the mysterious goal of his morning ride, he might as well let the stranger go, and pushed ahead, himself, for Dunraven.

The stream bent southward just at the point where he had first caught sight of the horseman, and around that point he knew the ranch to be. Very probably that was one of the ranchmen of whom Mrs. Lawrence had spoken,—churlish fellows, with a civil word for nobody, grim and repellent. Why, certainly! That accounted for his evident desire to avoid the cavalryman; but he need not have been in such desperate haste,—need not have kept at such unapproachable bounds, as though he shunned even being seen. That was the queer thing, thought Perry. He acted just as though he did not want to be recognized. Perhaps he'd been up to some devilment at the ranch.

This thought gave spur to his speed, and Nolan, responsive to his master's mood, leaped forward along the winding trail once more. The point was soon reached and turned, and the first object that caught Perry's eye was a long row of stakes stretching from the cottonwoods straight to the south up the gentle slope to the prairie, and indicating beyond all question the presence there of a stout and high and impassable wire fence. There are few things the cavalryman holds in meaner estimate.

"That marks the western limit," thought Perry to himself, "and doubtless reaches miles away to the south, from what I hear. Now, where does one enter?"

A little farther on he came upon a trail leading from the low bluffs to his left hand. It crossed the winding bridle-path on which he rode, though some of the hoof-tracks seemed to join, and wheel-tracks too. He had marked that between the fort and the point no sign of wheel appeared: it was a hoof-trail and nothing more. Now a light and little-travelled wagon-track came in from the north, and while one branch seemed to cross the Monce and to ascend the opposite slopes close along the wire fence, the other joined him and went on down the stream. This he decided to follow.

A ride of a few hundred yards brought him to a point where a shoulder of bluff twisted the trail well in towards the stream, and he, thinking to cross and reconnoitre on the other shore, turned Nolan in that way, and was suddenly brought up standing by the heaviest and most forbidding wire fence he had ever seen. Yes, there it stretched away through the cottonwoods, straight as a die, back to the angle whence started the southward course he first had noted, and, looking down stream, far as the eye could reach, he marked it, staked as though by the theodolite itself, straight as surveyor could make it, a rigid line to the southeast. Sometimes the stream lay on one side, sometimes on the other; so, too, the cottonwoods; but there, grim and bristling and impassable, over five feet high, and fairly snarling with its sharp and jagged teeth, this inhuman barrier lay betwixt him and the lands of Dunraven Ranch.

"Well," thought Perry, "I've often heard an Englishman's house was his castle, but who would have thought of staking and wiring in half a county—half a Texas county—in this hoggish way? How far down is the entrance, anyhow?"

Following the trail, he rode down-stream a full half-mile, and still there seemed no break. Nowhere on the other shore was there sign of bridle-path leading up the slopes. Turning to his left in some impatience, he sent Nolan at rapid lope across the intervening "bottom," and soon reached the bluffs, which rose perhaps forty or fifty feet above the stream. Once on the crest, the prairie stretched before him, northward, level as a floor, until it met the sky; but it was southward he longed to look, and thither quickly turned. Yes, there it lay,—Dunraven Ranch, in all its lonely majesty. From where he gazed the nearest building stood a good long mile away. That it was the homestead he divined at once, for a broad veranda ran around the lower story, and white curtains were visible at the dormer-windows of the upper floor. Back of it and on the eastern flank were other buildings, massive-looking, single-storied affairs,—evidently stables, storehouses, and corrals. There was a tall windmill there,—an odd sight in so remote a region,—and a big water-tank. Perry wondered how it ever got there. Then at the southwest angle was a building that looked like an office of some kind. He could see horses tethered there, and what seemed to be human figures moving about. Beyond it all, to the east and south, were herds of grazing cattle, and here and there in the dim distance a horseman moved over the prairie. This reminded him of the stranger who had given him the slip; and he gazed westward in search of him.

Far up the valley, between him and the distant post, he could plainly see a black object just descending the slopes from the southern prairie to the stream. Not another was in sight that his practised eye did not know to be cattle. That, then, was his horseman, once more going fort-wards in the valley, after having made a three- or four-mile *détour* to avoid him. "Now, what sort of a Christian is that fellow?" thought Perry, as he gazed at the distant speck. "Going to the fort, too. By thunder! I'll find out who *he* is, anyhow. Now I'm going to the ranch."

Down the slopes he rode. Down the winding trail once more he trotted, peering through every gap among the cottonwoods, slaking Nolan's thirst at a little pool in the stream, and then, after another long half-mile, he came to a sudden turn to the right. The road dipped and twisted through the stream-bed, rose to the other side, wound through the cottonwoods and then out on the open turf. Huzza! There it stretched up the slopes straight away for the south, straight through a broad gap between two heavy gate-posts standing on the stake-line of that rigid fence. Nolan broke into a brisk canter and gave a neigh of salutation; Perry's eyes glistened with anticipation as he bent over his charger's neck, keenly searching the odd-looking structure growing on his vision as they neared the fence. Then, little by little, Nolan's eager stride shortened and grew choppy. Another moment, and horse and rider reined up short in disappointment. Between the gate-posts swung a barrier of cobweb lightness, slender and airy as ever spider wove, but bristling with barbs, stiff as "bullfinch" and unyielding as steel. One glance showed Perry that this inhospitable gate was firmly locked.

For a moment he sat in saddle, studying the situation, while Nolan poked his head over the topmost strand of wire and, keeping at respectful distance from the glittering barbs, gazed wistfully over the enclosed prairie in search of comrade quadruped who could tell him what manner of place this was. Meantime, his rider was intently eying the heavy padlock that was secured on the inner side of the gate. It was square in shape, massive and bulky,—something utterly unlike anything he had ever seen among the quartermaster's stores. Dismounting, and holding Nolan well back from the aggressive fence with one hand, he gingerly passed the other through the spike-fringed aperture and turned the padlock so as to get a better view. It was of English make, as he surmised, and of strength sufficient to resist anything short of a trip-hammer. Evidently no admission was to be gained here, he reasoned; and yet it was through here that that horseman had come but an hour before. Here were the fresh hoof-prints in the trail, and it was evident that the rider had dismounted, opened the gate, led his horse through, closed and fastened it, then remounted and ridden away. Perry was plainsman enough to read this from the hoof-prints. Studying them carefully, a look of surprise came into his face: he bent down and closely examined the two or three that were most clearly defined upon the trail, then gave a long whistle as a means of expressing his feelings and giving play to his astonishment:

"Johnny Bull holds himself too high and mighty to have anything to do with us blarsted Yankees, it seems, except when he wants his horses shod. These shoes were set at the post blacksmith-shop, or I'm a duffer," was the lieutenant's verbal comment. "Now, how was it done without the quartermaster's knowing it? That's the cavalry shoe!"

Pondering over this unlooked-for revelation, Mr. Perry once more mounted, and turned his disappointed steed again down-stream. He had determined to follow the fence in search of another opening. A mile he rode among the cottonwoods and across low grassy points, and still that inflexible barrier stretched grimly between him and the open prairie to the south. Once, up a long shallow "break," he caught sight of the roofs of some of the ranch-buildings full a thousand yards away, and realized that he had passed to the east of them and was farther from the goal of his ambition than when he stood at that bristling gate. At last, full half a mile farther on, he saw that a wire fence ran southward again across the prairie, as though marking the eastern boundary of the homestead-enclosure, and, conjecturing that there was probably a trail along that fence and an opening through, even if the southeastward line should be found fenced still farther, he sent Nolan through the Monee to the open bank on the northern side, cantered along until the trail turned abruptly southward, and, following it, found himself once more at the fence just where the heavy corner-post stood deeply embedded in the soil. Sure enough, here ran another fence straight up the gentle slope to the south, a trail along its eastern side, and a broad cattle-gap, dusty and tramped with the hoofs of a thousand steers, was left in the fence that, prolonged down-stream, spanned the northern boundary. Inside the homestead-lot all was virgin turf.

Following the southward trail, Perry rode briskly up the long incline. It was east of this fence he had seen the cattle-herds and their mounted watchers. He was far beyond the ranch-buildings, but felt sure that, once well up on the prairie, he could have an uninterrupted view of them and doubtless meet some of the ranch people and satisfy himself what there was in the stories of their churlish and repellent demeanor. The sun was climbing higher all this time, and he, eager in pursuit of his reconnoissance, gave little heed to fleeting minutes. If fair means could accomplish it, he and Nolan were bound to have acquaintance with Dunraven Ranch.

Ten minutes' easy lope brought him well up on the prairie. There —westward now—was the mysterious clump of brown buildings, just as far away as when he stood, baffled and disappointed, by the gate-way on the Monee. Here, leading away towards the distant buildings, was a bridle-path. Here in the fence was a gap just such as he had encountered on the stream, and that gap was barred and guarded by the counterpart of the first gate and firmly secured by a padlock that was the other's twin. Mr. Perry's comment at this point of his explorations was brief and characteristic, if not objectionable. He gave vent to the same low whistle, half surprise, half vexation, that had comforted his soul before, but supplemented the whistle with the unnecessary remark, "Well, I'll be damned!"

Even Nolan entered his protest against such incredible exclusiveness. Thrusting his lean head far over the topmost wire as before, he signalled long and shrill,—a neigh that would have caught the ear of any horse within a mile,—and then, all alert, he waited for an answer. It came floating on the rising wind, a responsive call, a signal as eager and confident as his own, and Nolan and Nolan's rider whirled quickly around to see the source from whence it rose. Four hundred yards away, just appearing over a little knoll in the prairie, and moving towards them from the direction of a distant clump of grazing cattle, another horse and rider came trotting into hailing-distance; and Perry, his bright blue eyes dilating, and Nolan, his dainty, sensitive ears pricked forward, turned promptly to meet and greet the new arrivals.

For fifty yards or so the stranger rode confidently and at rapid trot. Perry smilingly watched the out-turned toes, the bobbing, "bent-over" seat, and angular elbows that seemed so strange and out of place on the broad Texan plain. He could almost see the "crop" in the free hand, and was smiling to himself at the idea of a "crop" to open wire gates, when he became aware of the fact that the stranger's mien had changed; confidence was giving place to hesitancy, and he was evidently checking the rapid trot of his horse and throwing his weight back on the cantle, while his feet, thrust through to the very heels in the gleaming steel stirrups, were braced in front of the powerful shoulders of the bay. The horse wanted to come, the rider plainly wanted to stop. Another moment, and Perry could see that the stranger wore eyeglasses and had just succeeded in bridging them on his nose and was glaring at him with his chin high in air. They were within two hundred yards of each other by this time, and, to Perry's astonishment, the next thing the stranger did was to touch sharply his horse with barbed heel, whirl him spitefully about, and go bobbing off across the prairie at lively canter, standing up in his stirrups, and bestriding his steed as though his object were not so much a ride as a game of leap-frog.

It was evident that he had caught sight of Perry when Nolan neighed, had ridden at once to meet him, expecting to find some one connected with the ranch, and had veered off in disgust the moment he was able to recognize the uniform and horse-equipments of the United States Cavalry.

IV.

Sweet-tempered a fellow as Mr. Perry confessedly was, there was something in the stranger's conduct that galled him inexpressibly. The tenets of "society," the formalities of metropolitan life, have no recognition whatsoever on the wide frontier when once the confines of the garrison are passed. Out on the broad expanse of the Plains the man who shuns the greeting of his fellow is set down at once as a party whose antecedents are shadowy and whose character is suspicious; and never before in his experience of several years and his wanderings from the Yellowstone to the Washita had Ned Perry met a frontiersman who fled at sight of him, except one horse-thief. From his handsome mount, his garb, and his general appearance, Perry set this stranger down as one of the Englishmen residing at the ranch. It was not fear of arrest and capture that sent *him* scowling away across the prairie; it was deliberate intent to avoid, and this was, to Perry's thinking, tantamount to insult. One moment he gazed after the retreating form of the horseman, then clapped his forage-cap firmly down upon his head, shook free the rein, and gave Nolan the longed-for word. Another instant, and with set teeth and blazing, angry eyes he was thundering at headlong speed, swooping down upon the unconscious stranger in pursuit. Before that sunburned, curly-haired, bulkily-framed young man had the faintest idea of what was impending, Mr. Perry was reining in his snorting steed alongside and cuttingly accosting him:

"I beg your pardon, my good sir, but may I ask what you mean by trotting away when it must have been evident that I wanted to speak with you?"

The stranger turned slightly and coolly eyed the flushed and indignant cavalryman. They were trotting side by side now, Nolan plunging excitedly, but the English horse maintaining his even stride; and stronger contrast of type and style one could scarcely hope to find. In rough tweed shooting-jacket and cap, brown Bedford cords fitting snugly at the knee but flapping like shapeless bags from there aloft to the waist, in heavy leather gaiters and equally heavy leather gloves, the stocky figure of the Englishman had nothing of grace or elegance, but was sturdy, strong, and full of that burly self-reliance which is so characteristic of the race. Above his broad, stooping shoulders were a bull neck, reddened by the sun, a crop of close-curling, light-brown hair, a tanned and honest face lighted up by fearless gray eyes and shaded by a thick and curling beard of lighter hue than the hair of his massive head. He rode with the careless ease and supreme confidence of the skilled horseman, but with that angularity of foot and elbow, that roundness of back and bunching of shoulders, that incessant rise and fall with every beat of his horse's powerful haunch, that the effect was that of neither security nor repose. His saddle, too, was the long, flat-seated, Australian model, pig-skin, with huge rounded leathern cushions circling in front and over the knees, adding to the cumbrousness of his equipment and in no wise to the comfort; but his bit and curb-chain were of burnished steel, gleaming as though fresh from the hands of some incomparable English groom, and the russet reins were soft and pliable, telling of excellent stable management and discipline.

Perry couldn't help admiring that bridle, even in his temporary fit of indignation.

As for him,—tall, slender, elegantly made, clothed in the accurately-fitting undress "blouse" of the army and in riding-breeches that displayed to best advantage the superb moulding of his powerful thighs, sitting like centaur well down in the saddle, his feet and lower legs, cased in natty riding-boots, swinging close in behind the gleaming shoulders of his steed, erect as on parade, yet swaying with every motion of his horse, graceful, gallant, and to the full as powerful as his burly companion, the advantage in appearance was all on Perry's side, and was heightened by Nolan's spirited action and martial trappings. Perry was an exquisite in his soldier taste, and never, except on actual campaign, rode his troop-horse without his broidered saddle-cloth and gleaming bosses. All this, and more, the Englishman seemed quietly noting as, finally, without the faintest trace of irritability, with even a suspicion of humor twinkling about the corners of his mouth, he replied,—

"A fellow may do as he likes when he's on his own bailiwick, I suppose."

"All the same, wherever I've been, from here to Assiniboia, men meet like Christians, unless they happen to be road-agents or cattle-thieves. What's more, I am an officer of a regiment just arrived here, and, from the Missouri down, there isn't a ranch along our trail where we were not welcome and whose occupants were not 'hail-fellow-well-met' in our camps. You are the first people to shun us; and, as that fort yonder was built for your protection in days when it was badly needed, I want to know what there is about its garrison that is so obnoxious to Dunraven Ranch,—that's what you call it, I believe?"

"That's what—it is called."

"Well, here! I've no intention of intruding where we're not wanted. I simply didn't suppose that on the broad prairies of the West there was such a place as a ranch where one of my cloth was unwelcome. I am Mr. Perry, of the —th Cavalry, and I'm bound to say I'd like to know what you people have against us. Are you the proprietor?"

"I'm not. I'm only an employee."

"Who *is* the owner?"

"He's not here now."

"Who *is* here who can explain the situation?"

"Oh, as to that, I fancy I can do it as well as anybody. It is simply because we have to do pretty much as you fellows,—obey orders. The owner's orders are not aimed at you any more than anybody else. He simply wants to be let alone. He bought this tract and settled here because he wanted a place where he could have things his own way,—see people whom he sent for and nobody else. Every man in his employ is expected to stick to the ranch so long as he is on the payroll, and to carry out his instructions. If he can't, he may go."

"And your instructions are to prevent people getting into the ranch?"

"Oh, hardly that, you know. We don't interfere. There's never any one to come, as a rule, and, when they do, the fence seems to be sufficient."

"Amply, I should say; and yet were I to tell you that I had business with the proprietor and needed to ride up to the ranch, you would open the gate yonder, I suppose?"

"No: I would tell you that the owner was away, and that in his absence I transacted all business for him."

"Well, thank you for the information given me, at all events. May I ask the name of your misanthropical boss? You might tell him I called."

"Several officers called three years ago, but he begged to be excused."

"And what is the name?"

"Mr. Maitland—is what he is called."

"All right. Possibly the time may come when Mr. Maitland will be as anxious to have the cavalry around him as he is now to keep it away. But if *you* ever feel like coming up to the fort, just ride in and ask for me."

"I feel like it a dozen times a week, you know; but a man mustn't quarrel with his bread-and-butter. I met one of your fellows once on a hunt after strayed mules, and he asked me in, but I couldn't go. Sorry, you know, and all that, but the owner won't have it."

"Well, then there's nothing to do for it but say good-day to you. I'm going back. Possibly I'll see some of your people up at Rossiter when they come to get a horse shod."

"A horse shod! Why, man alive, we shoe all our horses here!"

"Well, that fellow who rode out of your north gate and went up towards the fort about an hour or so ago had his horse shod at a cavalry forge, or I'm a duffer."

G*

A quick change came over the Englishman's face: a flush of surprise and anger shot up to his forehead: he wheeled about and gazed eagerly, loweringly, back towards the far-away buildings.

"How do you know there was—— What fellow did you see?" he sharply asked.

"Oh, I don't know who he was," answered Perry, coolly. "He avoided me just as pointedly as you did,—galloped across the Monee and out on the prairie to dodge me; but he came out of that gate on the stream, locked it after him, and went on up to the fort; and his horse had cavalry shoes. Good-day to you, my Britannic friend. Come and see us when you get tired of prison-life." And, with a grin, Mr. Perry turned and rode rapidly away, leaving the other horseman in a brown study.

Once fairly across the Monee, he ambled placidly along, thinking of the odd situation of affairs at this great prairie-reservation, and almost regretting that he had paid the ranch the honor of a call. Reaching the point where the wagon-tracks crossed the stream to the gate-way in the boundary fence, he reined in Nolan and looked through a vista in the cottonwoods. There was the Englishman, dismounted, stooping over the ground, and evidently examining the hoof-prints at the gate. Perry chuckled at the sight, then, whistling for Bruce, who had strayed off through the timber, he resumed his jaunty way to the post.

In the events of the morning there were several things to give him abundant cause for thought, if not for lively curiosity, but he had not yet reached the sum total of surprises in store for him. He was still two miles out from the fort, and riding slowly along the bottom, when he became aware of a trooper coming towards him on the trail. The sunbeams were glinting on the polished ornaments of his forage-cap and on the bright yellow chevrons of his snugly-fitting blouse. Tall and slender and erect was the coming horseman, a model of soldierly grace and carriage, and as he drew nearer and his hand went up to the cap-visor in salute a gesture from his young superior brought an instant pressure on the rein, and horse and man became an animated statue. It was a wonderfully sudden yet easy check of a steed in rapid motion, and Mr. Perry, a capital rider himself, could not withhold his admiration.

"Where did you learn that sudden halt, sergeant?" he asked. "I never saw anything so quick except the Mexican training; but that strains a horse and throws him on his haunches."

"It is not uncommon abroad, sir," was the quiet answer. "I saw it first in the English cavalry; and it is easy to teach the horse."

"I must get you to show me the knack some day. I've noticed it two or three times, and would like to learn it. What I stopped you for was this: you've been stable-sergeant ever since we got here, have you not?"

"Yes, sir."

"Then if anybody besides members of the troop had horses shod at our forge you would be pretty apt to know it?"

"I know that no one has, sir." And a flush was rising to the young sergeant's face and a pained look hovering about his bright blue eyes. Yet his manner was self-restrained and full of respect.

"Don't think I'm intimating anything to the contrary, Sergeant Gwynne. No soldier in the regiment more entirely holds the confidence of his captain—of all the officers—than you. I was not thinking of that. But somebody down there at that big ranch below us has had his horse shod by a cavalry farrier,—it may have been done while the Eleventh were here,—and, while I knew you would not allow it at our forge, I thought it possible that it might be done in your absence."

"It's the first time I've been out of sight of the stables since we came to the post, sir, and the captain gave me permission to ride down the valley this morning. May I ask the lieutenant why he thinks some ranchman is getting his shoeing done here at the post?"

"I've been down there this morning, and met a man coming up. He avoided me, and rode over to the south side, and so excited my curiosity; and as they keep that whole place enclosed in a wire fence, and he had evidently come out of the north gate, I was struck by the sight of the hoof-prints: they were perfectly fresh there on the trail, and plain as day. There's no mistaking the shoe, you know. By the way, he rode up to the fort, and probably entered at your side of the garrison: did you see him?"

"No, sir, and, except for breakfast,—just after reveille,—I have been at stables all the morning. I was there when the lieutenant got his horse."

"Yes, I remember. Then no one rode in from the valley?"

"No civilian,—no ranchman, sir. The only horsemen I've seen were some Cheyenne scouts during the last two hours, and Dr. Quin, —just before sick-call."

"Dr. Quin!—the post surgeon! Are you sure, sergeant?"

"Certainly, sir. The doctor rode into the post just about an hour after the lieutenant left,—coming up the valley too. He went right around to his own stable, over towards the hospital."

A look of amaze and stupefaction was settling on Perry's face. Now for the first time he recalled Mrs. Lawrence's intimations with regard to the doctor, and his connection with the signal-lights. Now for the first time it occurred to him that the secret of those cavalry hoof-prints at the gate was that no ranchman, but an officer of the garrison had been the means of leaving them there. Now for the first time it flashed upon him that the Englishman's astonishment and concern on hearing of those hoof-tracks indicated that the story of a mystery at Dunraven in which the doctor was connected amounted to something more than garrison rumor. Now for the first time an explanation occurred to him of the singular conduct of the horseman who had dodged him by crossing the Monee. Never in his young life had he known the hour when he was ashamed or afraid to look any man in the eye. It stung him to think that here at Rossiter, wearing the uniform of an honorable profession, enjoying the trust and confidence of all his fellows, was a man who had some secret enterprise of which he dared not speak and of whose discovery he stood in dread. There could be little doubt that the elusive stranger was Dr. Quin, and that there was grave reason for the rumors of which Mrs. Lawrence had vaguely told him.

For a moment he sat, dazed and irresolute, Nolan impatiently pawing the turf the while; then, far across the prairie and down the valley there came floating, quick and spirited, though faint with distance, the notes of the cavalry trumpet sounding "right, front into line." He looked up, startled.

"They're out at battalion drill, sir," said the sergeant. "They marched out just as I left stables."

"Just my infernal luck again!" gasped Perry, as he struck spur to Nolan and sent him tearing up the slope: "I might have known I'd miss it!"

V.

That evening a group of cavalry officers came sauntering back from stables, and as they reached the walk in front of officers' row a dark-featured, black-bearded, soldierly-looking captain separated himself from the rest and entered the colonel's yard. The commanding officer happened to be seated on his veranda at the moment, and in close confabulation with Dr. Quin. Both gentlemen ceased their talk as the captain entered, and then rose from their seats as he stepped upon the veranda floor.

"Good-evening, Stryker," said the colonel, cheerily. "Come in and have a seat. The doctor and I were just wondering if we could not get you to take a hand at whist to-night."

"I shall be glad to join you, sir, after parade. I have come in to ask permission to send a sergeant and a couple of men, mounted, down the Monee. One of my best men is missing."

"Indeed! Who is that? Send the men, of course."

"Sergeant Gwynne, sir. The first time I ever knew him to miss a duty."

"Your stable-sergeant, too? That *is* unusual. How long has he been gone?"

"Since battalion drill this morning. He was on hand when the men were saddling, and asked permission to take his horse out for exercise and ride down the valley a few miles. I said yes, never supposing he would be gone after noon roll-call; and we were astonished when he failed to appear at stables. Perry says he met him two miles out."

"The two culprits!" said the colonel, laughing. "Poor Perry is down in the depths again. He rode up to me with such a woebegone look on his face at drill this morning that I could hardly keep from laughing in front of the whole line. Even the men were trying hard not to grin: they knew he had turned up just in the nick of time to save himself an 'absent.' What do you suppose can have happened to Gwynne?"

"I cannot imagine, sir, and am inclined to be worried. He would never willingly overstay a pass; and I fear some accident has happened."

"Is he a good rider?" asked the doctor.

"None better in the regiment. He is a model horseman, in fact, and, though he never alludes to nor admits it, there is a general feeling among the men that he has been in the English cavalry service. Of course there is no doubt of his nationality: he is English to the backbone, and, I fancy, has seen better days."

"What made them think he had been in the cavalry service abroad?"

"Oh, his perfect knowledge of trooper duties and management of horses. It took him no time to learn the drill, and he was a sergeant before he had been with me two years. Then, if you ever noticed, colonel," said Captain Stryker, appealing to his chief, "whenever Gwynne stands attention he always has the fingers of both hands extended and pointing down along the thigh, close against it,—so." And Stryker illustrated. "Now, you never see an American soldier do that; and I never saw it in any but English-trained soldiers. He has quit it somewhat of late, because the men told him it showed where he was drilled,—we have other English 'non-coms.,' you know,—but for a long time I noticed that in him. Then he was enlisted in New York City, some four years ago, and all his things were of English make,—what he had."

"What manner of looking fellow is he?" asked the doctor. "I think I would have noted him had I seen him."

"Yes, you Englishmen are apt to look to one another," said the colonel, in reply, "and Gwynne is a particularly fine specimen. He has your eyes and hair, doctor, but hasn't had time to grow grizzled and bulky yet, as you and I have. One might say that you and the sergeant were from the same shire."

"That would help me very little, since I was only three years old when the governor emigrated," answered the doctor, with a quiet smile. "We keep some traces of the old sod, I suppose, but I've been a Yankee for forty years, and have never once set eyes on Merrie England in all that time.—Did the sergeant say where he wanted to go?" And the questioner looked up sharply.

"Nowhere in particular,—down the valley was all. I remember, though, that Mr. Parke said he seemed much exercised over the name of that ranch down the Monee,—I've forgotten what they call it.—Have you heard it, colonel?"

"Seems to me I have, but I've forgotten. *You* have, doctor, have you not?"

"Heard what, colonel?"

"The name of that ranch down the Monee,—an English ranch, they tell me, about seven miles away."

"Oh, yes!—that one! They call it Dunraven Ranch.—Did the sergeant take any of the hounds with him, captain? It occurs to me he might have been running a coyote or a rabbit, and his horse have stumbled and fallen with him. There is no end of prairie-dog holes down that way."

"No, the dogs are all in. I wouldn't be surprised if he had gone to the ranch. That's an English name, and they are all Englishmen down there, I hear. Very possibly that is the solution. They may have tempted him to stay with English hospitality; though it would astonish me if he yielded. I'll tell the men to inquire there first, colonel, and will go and send them now." And, bowing to his commander, Captain Stryker turned and left the porch.

The doctor rose, thrust his hands deep in his pockets, paced slowly to the southern end of the veranda, and gazed down the distant, peaceful valley, an anxious cloud settling on his brow. The colonel resumed once more the newspaper he had dropped upon the floor. After a moment Dr. Quin came slowly back, stood in front of the entrance a few seconds looking irresolutely at the soldier sprawled at full length in his reclining-chair, stepped towards him with a preparatory clearing of his throat as though about to speak, and then, suddenly and helplessly abandoning the idea, he plunged down the short flight of steps, hurried out of the gate, and disappeared around the fence-corner in the direction of the hospital. Immersed in his paper, the colonel never seemed to note that he had gone; neither did he note the fact that two ladies were coming down the walk. Possibly the vines clustering thickly all over the front of his veranda were responsible for this latter failure on his part, since it took more than a newspaper, ordinarily, to render the gallant dragoon insensible to the approach of the opposite sex. They saw *him*, of course, despite the shrouding vines, and, with perfectly justifiable appreciation of the homage due them, were mutually resolved that he should come out of that reclining pose and make his bow in due form. No words were necessary between them. The understanding was tacit, but complete.

The soft swish of trailing skirt being insufficient to attract his attention as they arrived nearly opposite the shaded veranda, a silvery peal of laughter broke the stillness of the early evening. Mrs. Belknap's laugh was delicious,—soft, melodious, rippling as a canary's song, and just as spontaneous. Neither lady had said anything at the moment that was incentive of merriment; but if Mrs. Lawrence had given utterance to the quaintest, oddest, most whimsical conceit imaginable, Mrs. Belknap's laugh could not have been more ready, and her great, dark eyes shot a sidelong glance to note the effect. Down went the paper, and up, with considerable propping from his muscular arms, came the burly form of the post commander. Two sweet, smiling faces beamed upon him through an aperture in the leafy screen, and Mrs. Belknap's silvery voice hailed him in laughing salutation:

"Did we spoil your siesta, colonel? How *can* I make amends? You see, you were so hidden by the vines that no one would dream of your being there in ambush."

"Oh, indeed, I assure you I wasn't asleep," answered the colonel, hastily. "Won't you come in, ladies, and sit here in the shade awhile? You've been calling, I suppose?"

"Yes,—calling, on the entire social circle of Fort Rossiter. Congratulate us, colonel: we have actually accomplished the feat of visiting every woman in society. We have made the rounds of the garrison. We owe no woman anything,—beyond a grudge or two,—and it has only taken forty-five minutes, despite the fact that everybody was at home."

"Well, come in, Mrs. Belknap; *do* come in, Mrs. Lawrence. I assure you that, though everybody must have been enchanted to see you, nobody is half as glad as I am. You must be tired after such a round of visits." And the colonel plunged heavily down the steps and hospitably opened the gate.

"We thought we would stroll around until parade," said Mrs. Lawrence, hesitatingly, "and then sit down and watch it somewhere."

"No place better than this," promptly answered the colonel. "You can sit behind the vines on that side and see, or, what we would infinitely prefer, sit here at the entrance and be seen. Meantime, I've been unpacking some photograph-albums this afternoon, and you can amuse yourselves with those while I put on my harness. Come!"

The colonel's collection of photographs was something the ladies had already heard a great deal of. One of the most genial and popular officers in the army, he had gathered together several large albums full of pictures of prominent men and attractive and distinguished women, —not only those with whom he had been associated in his long years of service, but men eminent in national and state affairs, and women leaders in society in many a gay metropolis. Both the ladies had hoped to see this famous collection the evening before, but the colonel had not then unpacked the albums, and they were disappointed. Now, however, the prospect was indeed alluring, and neither could resist. When the first call sounded for parade a few moments after, and the commanding officer was getting himself into his full-dress uniform, the two pretty heads were close together, and two pairs of very lovely eyes

—one dark and deep and dangerous, the other a clear and honest gray—were dilating over page after page of photographed beauty. There was no need to puzzle over the identity of the originals: under each picture the thoughtful colonel had carefully written the name and address. Absorbed in this treat, they could barely afford time to look up and smile their thanks as the colonel passed, clanking forth at the sounding of adjutant's call, and were too completely engrossed in their delightful occupation to notice what took place at parade.

The long, slender line had formed,—the infantry companies on the right and left flanks, their neat and tasteful dress of blue and white contrasting favorably with the gaudy yellow plumage of the four dismounted troops of the cavalry. Company after company had taken the statuesque pose of "parade rest" and its captain faced to the front again, the adjutant was just about moving to his post on the prolongation of the front rank, and the colonel settling back into the conventional attitude of the commanding officer, when from outside the rectangular enclosure of the parade-ground—from somewhere beyond the men's barracks—there came sudden outcry and commotion. There were shouts, indistinguishable at first, but excited and startling. Some of the men in ranks twitched nervously and partially turned their heads, as though eager to look behind them and see what was wrong; whereat stern voices could be heard in subdued but potent censure: "Keep your eyes to the front, there, Sullivan!" "Stand fast, there, centre of Third Company!" The guard, too, paraded in front of its quarters some distance behind the line, was manifestly disturbed, and the voice of the sergeant could be heard giving hurried orders. Every man in the battalion seemed at the same instant to arrive at one of two conclusions,—prisoners escaping, or fire over at the stables,—and all eyes were fixed on the imperturbable form of the commanding officer, as though waiting the signal from him to break and go to the rescue. But there the colonel stood, placid, calm, and apparently utterly unconscious of the distant yet nearing clamor. The adjutant hesitated a moment before proceeding further, and glanced appealingly at his chief; whereupon there came from the blue and gold and yellow statue out on the parade, in half-reproachful tones, the quiet order, "Go on!" and the adjutant, recalled to his senses and with evident expression of his sentiments to the effect that if others could stand it *he* could, brusquely turned his head towards the band and growled, "Sound off!" The boom and crash of drum and cymbal and the blare of brazen throats drowned for a moment the sound of the turmoil without. The next thing the battalion heard, or saw, was a riderless horse tearing full tilt out on the parade and sweeping in a big circle from the right of the line down towards the point where the colonel stood. Following him came a pair of Cheyenne scouts, their ponies scampering in pursuit, but veering off the green as their riders realized that they were intruding on the ceremony of the day. Relieved of his pursuers, the fugitive speedily settled down into a lunging trot, and with streaming mane and tail, with head and ears erect, with falling bridle-rein and flapping stirrups, he circled rapidly the open space between the colonel and the line of battle, then came trotting back along the front, as though searching in the stolid rank of bearded faces for the friends he knew. Officer after officer he passed in review until he came to Stryker's troop, posted on the right of the cavalry, and there, with a neigh of recognition, he fearlessly trotted up to the captain's outstretched hand. Another minute, and two men fell out and made a temporary gap in the rank; through this a sergeant file-closer extended his white glove, relieved the captain of his charge, and led the panting steed away. The men retook their places; the captain again resumed his position in front of the centre of his company, dropped the point of his sabre to the ground, and settled back into "parade rest;" the band went on thundering down the line, countermarched, and came back to its post on the right, making the welkin ring with the triumphant strains of "Northern Route," the trumpets pealed the "retreat," the adjutant stalked his three yards to the front, faced fiercely to the left and shouted his resonant orders down the line, three hundred martial forms sprang to attention, and the burnished arms came to the "carry" with simultaneous crash, ranks were opened with old-time precision, the parade "presented" to the colonel with all due formality, the manual was executed just as punctiliously as though nothing unusual had happened; first-sergeants reported, orders were published, parade formally dismissed; the line of officers marched solidly to the front, halted, and made its simultaneous salute to the colonel, who slowly raised and lowered his white-gloved hand in recognition; and then, and not till then, was any one allowed to speak of what was uppermost in every mind,—that Sergeant Gwynne's horse had come in without him, and that the animal's right flank was streaming with blood.

Ten minutes later, Lieutenant Perry, in riding-dress, came hurrying down to the colonel's quarters, where two or three officers were now gathered at the gate. The ladies had put aside the albums, and with anxious faces were scanning the little group, as though striving to gauge from their gestures and expression the extent of the calamity or the possible degree of danger. But Mrs. Lawrence looked fairly startled when her husband's voice was heard for the first time above the general hum of consultation :

"Colonel Brainard, Mr. Perry is coming, I see, and I presume there is no time to be lost. You have asked if none of us who were stationed here ever visited the ranch, and the answer was no. May I suggest that Dr. Quin could perhaps tell something of its inhabitants?"

"Where is the doctor?" asked the colonel, turning suddenly. "Orderly, go and give my compliments to the post surgeon and say I wish to see him here a moment.—All ready, Perry? You have made quick work of it."

"All ready, sir. At least, I will be the moment my horse gets here. There go the men running to the stables now."

"Captain Stryker will send a sergeant and four men to report to you, and you are to go direct to Dunraven Ranch. The rest of the troop, with the Cheyennes, will scout the prairie to the east and south. 'Twill soon be too dark to trail, but three of the Indians are going back on the horse's track as far as they can. The adjutant is writing a note to the proprietor of the ranch,—I don't know his name——"

"His name is Maitland, sir."

"Is it? Have you been there?"

"I've been around one end of it, outside, but nowhere near the buildings. It's all fenced in, sir, and the gates kept locked."

"What an incomprehensible proceeding for Texas! Wait a moment while I speak to Mr. Farnham : he's writing here at my desk. —Gentlemen, come in on the porch and sit down, will you not?"

But they excused themselves, and hastened away to remove their full dress. Captain Lawrence had no need to call his wife. She bade her companion good-evening, thanked the colonel with a smiling glance for the pleasure the photographs had given her, and added a word of earnest hope that they might find the sergeant uninjured. Then she joined her husband, and together they walked quickly away. Mrs. Belknap and Mr. Perry were left for the moment alone.

"Can you walk home with me?" she asked, in her low, modulated tones, the great, heavily-lashed, swimming dark eyes searching his face.

"I have not seen you since they broke in upon our talk last evening, and there is something I want to ask you."

"I'm sorry, Mrs. Belknap, but I'm on duty, you see," was the young fellow's answer as he gave a tug to the strap of his cartridge-belt. "Can't you ask me here?"

"How can I?"—and the eyes were full of pathetic disappointment,—"when they may come out any moment? You did not finish telling me about—about the tassel last night. I believe you were glad when they interrupted us. Were you not?"

"Nonsense, Mrs. Belknap! I was having too good a time,—lots of fun."

"Yes," was the reproachful answer, "that is what it was—to you,—mere fun. And now you are going away again, after promising to come in this evening."

"I have to go, Mrs. Belknap. Why, I *want* to go. Haven't you heard what has happened,—about Sergeant Gwynne?"

"Oh, yes, it is your duty, of course; but how unlucky!" And the pretty face was drooping with its weight of disappointment and sadness. She leaned against the railing near his gauntlet-covered hand, the dark eyes pensively downcast, the dark lashes sweeping her soft, flushing cheek. "And to-morrow you are on guard," she presently continued.

"Yes, unless some one has to go on for me,—in case we are not back in the morning in time."

"Then it's good-by, I suppose," she said, lifting her eyes once more to his. "After to-morrow there will be little chance of seeing you. Mrs. Page will be here by that time."

Mr. Perry looked at his fair companion with a glance that told of much perturbation of spirit. Mrs. Page was an old and cherished friend of Mrs. Belknap's,—so the latter had always said,—and now she was coming to visit her from a station in the Indian Territory. Just why *her* coming should prevent his seeing Mrs. Belknap or her seeing him was more than the tall subaltern could understand. On the brink of an unpardonable solecism, on the very ragged edge of a blundering inquiry, he was saved—in her estimation—by the sudden return of the orderly and the reappearance of the colonel.

"I've been to the hospital, sir, and to the doctor's quarters: he's not there. They say that's him, sir, riding off yonder." And the orderly pointed to a faint speck just visible in the waning twilight, far away southeastward beyond the Monee.

VI.

Twilight still hovered over the broad expanse of prairie when Lieutenant Perry and his little party, after a brisk canter down the valley, reached the barbed enclosure of Dunraven, and the young commander led unhesitatingly to the gate-way on the northern line. A sergeant of his troop and two private soldiers were his escort at the moment; a third man, by direction of Colonel Brainard, had been sent at the gallop in pursuit of the distant speck which the orderly had pronounced to be Dr. Quin, and the instructions which this messenger bore were to the effect that the post surgeon should ride by the most direct route and join Lieutenant Perry at the north gate of the ranch. In the few minutes which elapsed between the announcement of the doctor's departure on his solitary and unexpected ride and the arrival of the little mounted escort, Perry had time to tell the colonel something of the situation down the Monee and to make a rough sketch of the enclosure and the distant buildings. The direction taken by the doctor, up to the moment when the black speck disappeared from view in the waning light, would be very apt to lead him, if he rode far enough, to some point on the wire fence which spanned the western limit of Dunraven; but that point would be at least five or six miles south of the valley. Possibly there was no gate-way north of that,— certainly no trail was visible on the prairie,—but the more Mr. Perry thought of the matter as he rode away the more was he satisfied that somewhere far down that western line there was an entrance where Dr. Quin, at least, had the "open sesame." All the grazing thus far had been done north of the Monee; all the hunting and coursing, too, had been found best in every way far out to the north and east of the post; and so it happened that no one of the —th seemed to have acquired any knowledge of the English ranch. What the local infantry command was able to tell of it was purely hearsay. None of the officers had ever penetrated the charmed enclosure, and no one of the soldiers was known to have done so. Perry remembered hearing that the Eleventh while stationed there had made some scouts and expeditions out to the south, and that some of these had completely circled the broad lands of the estate, finding well-travelled roads leading from its southern boundaries to the settlements two days' journey farther towards the Gulf; but nowhere was there open or unguarded gap. Cattle with the Dunraven brand roamed the breaks and prairies far away towards the eastern streams, and crossed even the broad trail over which the great Texas "drive" of "long-horns," year after year, passed up across the valley of the Washita. Other cattle, of choicer breed, were carefully herded within the wire enclosure; but, thanks to the vigilance of the manager and the exertions of his few skilled assistants, none of their wandering chattels seemed ever to venture up-stream towards the fort, and all excuse for a visit there was apparently guarded against. These meagre points he had gathered from the remarks of one or two officers who had come to see him off, and, ignorant of his morning expedition, to offer suggestions as to his best course.

His orders were, in case nothing was seen or heard of Sergeant Gwynne while on the way thither, to enter the enclosure and make inquiries at the ranch itself. Meantime, the Cheyenne scouts had been hastily summoned from their lodges along the Monee just above the post and sent scurrying forth upon the prairie to trail the horse's footprints and so work back as far as possible before darkness interposed. Captain Stryker, too, and a dozen of his best men, had mounted and ridden forth in long, scattered line across the eastern plain; and these parties were all five miles out from the post before nightfall fairly hid them from view.

One thing the sergeant had to tell Mr. Perry which confirmed him in the belief that the sooner they got to Dunraven the quicker they would be at the scene of their comrade's mishap, whatever that might prove to be. He had had no time himself to visit the stables and examine the wounds on the horse's flank, but as they rode away from Rossiter he turned in the saddle and called the non-commissioned officer to his side.

"What sort of wound is it, sergeant, that made that horse bleed so,—bullet or knife?"

"It doesn't look like either, sir. There are several of them,—jagged scratches in the shoulder and along the flank, like thorns or nails——"

"Or barbed wire?" suggested the lieutenant, suddenly.

"Yes, sir, like as not; though we hadn't thought of that, not knowing of any fences hereabouts."

"You'll see fence enough presently. That's where we'll find Sergeant Gwynne, too. Let your horses out a little. I want to get there before dark, if possible."

It was dark in the timber, however, as they rode through and reined up at the gate-way. It would be half an hour at the very least, thought Perry, before the doctor could join them, if he came at all. It was by no means certain that the messenger had overtaken him, and, even if he had, was it probable that the doctor would be in great haste to come? His mysterious movements of the morning, his undoubted connection with the night-signals from the ranch, the fact that he had given his commanding officer no inkling whatever of these outside interests of his, all tended to make Perry distrustful of their post surgeon. He would not speak of it to a soul, or hint at the possibility of such a thing, until he had evidence that was indisputable, but the young officer was sorely perplexed by these indications of some secret and unlawful enterprise on the part of their new comrade, and he doubted his sympathy in the mission on which they had been hurried forth.

Dismounting to examine the gate while still pondering this matter over in his mind, Perry found it locked as securely as he had left it in the morning. The sergeant and his men dismounted, too, at a low-spoken word from their officer, and stood at the heads of their panting horses, looking in silent surprise at the strong and impervious barrier that crossed their track.

"The gate is locked and the fence impassable, sergeant," said Mr. Perry. "We cannot get our horses through or over unless we hack down a post or two. You can't cut such wire as this with any tool we've got. I'll leave Nolan here with you and go on to the ranch on foot: it lies about half a mile to the south. If the doctor comes, he can follow me. If I do not come or send back in half an hour from this, you three come after me, for I'll need you."

With that, slowly and carefully, and not without a muttered malediction on the stinging barbs, Mr. Perry wriggled through between the middle wires, and finally stood within the enclosure, readjusting his waist-belt and holster. Then he took his revolver from its leathern case, carefully tried the hammer and cylinder, saw that each chamber was loaded, and turned once more to the sergeant.

"Your pistols all right?"

"All right, sir,—fresh loaded when we started."

"I don't know that they'll be necessary at all, sergeant, but this is a queer place, from what I've heard and the little I've seen. Keep your eyes and ears open. Captain Stryker and some of the men may come down into the valley if they find no trace of Gwynne up on the prairie. Watch for the doctor, too."

Then, through the deepening twilight he strode, following the trail that led southward up the slopes. Five minutes' brisk walk along the springy turf brought him to the crest and in view of the lights at the ranch-buildings, still some six or seven hundred yards away. All through the eastern sky the stars were peeping forth, and even through the gleam of the twilight in the west two brilliant planets shone like molten gold. All was silence and peace on every hand, and, but for those guiding, glimmering lights at the south, all would have told of desolation. Behind him in the valley waited his faithful men. Far beyond the Monee, out on the northern prairie, he knew that comrades were scouring the face of the earth in search of their missing brother. Up the stream, somewhere behind them, the Cheyennes were patiently trailing the hoof-tracks as long as the light should last; he knew that search must be at an end by this time, and that some of their number, at least, would be riding down to join his men. Whoever found the sergeant was to fire three shots in air: the signal could be heard a long way in that intense stillness, and that signal was to recall the searching-parties. Every step brought him deeper into the darkness of the night, yet nearer and nearer those twinkling lights ahead. Already he could distinguish those in the main building, the homestead, from those more distant still, in the store-rooms and office. Far over among the stables and corrals he heard the deep baying of hounds, and he wondered if it was to be his luck to encounter any enterprising watch-dogs. An English bull-terrier would be a lively entertainer, thought he, with instinctive motion towards the flap of his holster; and it would be a wonder if a ranch that surrounded itself with fifty miles of barbed wire fencing were not further environed by a pack of watch-dogs of the most approved and belligerent breed. Once having passed the distant barrier of that gate on the Monee, however, his way was unimpeded, and, to all appearance, utterly unmarked; he had arrived within fifty yards of the foremost building, the homestead, before he was brought to a halt. Then he stopped short, surprised, half credulous, and all attention, listening to the "concord of sweet sounds" that came floating from the open casement somewhere along the east front of the big, gloomy house.

"One part of the story verified, by Jove! It's a piano,—and well played, too."

Full a minute he stood there listening. Perry was a dancer whose nimble feet moved blithely to any measured, rhythmical strains, and a soldier whose soul was stirred by martial music, but with Chopin and Mendelssohn, Bach and Rubinstein, he had but slight acquaintance. That any one should be playing a piano here on the borders of the Llano Estacado was in itself sufficient cause for wonderment; that the invisible performer was playing—and playing with exquisite taste and feeling—one of the loveliest of the "Lieder ohne Worte," the Spring Song, was a fact that conveyed no added astonishment to his soul: he never knew it until one sweet night long after.

However, matters more pressing than music demanded Mr. Perry's attention just here. He had reached Dunraven, after all. Neither dog nor man had challenged. Once within those barbed and frowning barriers, all the encircling objects spoke of security and rest. Far away towards the corrals he heard the sound of voices in jolly conversation; a rich, melodious laugh rang out on the cool evening air; he heard some one shouting genial good-night to somebody else, and then the slam of a distant door. Presently a light popped out from a window in what he believed to be a storehouse, and all was still again. Even the piano had ceased. Now was his time, thought Perry; and so, boldly mounting the steps, he stood upon a dark portico and strode to the black shadow in the wall before him where he knew the main door-way must be. It was his intention to knock or ring. Up-stairs dim lights were shining through the open windows, but on this front of the ground-floor all was darkness. His gauntleted hand felt all the face of the door in search of knob or knocker, but nothing of the kind was there; neither was there such a thing on either door-post. Just as he decided to hammer with his clinched fist, the piano began again. He waited for a pause, but none came. This time the music was vehement and spirited, and no banging of his on oaken door-way would be audible against such rivalry. Uncertain what to do, he concluded to reconnoitre the eastern front. A few steps brought him to the corner, and there lay the veranda before him, bathed at its farther end in a flood of light that streamed from one opened venetian window, and through this curtained aperture poured the grand tones of the melody. "That fellow can rattle more music out of a piano than any man I ever heard," muttered Mr. Perry to himself, as he strode down the wooden gallery. "Wonder if it's that boss cow-puncher I met this morning." Another moment, and he stood at the open window, rooted to the spot, and with his frank blue eyes fairly starting from their sockets in amazement at the sight that met them, all unprepared.

Across a spacious room, hung with rich curtains, carpeted with costly rugs of Oriental make, furnished with many a cosey chair and couch, and tables covered with dainty *bric-à-brac,* and shelves with tempting books, lighted by several large and beautiful astral lamps, some with colored shades of crimson and gold and delicate tint of blue, there stood close to the opposite wall a large piano of the class known as the "grand," rare enough among the railway towns west of the Mississippi States, but utterly unlooked for here, a week's long march from the nearest of the Texan railways. That in itself were sufficient cause for much surprise, notwithstanding the measure of preparation he had had in Mrs. Lawrence's remarks.

The sight that wellnigh took his breath away was something far more than the interior of a luxurious and beautifully-appointed room. *Nothing* that had been said or hinted prepared him in the faintest degree for the apparition, facing him, seated at the piano, of a performer utterly unlike the "cow-puncher" whom he had met in the morning. The "fellow" now bending over the key-board was a young, exquisitely fair, and graceful woman. Even as he stood there in the full glare of the parlor lights, she lifted up a pair of soft, shaded, lustrous eyes and saw him.

The music stopped with sudden shock. Tannhäuser was undone. The firm, white, shapely hands fell nerveless in her lap; a pallor as of faintness shot over the wild-eyed face, only to be instantly succeeded by a flush that surged up to the very brows. Startled she might have been for an instant; scared,—not a bit of it! One instant only of hesitation, then she rose and swept gallantly forward to meet him.

Instinctively Perry's hand went up to the visor of his forage-cap and bared the bright, curling crop of hair. Speechless with amaze, he could only bow before her and wait her question; but it was a moment before she could speak. Brave as she was, the sudden apparition of a stranger staring in upon her solitude from an open casement was a shock that served to paralyze the vocal cords. He could see that she was making gallant effort to control the tremor that had seized upon her and to inquire the purpose of his coming. He could see, too, that the sight of the uniform had reassured her, and that there was neither indignation nor displeasure in her beautiful eyes. Reserve, of course, he expected.

"Did you wish to see any one?" was finally the form her question took; and Perry had time to comment to himself, "English, by Jove!" before he answered,—

"I did; but let me first ask your pardon for this intrusion. I had no idea there was a woman at Dunraven. My knocking at the front brought no answer, and, hearing the piano, I followed the veranda. Believe me, I am as surprised as you could possibly have been."

Perry's voice was something greatly in his favor. It was modulated and gentle when in conversation, and with even a caressing tone about it when he spoke to women. Evidently the sound was not unwelcome to this one. She stood erect, her fingers interlacing as she clasped her hands in front of her and looked him well over with her brave eyes. The color ebbed and flowed through the creamy whiteness of her face, but the roses were winning every moment,—the red roses of the house of Lancaster.

"And—you wished to see—whom?" she presently asked, with courtesy in every word.

"Why, I hardly know," answered Perry, with a smile that showed his white teeth gleaming through the curling blond moustache. "A sergeant of my troop has been missing since morning. His horse came back to the fort just as we were on parade at sunset, bleeding and without his rider. We have searching-parties out all over the prairie, and I was ordered to come here to the ranch to make inquiries."

She hesitated a moment,—thinking.

"My father is at home, but I fear he is not well enough to see you. Mr. Ewen is with him, and he might know. Will you—would you step in one moment, and I will go and ask?"

"Thank you very much. I wish you would not trouble yourself. I presume I can go over to those stable-buildings, or wherever it is the men sleep: they would be most apt to know if our sergeant has been seen."

"Oh, no! it is no trouble; besides, they are all asleep over there by this time, I fancy. They have to be out so very early, don't you know?"

But Perry had stepped inside even as he offered to go elsewhere,—a fact that the girl had not been slow to notice, for a quizzical little shadow of a smile hovered for an instant at the corners of her pretty mouth. "Pray sit down," she said, as she vanished into an adjoining room, leaving Ned Perry standing gazing after her, spell-bound.

He listened to the swish of her trailing skirts through the dimly-lighted room beyond, through an invisible hall-way, and then to the quick pit-a-pat of her feet up some uncarpeted stairway. He heard her moving quickly, lightly, along the corridor of the upper story until the foot-falls were lost at the rear of the house, then a distant tap upon a door-way, and a soft voice, barely audible, calling, "Papa." He heard her speak again, as though in response to inquiry from within; he heard her raise her voice, as though to repeat an answer to a previous question, and this time her words were distinct. "An officer from the fort," she announced; and then followed sensation.

He heard a door quickly opened; he heard men's voices in low, eager, excited talk; he heard her sweet tones once more, as though in expostulation, saying something about the sergeant, lost or wounded, and they were merely inquiring for him; he heard a stern, harsh injunction of "Silence! that will do!" some quick, hurrying footsteps, a man's spurred boots descending some staircase at the back of the house, a colloquy aloft in fainter tones, and then—closing doors and silence. He waited five—ten minutes, and still no one came; but the murmur of voices in subdued but earnest controversy was again audible on the second floor, and at last a door was opened and he heard the same stern tones that had commanded her silence before, and this time they said,—

"That is entirely my affair! I will see the gentleman myself, and let him know my opinion of this impudent and—and—burglarious intrusion."

"Whew!" whistled Mr. Perry to himself at sound of these menacing words. "This is bearding the lion in his den with a vengeance! Now trot out your 'Douglas in his hall,' and let's see what it all means. I've seen the girl, anyhow, and he can't take *that* back, even if he turns me out."

He heard a heavy step, accented by the sharp, energetic prodding of a cane; it came slowly along the hall, slowly and majestically down the stairs, slowly into the lower front room, and presently there loomed forth from the darkness into the broad glare of the astrals at the hanging *portières* the figure of a tall, gray-haired, spectacled, slimly-built, and fragile-looking Englishman, erect as pride and high spirit could hold a man against the ravages of age and rheumatism; sharp, stern, and imperious of mood, as every glance and every feature plainly told; vehement and passionate, unless twitching lips and frowning brows and angry, snapping eyes belied him; a man who had suffered much, unless the deep lines and shadows under eyes and mouth meant nothing but advancing years; a man who entered full of wrath and resentment at this invasion of his privacy,—this forcing of his guarded lines; and yet—a gentleman, unless Ned Perry's instincts were all of little worth.

The young soldier had been standing by a centre-table, coolly scanning the pictures on the walls, and determining to present a rather exaggerated picture of nonchalance as reward for the hostile language of the proprietor of Dunraven. He expected to hear an outburst of invective when that gentleman reached the room; but no sooner had he passed the *portière* than he halted short, and Mr. Perry, turning suddenly, was amazed at the pale, startled, yet yearning look in his quivering face. The moment the young man confronted him there came as sudden a change. It was with evident effort that he controlled himself, and then, after brief searching study of Perry's face, accosted him,— coldly and with sarcastic emphasis:

"To what circumstance do I owe the honor of this intrusion?"

"I regret you so consider it, Mr. Maitland,—as I believe you to be——" The old gentleman bowed with stately dignity. "One of our men, a sergeant, rode down this way quite early this morning and failed to return. His horse came back, bleeding, at sunset, and we feared some accident or trouble. Searching-parties are out all over the prairies, and the colonel ordered me to inquire here."

"Does your colonel take us for banditti here, and ascribe your desertions and accidents to our machinations?"

"Far from it, sir, but rather as a hospitable refuge to which the injured man had been conveyed," answered Perry, with a quiet smile, determined to thaw the *hauteur* of Dunraven's lord if courtesy of manner could effect it.

"He is utterly mistaken, then," answered the Englishman, "and I resent—I resent, sir, this forcing of my gates after the explicit understanding we had last year. As a soldier I presume you had to obey your orders; but I beg you to tell your colonel that his order was an affront to me personally, in view of what has passed between us."

"Nothing has passed between you, Mr. Maitland," answered Perry, a little tartly now. "We have reached Fort Rossiter only within the last fortnight, and know nothing whatever of your understandings with previous commanders. Permit me to ask you one question, and I will retire. Have you heard anything of our sergeant?"

"Nothing, sir. I would hardly be apt to hear, for my people here are enjoined to keep strictly to our limits, and all we ask of our neighbors is that they keep to theirs. I presume you have destroyed my fences, sir, in order to effect an entrance."

"Upon my word, Mr. Maitland, you make me rather regret that I did not; but I had the decency to respect what I had happened to hear of your wishes, and so left my horse and my men outside, and footed it a good half-mile in the dark——"

"Ah! that sounds very like it!" replied Mr. Maitland, with writhing lips, for at this moment there came the dull thunder of rapidly-advancing hoof-beats, and before either man could speak again three troopers with a led horse—all four steeds panting from their half-mile race—reined up in front of the eastern portico in the full glare of the lights, and the sergeant's voice was heard eagerly hailing his lieutenant.

"My luck again!" groaned Perry. "I told them to come in half an hour if they didn't hear from me, and of course they came."

VII.

For a moment there was silence in the brightly-illuminated room. With flushed face and swollen veins and twitching, clutching hands, old Maitland stood there glaring at the young officer. Before Perry could speak again, however, and more fully explain the untoward circumstance, there came a rush of hurrying footsteps without, and the sound of excited voices. The next minute they heard an eager, angry challenge, and Perry recognized the voice of the overseer or manager whom he had met in the morning.

"What do you fellows want here?" was his brusque and loud inquiry as he sprang from the piazza and stood confronting the sergeant, who was quietly seated in the saddle, and the question was promptly echoed by three or four burly men who, in shirt-sleeves and various styles of undress, came tumbling in the wake of their leader and stood now a menacing group looking up at the silent troopers.

If there be one thing on earth that will stir an Irishman's soul to its inmost depths and kindle to instant flame the latent heat of his pugnacity, it is just such an inquiry in the readily recognized accent of the hated "Sassenach." Perry recognized the danger in a flash, and, springing through the open casement, interposed between the hostile parties.

"Not a word, Sergeant Leary. Here, Mr. Manager, these men simply obeyed orders, and I am responsible for any mistake. No harm was intended——"

"Harm!" broke in one of the ranchmen, with a demonstratively loud laugh. "Harm be blowed! What harm could you do, I'd like to know? If the master'll only say the word, we'd break your heads in a minute."

"Quiet, now, Dick!" interposed the overseer; but the other hands growled approval, and Perry's eyes flashed with anger at the insult. What reply he might have made was checked by the sight of Sergeant Leary throwing himself from the saddle and tossing his reins to one of the men. He knew well enough what that meant, and sprang instantly in front of him.

"Back to your horse, sir! Back, instantly!" for the sergeant's face was fierce with rage. "Mount, I say!" added the lieutenant, as the sergeant still hesitated, and even the sense of discipline could not keep the mounted troopers from a muttered word of encouragement. Slowly, wrathfully, reluctantly, the soldier obeyed, once turning furiously back as jeering taunts were hurled at him from among the ranchers, unrebuked by their manager. "Now move off with your men to the gate. Leave my horse, and wait for me there. Go!" added the young officer, sternly; and, with bitter mortification at heart and a curse stifled on his quivering lips, the Irishman turned his horse's head away and slowly walked him in the indicated direction.

"Now, Mr. Manager," said Perry, turning fiercely upon the younger Englishman, "I have done my best to restrain my men: do you look out for yours. You have allowed them to insult me and mine, and you may thank your stars that discipline prevailed with my people, though you have nothing of the kind here."

"Your men have cut down our fences, by your order, I presume," said the manager, coolly, "and it's lucky for them they got out of the way when they did. We have a right to protect our property and eject intruders, and——"

"I came here to inquire for a missing man,—a right even an Englishman cannot deny us on these prairies. We had excellent reason to believe him injured, and thought, not knowing you for the inhospitable gang you are, that he might have been carried in here for treatment: there *was* no other place. Your proprietor tells me he is not here. After what I've seen of your people, I have reason to be still more anxious about him. Scant mercy a single trooper would have had at their hands. Now I ask *you*, Do you know or have you heard of a cavalry soldier being seen around here during the day?"

Perry was standing holding his horse by the curb as he spoke, facing the parlor windows and confronting the angry group of ranchmen. Within, though nearer the window than he had left him, was the bent form of the owner of Dunraven, leaning on his cane and apparently impatiently striving to make himself heard as he came forward. Before the manager could answer, he was compelled to turn about and rebuke his men, two of whom were especially truculent and menacing. Finally he spoke:

"I have heard nothing, but I tell you frankly that if any of your men have been prowling around here it's more than probable some one has got hurt. Has there been any trouble to-day, men?" he asked.

"By God, there *will* be if this ranch isn't cleared in five minutes," was the only answer.

"Don't make an ass of yourself, Hoke," growled the manager. "They are going quick enough."

"I *am* going," said Perry, swinging lightly into saddle; "and mind you this, sir: I go with well-warranted suspicion that some of these bullies of yours have been responsible for the non-appearance of my stable-sergeant. If he is not found this night, you may confidently look for another visit. I say that to you also, Mr. Maitland; and you owe it to our forbearance that there has been no bloodshed here to-night."

Old Maitland's tremulous tones were heard but a second in reply when he was interrupted by a coarse voice from the crowd of ranchmen, by this time increased to nearly a dozen men. Some of them were gathering about Perry as he sat in the saddle, and an applauding echo followed the loud interruption,—

"Give the swell a lift, Tummy: 'twill teach him better manners."

Almost instantly Perry felt his right foot grasped and a powerful form was bending at the stirrup. He had heard of the trick before. Many a time has the London cad unhorsed the English trooper, taken unawares, by hurling him with sudden lift from below. But Perry was quick and active as a cat. Seat and saddle, too, were in his favor.

He simply threw his weight on the left foot and his bridle-hand upon the pommel, let the right leg swing over the horse's back until released from the brawny hand, then back it came as he settled again in the saddle, his powerful thighs gripping like a vise; at the same instant, and before his assailant could duck to earth and slip out of the way, he had whipped out the heavy Colt's revolver and brought its butt with stunning crash down on the ranchman's defenceless head.

There was instant rush and commotion. In vain old Maitland feebly piped his protests from the veranda; in vain the overseer seized and held back one or two of the men and furiously called off the rest. Aided by the darkness which veiled them, the others made a simultaneous rush upon the young officer and sought to drag him from his plunging horse. Perry held his pistol high in air, threatening with the butt the nearest assailant, yet loath to use further force. He was still in the broad glare of the parlor lights,—a conspicuous mark; eager hands had grasped his bridle-rein at the very bit, and he could not break away; and then missiles began to fly about his devoted head, and unless he opened fire he was helpless. While two men firmly held Nolan by the curb, half a dozen others were hurling from the ambush of darkness a scattering volley of wooden billets and chunks of coal. He could easily have shot down the men who held him. It was sore temptation, for already he had been struck and stung by unseen projectiles; but just as the manager sprang forward and with vigorous cuffs induced the men to loose their hold on his rein, there came three horsemen charging full tilt back into the crowd, scattering the assailants right and left; and, this time unrebuked, Sergeant Leary leaped from the saddle and with a rage of fierce delight pitched headlong into battle with the biggest ranchman in his way. And this was not all; for behind them at rapid trot came other troopers, and in a moment the open space was thronged with eager, wondering comrades,—full half of Stryker's company,—in whose overwhelming presence all thought of promiscuous combat seemed to leave the ranchmen. They slipped away in the darkness, leaving to their employers the embarrassment of accounting for their attack. Leary was still fuming with wrath and raging for further battle and shouting into the darkness fierce invective at the vanished head of his opponent. He turned on the overseer himself, and but for Perry's stern and sudden prohibition would have had a round with him, but was forced to content himself with the information conveyed to all within hearing that he'd "fight any tin min" the ranch contained if they'd only come out where the lieutenant couldn't stop him. The troopers were making eager inquiry as to the cause of all the trouble, and, fearing further difficulty, Perry promptly ordered the entire party to "fall in." Silence and discipline were restored in a moment, and as the platoon formed rank he inquired of a sergeant how they came to be there. The reply was that it had grown so dark on the prairie that further search seemed useless, Captain Stryker and most of the men had been drawn off by signals from the Cheyennes up the valley towards the post, and these men, who had been beyond Dunraven on the northern prairie, were coming back along the Monee trail when they saw the lights and heard voices over at the lower shore. There they found Leary, who was excited about something, and before they had time to ask he suddenly shouted, "They're killin' the lieutenant. Come on, boys!" and galloped off with his own party: so they followed. Perry quietly ordered them to leave a corporal and four men with him, and told the senior sergeant to march the others back to the post: he would follow in five minutes. Then he turned to the manager:

"You will have to put up with my keeping some of my men with me, in view of all the circumstances," he said, coldly. "But after this exhibition of lawlessness on the part of your people I do not propose to take any chances. I want to say to you that it is my belief that some of those ruffians you employ can tell what has become of our missing man, and that you will do well to investigate to-night. As to you, Mr. Maitland," he said, turning to the old gentleman, who had sunk into a low easy-chair, "much as I regret having disturbed your privacy and—that of the—ladies of your household, you will admit now that justice to my men and to the service demands that I should report my suspicions and my reception here to the commanding officer at Fort Rossiter."

There was no reply.

"I wish you good-night, sir," said Perry; but his eyes wandered in to the lighted parlor in search of a very different face and form,—and still there was no answer.

The manager came back upon the piazza and stepped rapidly towards them. Perry quickly dismounted and bent down over the crouching figure.

"Why, here!" he suddenly exclaimed, "your employer is faint, or —something's gone wrong."

"Hush!" was the low-spoken, hurried answer of the Englishman. "Just bear a hand, will you, and help me lift him to yonder sofa?"

Easily, between them, they bore the slight, attenuated form of the old man into the lighted parlor. A deathly pallor had settled on his face. His eyes were closed, and he seemed fallen into a deep swoon. Perry would have set a cushion under his head as they laid him down on a broad, easy couch, but the manager jerked it away, lowering the gray hairs to the very level of the back, so that the mouth gaped wide and looked like death itself.

"Just steady his head in that position one minute, like a good fellow. I'll be back in a twinkling," said the manager, as he darted from the room and leaped hurriedly up the hall stairway.

Perry heard him rap at a distant door apparently at the southwest angle of the big house. Then his voice was calling, "Mrs. Cowan! Mrs. Cowan! would you have the goodness to come down quick? the master's ill."

Then, before any answer could be given, another door opened aloft, and trailing skirts and light foot-falls came flashing down the stairway. Almost before he could turn to greet her, *she* was in the room again, and with quick, impulsive movement had thrown herself on her knees by his side.

"Oh, papa! *dear* father! I was afraid of this! Let me take his head on my arm, *so*," she hurriedly murmured; "and would you step in the other room and fetch me a little brandy? 'Tis there on the sideboard."

Perry sprang to do her bidding, found a heavy decanter on the great oaken buffet, half filled a glass, and brought it with some water back to the lounge. She stretched forth her hand, and, thanking him with a grateful look from her sweet, anxious eyes, took the liquor and carried it carefully to her father's ashen lips.

"Can I not help you in some way? Is there no one I can call?" asked the young soldier, as he bent over her.

"Mr. Ewen has gone for her,—our old nurse, I mean. She does not seem to be in her room, and I fear she has gone over to her son's,— a young fellow at the storehouse. Mr. Ewen has followed by this time."

She dipped her slender white fingers in the water and sprinkled the forehead and eyelids of the prostrate man. A feeble moan, followed by a deep-drawn sigh, was the only response. More brandy poured into the gaping mouth seemed only to strangle and distress him. No sign of returning consciousness rewarded her effort.

"If Mrs. Cowan would only come! She has never failed us before; and we so lean upon her at such a time."

"Pray tell me which way to go. Surely I can find her," urged Perry.

"Mr. Ewen must be searching for her now, or he would have returned by this time; and I dread being alone. I have never been alone with father when he has had such a seizure."

Perry threw himself on his knees beside her, marvelling at the odd fate that had so suddenly altered all the conditions of his unlooked-for visit. He seized one of the long, tremulous hands that lay so nerveless on the couch, and began rapid and vigorous chafing and slapping. Somewhere he had read or heard of women being restored from fainting-spells by just such means. Why should it not prevail with the old man? He vaguely bethought him of burnt feathers, and looked about for the discarded pillow, wondering if it might not be a brilliant idea to cut it open and extract a handful and set it ablaze under those broad and eminently aristocratic nostrils. Happily, he was spared excuse for further experiment. He felt that life was returning to the hand he was so energetically grooming, and that feeble but emphatic protest against such heroic treatment was manifest.

"I think he's coming to," he said. "He's trying to pull away. Shall I keep on?"

"Yes, do! Anything rather than have him lie in this death-like swoon."

Obediently he clung to his prize, rubbing and chafing hard, despite increasing tug and effort. Then came another feeble, petulant moan, and the hollow eyes opened just as rapid foot-falls were heard on the veranda without and Mr. Ewen rushed breathless and ruddy-faced into the room.

"Where on earth can that woman have gone?" he panted. "I cannot find her anywhere. Is he better, Miss Gladys?"

"Reviving, I think, thanks to Mr.——thanks to you," she said, turning her eyes full upon the kneeling figure at her side and sending Perry's heart up into his throat with delight at the gratitude and kindness in her glance. She was striving with one hand to unfasten the scarf and collar at the old man's neck, but making little progress.

"Let me help you," eagerly said Perry. "That, at least, is more in my line." And somehow their fingers touched as he twisted at the stubborn knot. She drew her hand away then, but it was gently, not abruptly done, and he found time to note that too, and bless her for it.

"I hate to seem ungracious, you know, after all that's happened," said Mr. Ewen, "but I fear 'twill vex him awfully if he should find you in here when he comes to. He has had these attacks for some time past, and I think he's coming through all right. See!"

Old Maitland was certainly beginning to open his eyes again and look vacantly around him.

"Better leave him to Miss Gladys," said the overseer, touching the young fellow on the shoulder. Perry looked into her face to read her wishes before he would obey. A flush was rising to her cheek, a cloud settling about her young eyes, but she turned, after a quick glance at her father.

"I cannot thank you enough—now," she said, hesitatingly. "Perhaps Mr. Ewen is right. You—you deserve to be told the story of his trouble, you have been so kind. Some day you shall understand,—soon,—and not think unkindly of us."

"Indeed I do not now," he protested.

"And—whom are we to thank?—your name, I mean?" she timidly asked.

"I am Mr. Perry, of the —th Cavalry. We have only come to Fort Rossiter this month."

"And I am Miss Maitland. Some day I *can* thank you." And she held forth her long, slim hand. He took it very reverently and bowed over it, courtier-like, longing to say something that might fit the occasion; but before his scattered senses could come to him there was another quick step at the veranda, and a voice that sounded strangely familiar startled his ears:

"Gladys! What has happened?" And there, striding to the sofa with the steps of one assured of welcome and thoroughly at home in those strange precincts, came Dr. Quin.

VIII.

It was very late that night—nearly midnight—when the colonel, seated on his veranda and smoking a cigar, caught sight of a cavalry sergeant hurriedly passing his front gate. The main searching-parties had long since come home, unsuccessful; Lieutenant Perry had returned and made report that the people at Dunraven denied having seen or heard anything of Gwynne, that both proprietor and manager had treated his visit as an affront, and that he had had much difficulty in preventing a fracas between his men and a gang of rough fellows employed at the ranch, that finally Mr. Maitland had fallen back in a swoon, and that he had left him to the care of Dr. Quin, who arrived soon after the occurrence. The colonel had been greatly interested and somewhat excited over the details of Perry's adventure as that young gentleman finally gave them, for at first he was apparently averse to saying much about it. Little by little, however, all his conversation with Maitland and Ewen was drawn out, and the particulars of his hostile reception. The colonel agreed with him that there was grave reason to suspect some of the ranch-people of knowing far more of Sergeant Gwynne's disappearance than they would tell; and finally, seeing Perry's indisposition to talk further, and noting his preoccupation and apparent depression of spirits, he concluded that between fatigue and rasped nerves the young fellow would be glad to go to bed: so he said, kindly,—

"Well, I won't keep you, Perry: you're tired out. I'll sit up and see the doctor when he gets back and have a talk with him, then decide what steps we will take in the morning. I'll send a party down the valley at daybreak, anyway. May I offer you some whiskey, or a bottle of beer?"

"Thank you, colonel, I believe not to-night. A bath and a nap will set me all right, and I'll be ready to start out first thing in the morning. Good-night, sir."

But Colonel Brainard could not go to sleep. The garrison had "turned in," all except the guard and Captain Stryker. That officer had returned an hour after dark, and, getting a fresh horse, had started out again, going down the south side of the Monee to search the timber with lanterns, the Cheyenne scouts having reported that Gwynne's horse had come up that way. He had been missed by Mr. Perry, who galloped up the trail to catch the platoon before it reached the post, and the colonel, now that he had heard the lieutenant's story, was impatiently awaiting his return. Up to within a few minutes of midnight, however, neither Stryker nor the doctor had come; dim lights were burning in both their quarters and at the guard-house. Everywhere else the garrison seemed shrouded in darkness. Catching sight of the yellow chevrons as they flitted through the flood of light that poured from his open door-way, the colonel instantly divined that this must be a sergeant of Stryker's troop going in search of his captain, and promptly hailed him:

"What is it, sergeant? Any news?"

"Yes, sir," answered the soldier, halting short. "Sergeant Gwynne's come back. I was going to the captain's to report."

"How did he get back. Isn't he injured?"

"He says he's had a fall, sir, and has been badly shaken up, but he walked in."

"Why, that's singular! Did he meet none of the searching-parties?—see none of their lights?"

"I can't make out, sir. He's a little queer,—doesn't want to talk, sir. He asked if his horse got in all right, and went and examined the scratches, and seemed troubled about them; but he doesn't say anything."

"Has he gone to the hospital?"

"No, sir: he'll sleep in his usual bunk at the stables to-night. He is only bruised and sore, he says. His face is cut and scratched and bound up in his handkerchief."

"Very well," said the colonel, after a moment's thought. "The captain will look into the matter when he gets back. You take your horse and ride down the south side of the valley and find the Cheyenne scouts. Captain Stryker is with them. Tell him the sergeant is home, safe."

"Very well, sir." And the trooper saluted, faced about, and disappeared in the darkness; while the colonel arose, and, puffing thoughtfully at his cigar, began pacing slowly up and down the piazza. He wished Stryker were home; he wished Captain Lawrence were officer of the day, and, so, liable to come out of his quarters again: he had heard just enough about that odd English ranch to make him feel disturbed and ill at ease. There had evidently been hostility between his predecessor and the proprietor of Dunraven, and very probably there had been bad blood between the men of the Eleventh Cavalry and the employees of the ranch: else why should there have been so unprovoked an assault upon the lieutenant this night? Then there were other things that gave him disquiet. Several officers had gathered upon the piazza during the early evening; they were mainly of his own regiment, but Captain Belknap and two of the infantry subalterns were there; Lawrence did not come. Of course the talk was about the incident of the evening, and, later, the rumors about Dunraven. All this was new to the cavalrymen: they had heard, as yet, nothing at all, and were not a little taken aback by the evident embarrassment and ominous silence of the three infantrymen, when the colonel turned suddenly on Belknap with the question,—

"By the way, captain, I had no time to ask Lawrence, and it really did not occur to me until after he had gone, but—what did he mean by saying that Dr. Quin could tell us something about the people at Dunraven?"

Belknap turned red and looked uncomfortably at his two comrades, as though appealing to them for aid. The younger officers, however, would say nothing at all, and the colonel promptly saw that he had stumbled on some piece of garrison gossip.

"Never mind," he said, with a kindly laugh. "I don't want to drag any stories out by the roots. The doctor can doubtless explain it all in good season."

"Well, Colonel Brainard," answered Belknap, bulkily, "to tell the truth, I really don't know anything about it, and I don't know any one who *does*, though I have heard some woman-talk about the post. The relations between Dr. Quin and some of the officers of the Eleventh were rather strained, and he is a somewhat reserved and secretive man. The stories were set afloat here last fall, and we *had* to hear more or less of them until the Eleventh went away this spring. We know only that Dr. Quin has been to Dunraven and the rest of us haven't. Possibly some of the Eleventh were piqued because they had no such luck, or perhaps their ladies did not like it because Quin wouldn't tell them anything about what he saw. At all events, he refused to talk on the subject at all, and allowed people to draw their own conclusions."

"He probably told his post commander," suggested Lieutenant Farnham, who, as acting adjutant of the post and an aspirant for the adjutancy of the regiment, thought it a good opportunity of putting in a word as indicative of what *he* considered the bounden duty of an officer under like circumstances.

"Well, no, I fancy not," replied Belknap. "About the only thing we really do know is that, in a somewhat angry interview last fall, Colonel Stratton forbade Dr. Quin's leaving the post or going to Dunraven without his express permission. I happened to be in the office at the time."

"Was it before or after that that he was said to go there so often?" asked Farnham.

"Well, both," answered Belknap, reluctantly. "But understand me, Mr. Farnham, I know nothing whatever of the matter."

"I should not suppose that Colonel Stratton would care to restrict his post surgeon from going thither if they needed his professional services," said Colonel Brainard, pleasantly.

"That was the point at issue, apparently," answered Belknap. "Colonel Stratton said that it was *not* on professional grounds that he went, and thereby seemed to widen the breach between them. Dr. Quin would not speak to the colonel after that, except when duty required it."

The conversation changed here, and little more was said; but Colonel Brainard could not help thinking of a matter that he carefully kept to himself. It was not his custom to require his officers to ask permission to leave the garrison for a ride or hunt when they were to be absent from no duty, and only by day. Here it was midnight, as he thought it over, and the doctor had not returned, neither had he mentioned his desire to ride away, although he had been with the colonel wellnigh an hour before parade. True, he had sent the doctor word to go and join Lieutenant Perry at the gate of Dunraven, and *that* would account for his detention; but he knew that the surgeon was several miles away from his post and his patients at the moment that message was sent.

Meantime, Perry, too, was having a communion with himself and finding it all vexation of spirit. All the way home the memory of that sweet English face was uppermost in his thoughts. He had been startled at the sight of a young and fair woman at Dunraven; he had felt a sense of inexplicable rejoicing when she said to him, "I am Miss Maitland;" it would have jarred him to know that she was wife; he was happy, kneeling by the side of the beautiful girl he had never seen before that very evening, and delighted that he could be of service to her. All this was retrospect worth indulging; but then arose the black shadow on his vision. How came Dr. Quin striding in there as though "native and to the manner born"?—how came he to call her "Gladys"? Perry had been pondering over this matter for full half an hour on the homeward ride before he bethought him of Mrs. Lawrence's remarks about the signal-lights. One thing led to another in his recollection of her talk. The doctor answered the signals,—no one else; the doctor and no one else was received at Dunraven; the doctor had declined to answer any questions about the people at the ranch,—had been silent and mysterious, yet frequent in his visits. And then, more than all, what was that Mrs. Lawrence had said or intimated, that Mrs. Quin, "such a lovely woman, too," had taken her children and left him early that spring, and all on account of somebody or something connected with Dunraven Ranch? Good heavens! It could not be "Gladys." And yet——

Instead of taking a bath and going to bed, Mr. Perry poked his head into Parke's bachelor chamber as he reached the little cottage they shared in common. No Gladys disturbed the junior's dreams, apparently, for he was breathing regularly, sleeping the sleep of the just; and so, finding no one to talk to and being in no mood to go to bed at an hour so comparatively early when he had so much to think about, Perry filled a pipe and perched himself in a big chair by the window-seat, intending to think it all over again. He was beginning to hate that doctor: he would have chafed at the idea of any bachelor's being before him in an acquaintance with Gladys Maitland, but a married man, knowing her so well as to make his wife jealous and himself indifferent to that fact,—knowing her so well as to drive "such a lovely woman, too," into taking her children and quitting the marital roof,—that was too much of a bad thing, and Perry was sore discomfited. He got up, impatient and restless, passed out to the little piazza in front of his quarters, and began pacing up and down, the glow from his corn-cob pipe making a fiery trail in the darkness. He would have been glad to go back to the colonel and keep watch with him; but there was one thing connected with his visit to Dunraven that he could not bear to speak of, especially as those words of Mrs. Lawrence recurred again and again to his memory. He had not said one word—he did not want to tell—of Gladys Maitland.

And so it happened that Perry, too, was awake and astir when the footsteps of the cavalry sergeant were heard on their way to Captain Stryker's quarters. Listening, he noted that the soldier had halted at the colonel's, held a brief conversation with that officer, and then turned back across the parade. Instantly divining that news had come of Sergeant Gwynne, Perry seized his forage-cap and hurried in pursuit. He overtook the trooper just beyond the guard-house, and went with him eagerly to the stables. A moment more, and he was bending over a soldier's bedside in a little room adjoining the forage-shed and by the light of a dim stable-lantern looking down into the bruised and battered features of the non-commissioned officer whom he had pronounced of all others at Rossiter the most respected and highly thought of by the cavalry garrison.

"Sergeant, I'm very sorry to see you so badly mauled," said Perry. "How on earth did it happen?"

Gwynne turned his head painfully until the one unbandaged eye could look about and see that none of the stable-guard were within hearing, then back again and up into the symphathetic face of his young superior.

"Lieutenant, I must tell you and the captain; and yet it is a matter I profoundly wish to keep as secret as possible,—the story of my day's adventure, I mean."

"You need not tell me at all if you do not wish to," said Perry; "though I think it is due to yourself that the captain should know how it was you were gone all day and that your horse and you both came back in such condition."

"I understand, sir, fully," answered Gwynne, respectfully. "I shall tell the captain the whole story, if he so desire. Meantime, I can only ask that no one else be told. If the men in the troop had an inkling of the true story there would be endless trouble; and so I have tried to account for it by saying my horse and I had an ugly fall while running a coyote through the timber. We did see a coyote, down near the ranch on the Monee, and I did have an ugly fall: I was set upon by three of those ranchmen and badly handled."

"Yes, damn them!" said Perry, excitedly and wrathfully. "I've had an experience with them myself to-night, while we were searching for you."

"So much the more reason, sir, why my mishap should not be told among the men. The two affairs combined would be more than they would stand. There are enough Irishmen here in our troop alone to go down and wipe that ranch out of existence; and I fear trouble as it stands."

"Whether there will be trouble or not will depend very much on the future conduct of the proprietor and manager down there. Of course we cannot tolerate for an instant the idea of their maintaining a gang of ruffians there who are allowed to assault officers or men who happen to ride around that neighborhood. You were not inside their limits, were you?"

"Yes, sir," said the sergeant, painfully, "I was: I had tied my horse outside and ventured in to get a nearer look at the buildings."

"What time did it happen?"

"This morning, sir; not more than an hour and a half after you spoke to me in the valley."

"Indeed! Then you must have lain there all day! Why, Gwynne, this will never do. I'll go and get the surgeon and have him look you over. You must have been brutally mauled, and must be utterly exhausted."

"Don't go, sir," said the sergeant, eagerly stretching forth a hand. "It—it isn't as you think, sir. I have been kindly cared for. They're not all ruffians down there, and the men who assaulted me will be fully punished. I've been quite as well nursed and fed and brandied and bandaged as though I'd been carried right to hospital. Indeed, I don't need anything but rest. I'll be all right in a day."

"But I think Dr. Quin ought to see you and satisfy us you are not injured."

"Be satisfied, sir. The doctor *has* seen me."

"Why, but how?—where? He was here all day, and only went away at sunset. He joined me at Dunraven about nine o'clock, and hadn't returned when I came in. Did he find you and bring you back?"

Gwynne hesitated painfully again:

"The doctor saw me this evening,—down near where I was hurt; but I got back here without his help, sir. Lieutenant," said the soldier, suddenly, "there are one or two things connected with this day's work that I cannot tell. Come what may, I must not speak of them, even to the captain."

Perry was silent a moment. Then he kindly answered,—

"I do not think any one here will press you to tell what you consider it might be ungrateful or dishonorable in you to reveal. I will do what I can to see that your wishes are respected. And now, if you are sure I can do nothing for you, good-night, sergeant." And the young officer held out his hand.

"Good-night, sir," answered Gwynne. He hesitated one moment. It was the first time since he entered service, nearly five years before, that an officer had offered him his hand. It was a new and strange sensation. It might not be "good discipline" to take advantage of it, but there were other reasons. Gwynne looked up in the frank blue eyes of his lieutenant and read something there that told a new story. Out came a hand as slender and shapely as that of the young officer, and the two were silently and firmly clasped.

"How can I question him?" said Perry to himself as he walked slowly homeward. "Is there not something I am holding back?—something I cannot speak of? By Jupiter! can his be the same reason?"

IX.

At just what hour the post surgeon returned to Fort Rossiter that night no one seemed to know. He was present at sick-call, and imperturbable as ever, on the following morning, and the few officers who were at head-quarters after guard-mounting were able to affirm that the colonel had been courteous as usual in his greeting to the medical officer, and that nothing whatever had been said about his being away so late the previous evening. Captain Stryker came home soon after midnight, had a brief talk with his colonel, and went over to the stables to inquire into Gwynne's condition before he went to bed. Parke came into Perry's room after morning stables, and told him, as he was yawning and stretching in bed, that the captain had had quite a long talk with Gwynne that morning, and that "something was up,"—he didn't know what. Later in the day Perry was sent for by Colonel Brainard, and found the commanding officer in consultation with Captain Stryker and two other troop-commanders. At their request he repeated the story of his adventure at Dunraven, beginning with his instructions to the men he left at the gate, and ending with old Maitland's swooning; and about an hour after he had finished he saw the adjutant with a small escort ride away down the valley, and rightly conjectured that the colonel had sent a letter to Dunraven inquiring into the cause of the assaults on two members of his command. Battalion drill kept him occupied all the morning; a garrison court convened at noon and sat until skirmish drill began at three P.M.; and so it happened that not until near parade did he find a moment's time to himself. He longed to see Mrs. Lawrence and question her as to the nature of the "Dunraven stories" she had mentioned; for what had been a matter of indifference to him then had suddenly become of vivid interest. There were ladies sitting on the Lawrences' gallery, he could plainly see, as the cavalry officers came tramping in from afternoon stables, but he could not hope to ask or hear anything about a matter so near his heart in the presence of so many sympathetic and interested listeners. He kept away towards his own gate, therefore, until he saw that there, leaning on the gate-post, and apparently awaiting him, stood Dr. Quin.

Perry would gladly have avoided the doctor: the antagonism he was beginning to feel for him was of a character that would hardly brook concealment. Cordial and joyous in manner as he was to almost every man, woman, and child he met, it was all the more noticeable that to the very few whom he held in dislike or distrust his bearing was cold and repellent in the last degree. Something told him the doctor was there to speak to him about their chance meeting at Dunraven. He did not want to speak to him at all, just now. Yet how could he hope to have these matters explained without a meeting and a talk? While the other officers strolled over and stopped, most of them, in front of the group of ladies at Lawrence's, Perry stalked straight across the parade and the boundary road, with his blue eyes fixed on the doctor's face.

The latter was studying him as he came, and doubtless read that expression of coldness and distrust: possibly he resented it. At all events, something prompted him to speak in a tone less cordial than he had ever employed towards Perry,—"a youngster whom I thoroughly approve of," as he said before he had known him a week. Still leaning on the gate-post, and resting his head on his hand, the doctor began:

"Mr. Perry, I have been to see you twice to-day, but could not find you, and I wanted to speak with you on a matter of some importance."

"You could have found me on drill or the court, if anything immediate was needed. I have been nowhere else, except to stables," said Perry, shortly.

"It was a personal matter,—a somewhat embarrassing one,—and I thought best to see you alone."

"Well, here I am, Dr. Quin: drive ahead and let us have it."

"I wanted to ask you if, while you were at the ranch last night, you saw anything of a large signet-ring, with a crest and motto engraved on the stone."

"I did not,—unless you mean the one Mr. Maitland wore."

"The very one! You noticed that, did you?"

"I noticed he had something of the kind on his left hand when he came down."

"And it was nowhere to be found after you went away. You may remember you were chafing and slapping that hand; and I thought you might have accidentally removed it at that time."

"The reflection is not a pleasant one, Dr. Quin," said Perry, with an angry light in the blue eyes.

"Pardon me, Mr. Perry: I put it awkwardly, but I mean no reflection whatever. Miss Maitland mentioned your efforts to restore the old gentleman to consciousness, and together we searched the sofa and the floor after we had put him safely to bed and discovered the loss of the ring. It is one to which he attaches peculiar value, and its loss has preyed upon him. While I know very well you could not have the ring, I was asked to ascertain if you remembered seeing it, and so establish the truth of Mr. Maitland's belief that it was on his finger when he went to that room."

"It was; but I do not recollect its being on his hand after he was carried to the sofa. It would surely have attracted my attention while chafing it."

"The parlor, hall, and piazza have been swept and searched, I am told by this note," and the doctor indicated a little missive he held in his hand, whereat Perry's face did not brighten, "and with no success. I was *asked* to inquire of you, and if it has annoyed you, as I infer by your manner, pray let that be my apology. Then I am to say you saw it when Mr. Maitland entered the room, but not again?"

"Precisely; unless you choose to add to your correspondent that the next time I am associated with missing property at Dunraven I would prefer to be questioned direct, and not through a third party."

A quiet smile shone for an instant on the doctor's grave face:

"I fear that I have not accomplished my mission very diplomatically, Mr. Perry, and am sorry to have vexed you. The colonel tells me, by the way, that I ought to say to you that the reason I was so long in reaching your party last night was that I was detained attending to another case,—one of our own men. Good-evening, sir." And, raising his forage-cap, the doctor walked slowly and with dignity away, leaving Perry too surprised to speak.

"The colonel told him to tell me!" was Perry's wondering soliloquy at last. "Then I suppose he must have told the chief some story to account for his being away." It was pretty evident from the young fellow's manner as he entered the house that the story was not one which struck him as being entitled to confidence or consideration.

On the table in his little sitting-room lay a dainty note. It was not the first he had received under that superscription, and he had not been slow to open and read them. If anything, the cloud upon his forehead seemed to deepen at sight of it. He picked it up, looked impatiently at the address, hesitated a moment, tossed it back on his desk, and went into the inner room. He would not read it now; it was almost parade-time; he had to bathe and change his dress, for after parade he was to dine at the quarters of an infantry friend, and Captain and Mrs. Lawrence were to be of the party. Already it was noted that when any of the few infantry people at the post gave a little tea or dinner at which only eight or ten were gathered together, the Belknaps were not invited on the same evening with Mr. Perry, and *vice versâ*. When Parke came in, whistling and singing and banging doors and making all manner of uncouth noise in the exuberance of his boyish spirits, he bolted into Perry's domain, as was his wont, and began a rattling comment on the events of the day.

"By the way," he broke in, suddenly, "we can't both go to-morrow; and I suppose you want to."

"Go where?"

"Why, out with the hounds: to-morrow's the day, you know."

Perry gave a whistle of perplexity. The colonel had promised the ladies that there should be a big run this very week. All the fleet hounds of the cavalry battalion were to be out, and all the officers who could be spared from the day's duties: a detachment was to go over into the valley of a stream some ten miles away, pitch tents in the shade, and there set luncheon for the entire party; horses were to be provided for all the ladies who cared to go mounted, buggies and "buckboards" were to convey the others, and it was to be a gala occasion. Antelope, coyote, or jack-rabbit,—any four-footed game the prairie afforded was to be "coursed" in due state and ceremony; the ladies "in at the death" were to be crowned and subsequently presented with trophies of the chase more sightly than the mask or brush *au naturel*. The affair had been gayly talked over that very evening of the colonel's dinner, but the events of the previous day and the perplexities of the one just closing had completely driven it all out of his head.

And yet he was engaged to ride with Mrs. Belknap,—the Amazon of Fort Rossiter! and for the first time in his life Ned Perry would have been glad of an excuse to get away from a gallop with an accomplished équestrienne.

"You don't mean to say you had forgotten it?" asked Parke, in amaze.

"Don't blow on me, there's a good fellow; but, after all my 'breaks' of yesterday,—getting an absent from drill and into a row at the ranch,—I declare it had slipped my memory. No, you go, Parke: I don't deserve to be let off anything, after yesterday. You've been sticking to duty like a brick ever since you joined, and Stryker ought to give you the preference."

"But you're engaged to ride with Mrs. Belknap," said Parke.

"Who told you so?"

"I heard her say so. Dana asked if he might have the pleasure, just a while ago, and she smilingly replied that it would have been delightful, but that you had asked her four days ago, when it was first planned."

"So I had; but I've been getting into scrapes ever since, and I oughtn't to go. By Jove! I'll write her a note now and say I can't get off. It's true enough. I wouldn't let such a fellow go if I commanded the troop. I'd make him stay in and attend roll-call a week."

"Well, Mrs. Belknap expects you," said Parke, dubiously. "Not but what Dana would be glad to take your place. Belknap can't go: he's too bulky to ride, and she'd leave him miles astern first run we had, sure."

Suddenly Perry bethought him of the note, and made a dive into the sitting-room, towel in hand and shirt-sleeves rolled to the elbows. It read,—

"MON AMI,—

"You go to the Spragues' to dine this evening, and there will be cards, and you will not be able to get away until very late. Will you not come in a little while before parade,—without fail? There is something I greatly want to see you about.

"Sincerely,

"F. E. B.

"Come early as possible after stables."

"Thunder and turf!" exclaimed Perry; "and there goes first call now! Here, Parke, you're dressed; run over and tell Mrs. Belknap

I just this instant read her note and I can't come : I'll get a late as it is."

"How can I, man?" shouted Parke, as he fled. "I've got to get into war-paint too.—Lucky thing for me," he added, in lower tone. "I don't want to be the one to tell the prettiest woman at Rossiter that her note that she sent here at noon wasn't opened until first call for parade."

Perry's dressing was completed at racing speed, but even then he was buckling his sabre-belt as the assembly sounded, and he had to go straight across to where his troop was forming,—a glittering rank of yellow plumes,—and so could only give a hurried sidelong glance towards Belknap's quarters. There was her bonnie ladyship pacing up and down the veranda; and he knew well he would have to account for his sins. All through parade his thoughts were divided between the fair face he had seen at Dunraven the night before and the dark one with the long, curving lashes sweeping those soft, peachy cheeks and half veiling those wonderful, liquid, speaking, side-glancing eyes. He saw Mrs. Belknap stroll forth a moment as though to join the group of ladies on the walk, then return to her slow, graceful, languid promenade up and down her piazza. He knew that he must hasten to her the instant the rank of officers dispersed and make his peace if possible, but as they marched to the front and saluted the commanding officer he signalled that he had something to say to them all, and, moving away to the edge of the parade-ground, so that the troops might not be detained on the line, he gathered his officers about him, a silent group under the little shade-trees that bounded the road-way, and took a letter from the breast of his uniform coat.

"Gentlemen," said he, "this will be of importance to some of you, and of interest to all. It explains something none of us understood, and contains matter that I deem it best you all should hear. It is a letter from the manager of Dunraven Ranch.—Mr. Adjutant, you read it."

And, clearing his throat, Mr. Farnham began:

"DUNRAVEN RANCH,
"Friday.

"COLONEL BRAINARD, —th Cavalry, Fort Rossiter:

"DEAR SIR,—Mr. Maitland is confined to his bed, and too ill to personally reply to your letter of this morning, which was duly received at the hands of your adjutant. He directs me to write as follows: that, while he regrets the boisterous conduct of some of his employees last evening and their assault on Mr. Perry, he considers that in view of the results—a broken head on the part of one of our people and no apparent damage to Mr. Perry—the matter should not be pressed. As to the other assault alluded to, he has no knowledge of it whatever, and can find no man who has.

"The distinct understanding between Mr. Maitland and the former commanding officer at Fort Rossiter was that none of the garrison should ever pass within our lines; and we agreed on the other hand that none of our people should ever trespass on the reservation. Mr. Maitland holds that it was the duty of Colonel Brainard's predecessor to acquaint him with the terms of this agreement, and the residents at Dunraven had no means of knowing that the invaders of last evening were not the very men whom the proper authorities had pledged themselves to restrain from such aggression.

"Mr. Maitland begs that Colonel Brainard will in future ratify and conform with the agreement formally entered into by his predecessor.

"Respectfully,
"P. EWEN, *Manager.*"

There was a moment of puzzled silence. The colonel looked quizzically around upon the circle of bronzed and soldierly faces under the black helmets. Captain Stryker's lips were twitching with amusement behind their black fringe of beard. No one spoke at first; but presently a deep-voiced troop-commander gave vent to his emotions:

"What a bombastic old crank! Who is he?"

"An Englishman,—the owner of the biggest ranch in this part of Texas," answered the colonel. "Captain Belknap, Captain Lawrence, have you any knowledge of the agreement of which he speaks?"

"Nothing beyond the vague talk we heard. Dr. Quin would be more apt to know what Colonel Stratton agreed to than we would," answered Belknap.

"I will ask the doctor this evening. Meantime, knowing no reason why such a policy of non-intercourse should be observed, I shall not recognize it. What is more, while you will caution your men to respect Dunraven bounds as they would other private property, let them show no hostility to the ranch-people who may have occasion to visit us. The man who brought this note tells me he was threatened and abused by some cavalrymen near the stables. Mr. Maitland professes to have no knowledge of another assault; but we have evidence that Sergeant Gwynne was beaten by three fellows on the Dunraven grounds yesterday. That matter is yet to be settled. Now one thing more: troop and company commanders will closely watch their men the next few nights,—keep a sharp lookout on the quarters until midnight, to see that no men slip away; after midnight the guard must attend to it. There is an element in the ranks that would be only too glad to go down to Dunraven some night and have satisfaction on their own account for yesterday's affairs. This must *not* be permitted. See to it, gentlemen. That is all for the present.—Mr. Perry, will you come with me a moment?"

Perry went. Mrs. Belknap saw him go, and believed herself slighted.

X.

The hounds were out, and all Fort Rossiter "society" was with them. The day was faultless,—neither too warm nor too cloudy; a brisk westerly breeze sent the cloud-shadows sailing steadily across the broad prairie sea and keeping the veils and skirts of the Amazons of the party a-flutter. Three there were of these, the rest of the sisterhood preferring to follow the hunt by buggy or buck-board, though frankly expressing their envy of the fortunate riders. Mounted on her own spirited little bay, admirably fitted as to habit, and sitting squarely and well, Mrs. Belknap would have been the centre of observation of all the cavalry officers even had she not been, as she incontestably was, the beauty of the garrison. The colonel had offered Mrs. Lawrence one of his own horses, and therefore was accorded the right of being her escort. Mrs. Sprague was similarly indebted for her "mount" to Captain Stryker; and a very bright and beaming little body she was as she rode over the springy turf at the side of the dark-haired troop-leader. She dearly loved fresh air, sunshine, space, healthful exercise of every kind, was the champion at tennis and an indomitable walker, but a ride was something better than all, and of course the rarest pleasure. The wife of a faithful and honest old subaltern who had reaped his four "fogies" for twenty years' service and was still looking forward to his captaincy, her opportunities for riding had been limited to those occasions when some thoughtful cavalryman would send his horse around with his compliments and an invitation to take a canter. The Eleventh were very busy during their stay at Rossiter, or very chary of their horseflesh. They never rode, said the infantry people, in speaking of them to their successors, while the —th were not only themselves in saddle hours each day, but they were constantly sending horses to the ladies; and—wonder of wonders!—*all* the infantry officers were invited to join in the hunt, and such as could go were provided with excellent mounts. And so it happened that a large and merry party had taken the field: the colonel with a dozen of his officers,—cavalry and infantry,—the ladies, the sergeant in charge of the hounds, with his two or three assistants, and the brace of orderlies, made a "field" that covered a goodly front as in dispersed order, chatting and laughing, they swept out eastward from the post, following in the wake of the master of the hounds and his long, lithe, fleet-limbed coursers themselves. Beautiful creatures were these hounds of the —th,—many of them black as jet, others a slaty blue, others a quakerish drab, but all with huge rounded chests, powerful shoulders and haunches, and wonderful limbs for speed. There were nearly two dozen of them, springily trotting along behind their huntsman, with lolling tongues and drooping head and tail. Yet eyes and ears were eager and alert, watching, waiting for the signal from anywhere along the extended front that should start them in a race that would leave the very gale behind. They are the coursers, the runners, the aristocrats of the chase, disdainful of the work being done by their humbler kindred,—the canine skirmishers who are bounding, bustling, scurrying, sniffing, scampering everywhere over the prairie to their front,— yet keenly observant of the results. All manner of dog—even volunteer whelp from the Cheyenne camp—is to be seen along that outer line,—spaniels, a lordly Newfoundland, all varieties of terrier and "curs of low degree," all, even an occasional bird-dog, scouting the prairie in desperate eagerness to snap and seize a rabbit or throttle a coyote, for down in their jealous hearts they well know that, once started, the quarry leaps for the far horizon, vanishes from their view like the "Split-the-Wind" of tradition, and leaves them, despite heroic effort, far, far behind, while the lithe-limbed greyhounds and the racers of the garrison horses alone can keep in sight of the chase.

"Hard lines on Perry, isn't it?" said Mr. Graham, as he trotted up beside Mrs. Belknap and took his place for the moment with her bevy of cavaliers. "First time he ever missed a hunt, I reckon."

"He needn't have missed this one," said Parke. "It was my week, and I told him to go; and Captain Stryker said so, too; but——"

Here Mr. Parke broke off suddenly and looked in mild wonderment in Dana's face, for that young gentleman had managed, unseen by Mrs. Belknap, to swing free his right foot and give the speaker's left a vehement kick. Too late, however. Mrs. Belknap had heard it.

"Are you cavalrymen *all* so little to be trusted?" she asked, with a brilliant smile upon her flushing face. Exercise and excitement had lent unusual sparkle to her eyes and color to her cheeks—"she is positively beautiful to-day," as Mrs. Lawrence confessed to the colonel at the moment.

"I had a note from Mr. Perry this morning saying he was grievously disappointed, but that some troop-duty had been assigned to him which could not be transferred and he must stay and finish it."

"What he said is true, Mrs. Belknap," promptly asseverated Mr. Dana. "The papers have all to be in readiness for muster on Monday, and the saddle-kits put in shape for inspection."

"*Only* in Captain Stryker's troop?" softly inquired the lady, with eyelids rising incredulously.

"No, of course not. One officer is back at the post from each troop. It happened to fall on Perry in his."

"I fancy I should prefer serving in some older captain's troop if I were Mr. Perry. It seems that while your other captains stay home and look after their companies, Captain Stryker has a subaltern attend to his while *he* comes a-hunting."

"On the other hand, we fellows have a dozen things to do in *our* troops that Captain Stryker does himself in his. It's as broad as it's long, Mrs. Belknap," said Dana. He did not fancy her criticising the methods of his cavalry associates, and was possibly a little piqued at the decided annoyance she showed at Perry's failure to attend. Meantime, Stryker, all unconscious of her censure, was chatting laughingly with Mrs. Sprague and exchanging shots with the colonel and Mrs. Lawrence. The four were getting on admirably together, and seemed too much absorbed in their own fun to note the fact that Mrs. Belknap and her knot of four or five satellites had been gradually edging away towards the right, and that the rest of the hunt was becoming widely scattered.

"It is time we stirred up a jack-rabbit at least," said the colonel. "Suppose we veer over towards the northeast a little. Whatever we do, we want no chase down there towards Dunraven: those wire fences would spoil it all."

"I wonder if those people never hunt?" said Mr. Farnham, who had joined the quartette: he always kept close to his colonel, as befitted an aspirant for the adjutancy. "Englishmen are generally game for all manner of sport."

"I can see horsemen out there on the prairie to the east of the ranch," said Stryker, whose eyes were keen, "and I could have sworn a moment ago that I saw a horsewoman."

"Nonsense, Captain Stryker!" exclaimed Mrs. Lawrence, yet with quick glance at Mrs. Sprague. "What *could* you have taken for a 'lady on a horseback'? Do you suppose there could be ladies at Dunraven and we not know it?"

"Hardly possible," answered the captain; "and therefore I doubted the evidence of my senses. Yet something very like a lady followed by a groom rode down the slope into the valley about ten minutes ago. She is out of sight in the timber now. If Perry were only with us I'd send him off there to see."

"Yes, we miss Perry on our hunts," said the colonel to his lady friends. "He is one of our best riders and most enthusiastic sportsmen. He *will* be out, will he not, Stryker?"

"Yes, sir. There is really no necessity for his staying in, and I so told him; but he felt that he ought to, at least until certain work was finished. Then he said he could ride eastward and join us. Hurrah! there they go!"

Far out to the front, straight to the east, "a gray streak with a white tip to it" went shooting into space as though launched from some invisible bow drawn by giant power. A big jack-rabbit, all legs and ears, had listened quivering and trembling to the sounds of the approaching hunt, until an enterprising terrier, foremost skirmisher of the line, fairly tumbled over him as he crouched behind a little bunch of weeds: then with one mighty leap and the accompaniment of a wild yelp from his discoverer he sprang forth into a race for his precious life. "Hoy! hoy!" yells the sergeant as he sights the quarry. "Hurrah!" shout the nearest huntsmen, and, with one simultaneous impulse, skirmishing curs, stealthy, springing hounds, eager steeds, and jubilant riders,—men and women,—away goes the entire field sweeping in pursuit. At first all is one mad rush until it is certain that the rabbit is a veteran who understands well the maxim that "a stern-chase is a long chase" all the world over. Let him keep it well in mind, fix his eyes on that one distant, shadowy butte on the eastern horizon, and bear away for that, straight as the flight of laden honey-bee, and his chance for life is fair: he has fifty yards the start of the nearest hound. Let him swerve or hesitate, and, like the original of the famous comparison, he is lost. The prairie is level as a floor, the turf firm and springy: not a prairie-dog has mined the sod or digged a pit for the unwary. "Magnificent ground!—couldn't have better!" shouts the colonel to Mrs. Lawrence, who is somewhat nervously tugging at her reins and leaning back in the saddle. "Let him go. There isn't a possibility of a stumble. Look at Mrs. Belknap!" he adds. He would not do so ordinarily, but he and his fair partner are being left hopelessly behind in the race, and, though his big charger rarely lands him among the foremost and the colonel does not attempt to vie with the light riders among the youngsters, he cannot bear "dragging." Mrs. Lawrence gives one glance in the indicated direction, sees Mrs. Belknap skimming like a bird across the grassy level, riding from the right front diagonally towards the frantic chase. Gentle as she is and unenvious of her rival's superiority in some respects, she *won't* be thought a coward. The color deepens on her cheek, her soft eyes flash, she bites her pretty red lips, and, to Lawrence's amaze, her riding-whip comes viciously down upon her courser's flank and her little hands give rein. Away she flies, out to the front, leaving her lord and master and his friend, her escort the colonel, thundering bulkily in her track, but losing ground with every stride. Delighted to have so light a rider, the colonel's second horse makes play for the very leaders. Here, close behind the master of the hounds, all eyes fixed on that bounding tuft of gray and white a few score yards ahead, bending over their horses' necks and keeping just enough pressure on the bit to prevent over-riding the huntsman, ride Parke and Graham, two "light weights," who have coursed many a mile of prairie. Just behind them, a little to their right, rides Mrs. Belknap, her veil fluttering straight out behind, her glorious eyes flashing, her dark skin flushed with triumph and the exhilaration of the dashing pace, her little hands wound about in the reins she holds so firmly. Splendidly she sits her fleet racer, and Dana has to urge and spur his clumsier troop-horse to keep in close attendance. These four are well in advance of all the others. Back of them, gallantly urging on her sturdy sorrel, comes Mrs. Sprague, with Stryker riding warily alongside and watching her "going" before he will satisfy himself that it is safe to trust her to her own guiding. Level as the prairie is here, he knows that a mile or so ahead there are "breaks" leading down into the valley of one of the innumerable tributaries of the Washita. *Then* the story may be different. He looks up in surprise at the thunder of hoofs close alongside, and Mrs. Lawrence, with excitement in her eyes, overtakes, then passes them on her way to the front. "See!" he points to his partner,—"see that dark shadow across the prairie out there. We cannot ride at this pace when we pass that hollow: the breaks set in still farther." He glances over his shoulder and signals to the nearest officer to follow Mrs. Lawrence and look out for her, and the gallant does his best, but all are at top speed; the colonel and the heavy weights—infantry and cavalry—are beginning to lose ground, and still that gray "puff-ball" far to the front seems inch by inch to be slipping away from his pursuers; still the long, lean greyhounds, looking almost flat against the sward in their wonderful strides, speed on in relentless chase, eager muzzles outstretched, eager eyes glaring on the bounding quarry, gleaming muscles working in the sunshine like the steel rods of the drivers of the "lightning express." A dozen of them are bunched in the track of the chase; others are farther out to right and left. Not an inch do the pursuers seem to have gained: straight as an arrow has been the flight so far, but now the "breaks" are just ahead, little ravines cut in here and there across the level. Will he keep his determined course, up hill and down, straight away to the east, or will he lose heart, tack, veer, double and twist? If he swerve he is a lost rabbit!

Far to the rear, yelping, panting, distracted by this time, the terriers and mongrels, the original leaders, have fallen. The field, too, is strung out nearly a mile deep at the end of the first six minutes' run, for some of the laggards have given up and are disposed to wait for the coming of the buggies and buck-boards. Here at the front all is tense excitement. All eyes are on the rabbit, for now or never will the crisis come. The horses are breathing heavily, but with no thought of slackening speed. "Watch him now as he sights that *arroyo!*" shouts Graham to Parke, for far out to the right front a ravine bursts off to the southeast, and one of its shallow contributors stretches obliquely across the rabbit's frenzied vision. "Veer that way; he'll take it, sure!" shouts the huntsman; and, sure enough, no sooner does he reach it than the gray victim darts down the winding shelter, as though hopeful that his sudden twist would throw his pursuers off the sight; scent the greyhound has none. The move is disastrous; "Hi!" shout the leading riders, waving the pursuit to the right front, and, obedient to signal,

T *

the foremost hounds sweep in long curve into the *coulée*, striking it many a yard farther down than where the harried chase first dived into its treacherous shadows. And now those hounds who were out on the right flank are up in line with the very leaders, and bounding along the level at the side of the ravine, yet keeping wary eye upon the chase. So, too, the horsemen. Making a deep curve in the ravine five hundred yards ahead, and confident that Bunny will blindly rush along his winding track, they strike out across the prairie, gaining twenty horse-lengths by the move; and now, with two or three of the oldest hounds, Parke, Dana, and Mrs. Belknap are darting on abreast of the chase. "Keep out there to the left, some of you!" shouts Dana. "He'll spring up the other side quick as he sees us. Drive him back." And, obedient to the signal of his waving hand, two of the leading troopers breast the slopes to the east, calling half a dozen hounds with them. Darting around a bend, Bunny's agonized eyes catch sight of the hounds and horses on the right bank, and like a flash he whirls, scampers up the opposite slope, and shoots out on the prairie again just in time to meet the hounds and troopers who have anticipated the move. Now he is wild and demoralized. Once more he dives into the ravine and sends the dust flying into the very faces of his pursuers, for now the leading hounds are so close that the foremost jaws are snapping the air at his every bound. A quick turn to the right and up the slope throws these leaders far—*too* far—beyond; they sweep around in long curve; but, though he has thrown them off, the hunted, senseless, helpless wretch has forgotten the trailers to the rear; they spring across the angle he has made, and are close as the original pursuers, and much the fresher. Wildly, madly now he twists and turns, first up one bank, then the other. Far to the rear the coming riders see the signs of his breaking down, mark the scurrying to and fro of horse and hound. "Come on!" they shout. "He's gone now, and we can be in at the death!" Mrs. Lawrence on one side of the ravine is as far to the front as Mrs. Belknap on the other. *One* of them *must* lose the brush: he cannot die on both sides at once. The dark beauty has had more than one rasping disappointment in the last two days: it would be intolerable now that, after all, Mrs. Lawrence, and not she, should prove the victor. Bunny makes one frantic rush up the slope to the right, and, with half a dozen hounds at his very heels, spins in front of her eyes, catches sight of two fresh antagonists confronting him, whirls suddenly about to the right, and almost dives under her horse's heaving barrel as he once more plunges into the ravine, down the rugged slope, up the gentle ascent to the other side. There half a dozen long, lean muzzles gleam close behind him; he falters, wavers; a sharp nose is thrust underneath him as he runs, a quick toss sends him kicking, struggling into air, and in another instant, with piteous but ineffectual squeak and pleading, he is the centre of a tumbling, snapping, fang-gnashing group of hounds, and his little life is torn out almost before Graham can leap from his saddle, beat them back with the visor of his cap, then, seizing the still quivering body by the legs that would have saved could that empty head only have directed, holds poor Bunny aloft in front of Mrs. Lawrence's snorting steed and proclaims her "Queen of the Chase."

And this, too, has Mrs. Belknap to see and strive to smile; while down in her heart she knows that it could not so have happened had Perry come.

XI.

Riding eastward just before noon, somewhat comforted in conscience because of his self-denial of the morning, Ned Perry scanned the distant prairie in search of the hunt. It was nearly luncheon-time, and he expected to find the party making its way to the little stream whither the baskets, boxes, and hampers had been despatched by wagon some hours before; but when he sighted the quartermaster driving homeward in his buggy he learned from that bulky veteran that rabbit after rabbit had been run, and that the whole party had finally decided to give dogs and horses a cool drink down in the Monee valley before starting northward across the prairie. "They must be getting down into the valley two or three miles east of the ranch just about now, and will go due north from there, unless they stir up more game along the Monee. If I were you," said the quartermaster, "I'd ride over to the lunch-stand. You won't get there much before the crowd."

Perry thanked him for the information, but, so far from accepting his advice, the younger officer turned his horse's head in the direction of Dunraven, and was speedily riding thither with an alacrity that he himself could hardly explain.

In his brief talk with the colonel after parade on the previous evening Perry had told him what he could of the characteristics of Messrs. Maitland and Ewen. The odd letter which had been sent by them had given the commanding officer cause for much thought, and he was desirous, evidently, of gathering from Perry's observations as complete an idea as was possible of their life and surroundings. And still Perry had found it impossible to volunteer any description of Miss Maitland; he could not bear to speak of her until — until he knew more of the doctor's purpose in his visits to the ranch. He had been detained by his commander just long enough to make it necessary for him to go direct to the Spragues' without leaving his helmet and sabre at home. They were waiting dinner for him as it was, but Mrs. Belknap took no note of that circumstance: what she saw was that he had avoided even passing within hail of her piazza both before and after parade.

Now, though conscious of no intention of avoidance, Perry rode forth to the meeting of this day with some little misgiving. In the first place, he knew that he must strive to make his peace with this slighted lady; and yet, in view of all he had seen and heard in the past forty-eight hours, how utterly dwarfed had that affair — his laughing flirtation with Mrs. Belknap — become! Had any one told him his attentions to her and her marked preference for his society were matters that people were beginning to talk of, — some with sly enjoyment, others with genuine regret, — he would have been grateful for the information, instead of resentful, as, with most men, would be the case ninety-nine times out of a hundred. But he knew nothing of this, and had too little experience to suspect the comments in circulation. She was most interesting — up to the day before yesterday; he loved to ride or dance with her; he enjoyed a chat with her more than he could tell. A most sympathetic and attentive listener was Mrs. Belknap, and her voice was low and sweet and full of subtly caressing tones. She had made him talk to her by the hour of his home, his hopes and ambitions, his profession and his prospects, and had held him in a silken bondage that he had no desire to escape.

And yet, as he rode out on the breezy plain this brilliant day, he found all thought of her distasteful, and his eyes, far from searching for the flutter of her trim habit in the distant riding-party, *would* go a-roaming over the intervening shades and shallows down in the Monee valley and seek the bare, brown walls of Dunraven far across the stream. It was odd indeed that he should have sought this, the longest way round, on his ride in quest of his companions from the fort.

Once again he looked at the isolated clump of buildings from his post of observation on the bluff; once again he saw across the stream and through the trees the barbed barrier that had caused both him and his men such laceration of flesh and temper; once again he saw the shallow valley winding away to the southeast, decked with its scrubby fringe-work of cottonwood and willow; but this time, three miles away its accustomed solitude was broken by groups of riders and darting black specks of dogs, all moving northward once more and already breasting the slopes. He should have turned away eastward and ridden across country to join them, but down here in the valley, only a short distance away, absorbed in watching the hunting-party, sat Mr. Ewen on a pawing and excited bay. Whatever coolness his rider might feel at this discovery, it was not shared by Nolan: he pricked up his ears and hailed his fellow-quadruped with cordial and unaffected pleasure, a neigh that the English-bred horse was so utterly uninsular as to whirl about and answer with corresponding warmth. Ewen caught at his heavy Derby and jerked it off his bullet head with an air of mingled embarrassment and civility, replacing it with similarly spasmodic haste. Perry coolly, but with a certain easy grace, raised his forage-cap in response to the salutation, and then, seeing the manager still looking at him as though he wanted to say something and did not know how to begin, gave Nolan his head and rode down to short hailing-distance.

"We meet on neutral ground out here, Mr. Ewen. I suppose your exclusive employer over yonder can hardly prohibit your answering civil inquiries after his health?" And, though he meant to be distant, Perry found himself smiling at the oddity of the situation.

"Do you know, I was just thinking about you," answered Ewen, "and wondering whether you were with that party down yonder? The old gentleman is better, thanks. He had two pretty bad nights, but is coming around slowly."

"And Miss Maitland,—how is she?"

"Rather seedy. She has had a good deal of care and vexation of late, I fancy, and this is no place for a young girl, anyhow."

"Well, you have some appreciation of the true character of Dunraven as a residence, after all!" answered Perry. "Now, if you can give me any good reason why she should live in this utterly out-of-the-way place, you will lift a weight from my mind."

"Oh, they don't live here, you know," spoke Ewen, hurriedly. "She comes here only when her father does. It is her own doing.

She goes with him everywhere, and will not leave him. She's all he has, don't you know?"

"I don't know anything about it. You Dunraven people seem averse to any expression of interest or courtesy from your fellow-men, but I'm free to say I should like to know what on earth there is in American cavalrymen to make them such objects of aversion to your master; and I would be glad to know how it is such a girl as that is dragged into such a hole as yonder."

Ewen sat in silence a moment, studying the young fellow's face.

"You deserve a better welcome there," he presently answered, "and I don't know that I can do better than to tell you the truth,—what I know of it. And let me tell you that if the old man knew of my speaking of it to any one, I'd lose the most lucrative but least attractive place I ever had. Do you see?"

"Then perhaps you had better not tell me. I do not care to pry into secrets."

"Oh, this is no secret. It was *that* that drove him here: everybody knew it in England. You were mighty shabbily treated at the ranch, and you requited it by preventing what would have been a bloody row and by lending us a helping hand. Even the old man recognizes that; and I think he'd be glad to say so to you, and see you, if you were not just what you are,—a cavalry officer."

"Why, what on earth can we have done? If any of our cloth have wronged Mr. Maitland in any way, it is our right to know it and take it up."

"It wasn't *your* cloth, old fellow," said Ewen, thawing visibly, "but it was the cavalry all the same that broke his heart and his pride, and made his life the wreck it is, and drove him from his home, shunning the sight of his fellow-men, all these years,—exiling *her*, too, in the prime of her young life. Mr. Perry, there are only three or four of us at Dunraven who know the story, but *we* have only sympathy and pity—no blame—for him, though he is the harshest master I ever served."

"How did it happen?" asked Perry.

"All through his son. There had been more of them, but there was only the one—Archie—when the Lancers were ordered to South Africa. He was a youngster, only seventeen, they tell me, and he had just been gazetted to his cornetcy. The old man was all wrapped up in him, for of the three boys the eldest had died only the month before the regiment was ordered on foreign service and the second had been killed in India. Both these two who were gone had made themselves famous among their comrades by their fearlessness and high character, and the old man, of course, could not ask Archie to quit the service just when orders for dangerous duty came. The boy went to the Cape with his corps, and got into the thick of the Zulu war just at the time of the massacre of the 24th at Isandlwhana and the fight at Rorke's Drift. I was at home then, and all England was quivering with grief over such needless sacrifice as was made of that regiment, and all ready to fall down and worship such fellows as Chard and Bromhead, who made the superb fight almost at the same time. They say old Maitland wanted to go himself, as volunteer or something, with Lord Chelmsford, but it couldn't be done. *His* father had fought at Alma and Inkerman, and his grandfather had led the Guards at Waterloo. The whole tribe were soldiers, you know; and now Archie was with the Lancers in Zululand, and the Lancers were going to wipe out the disasters of the first fights of the campaign, and Archie was to uphold the grand old fighting name and come home covered with glory. He was the heir now, and Miss Gladys was but a little girl. I have heard it all from Mrs. Cowan: she was their housekeeper in those days, and a sort of companion, too, to Mrs. Maitland, who was very delicate. The old man was very fiery and proud, and full of fierce denunciation of everything that had gone wrong in the campaign; and he offended some people by the way he condemned some officer who was a friend of theirs, and there were others who thought he talked too much; but he fairly boiled over when the news came of how the Prince Imperial had been abandoned by his escort, and that a British officer and a dozen men had run two miles at top speed from a beggarly little squad of niggers before they dared look round to see what had become of their prince, whom they had left to fight the gang alone. That was old Maitland's text for a month. If any son of his had ever been of that party he would disown, disgrace, deny him, forbid him his sight, cut him off forever. And right in the midst of it all—a judgment, some people said—there came the awful news that Cornet Maitland of the Lancers was to be court-martialled for misbehavior in face of the enemy. Of course the old man only raged at first,—said it couldn't be true,—'twas all some foul invention or ridiculous blunder; but he ran up to London and saw somebody at the Horse-Guards,—that's our War Office, you know,—and came back looking a century older and simply crushed to earth. Mrs. Cowan says they showed him the official report of a general officer who was called upon to explain why he had not sent certain troops to the relief of an advanced and threatened post, and he replied that he had sent the order by Cornet Maitland of the Lancers, had given him an escort of a dozen men and strict injunctions to push through by night, at all hazards, though the way was beset with Zulus, and that he neither went through nor returned, but was found hiding at a kraal two days after, only twenty miles away. The escort returned, and after much cross-examination had told the story, separately and collectively, that the young officer had become utterly unnerved towards midnight by the reports from scouting-parties and others, had declared to them that it was simply madness to attempt to push through,—they would be massacred to a man,—and, though they announced that they were stanch and ready, he refused, and ordered them to bivouac where they were for the night; and in the morning he had disappeared. They declared they supposed he had gone back to camp, and, after waiting a day, they returned, reporting him lost. When found at the kraal he was delirious with fever, or pretended to be, said the general, and he was brought in under arrest, and the trial was to proceed. I don't know how it turned out. He was not court-martialled, but permitted to return to England. It was said he told a very different story,—that he had begged the brigade major who detailed the escort to let him have half a dozen of his own Lancers instead of the pack of irregulars they gave him; he did not trust them, and feared they would abandon him as they had the Prince; but the staff-officer said the order couldn't be changed,—these men knew the country, and all that sort of thing, you know; and there was one fellow in the Lancers who stuck to it that he believed Maitland had tried his best to get through alone. But 'twas all useless: somebody had to be held responsible, and the failure was all heaped on him. Meantime, there had been fury at home; old Maitland had written casting him off, repudiating,—cursing him, for all I know,— and the next thing there came a messenger from the captain of his ship at Southampton. They brought his watch, his ring, his sword and portmanteaus, and a letter which was written on receipt of that his father sent him,—a long letter, that the old man never read to any living soul, but broods over to this day. The young fellow bade them all good-by; he would not live to disgrace them further, if that was what was thought of him at home, and leaped overboard from the steamer the night after she weighed anchor,—no one aboard could tell just when, but he was writing in his state-room as she cleared the harbor, and the steward saw him undressing at nine o'clock. In the morning everything about his belongings was found in perfect order,—his letter to the captain of the ship, the portmanteaus, watch, ring, clothing, etc., just as he described in that letter,—and he was no more seen. It was the conviction of all that he must have leaped overboard in the darkness when far out at sea.

"Then Mrs. Maitland bowed her head and never lifted it again. Then, all alone, and fiercely rejecting anything like sympathy, old Maitland took to travel,—came here to America, wandered around the world, shunning men as he would these prairie-wolves; and when he had to go to England he would see no one but the attorneys and solicitors with whom he had business. Here at Dunraven he is more content than anywhere, because he is farther from the world. Here Gladys is queen: 'twas she who named it, two years ago, for her mother was a connection of the earl's. But Maitland even here hates to have his name mentioned; and that is why I say he refers all business to me and keeps himself out of everything. Do you see what a weight he carries?"

Mr. Ewen had grown red with the intensity and rapidity of his talk. He removed his hat and mopped his face and brow with a big silk handkerchief, and then glanced again at Perry, who had listened with absorbed interest and who was now silently thinking it over, looking curiously at Ewen the while.

"Have I bored you half to death?" asked the Englishman, somewhat ruefully. "I never told that story before, but it has been smouldering for years."

"*Bored?* No! I never was more interested in my life. I was thinking what a different sort of fellow you were from the man I met out yonder the other day. Did they never do anything to clear the matter up? In our country it never would have been allowed to rest there."

"It was too far gone; and when the boy killed himself the thing was used by all the government papers—you'd call them 'administration organs'—as a confession of judgment. When the Lancers came home there was some talk, but it was soon hushed. Maitland had shut up the old place by that time and gone no one knew where, but I read it in one of the London papers,—*Truth*, I think,—a story that two of the irregulars had quarrelled with their fellows and after the war was over told a tale that made a sensation in Cape Colony. They said that the young officer was a maligned man; that up to midnight he had pushed on, but every scout and patrol they met warned them that thousands of Zulus were ahead, and that it was madness to try. The men began whispering among themselves, and begged the sergeant to attempt to dissuade the Lancer officer; and he did, and they all began to talk, but he refused to listen. At last they halted at a little stream and flatly refused to go a step farther. He ordered, begged, and implored. He promised heavy reward to any one of their number who would come and show him the way. Then they heard the night cries or signals of some war-parties across the fields, and the sergeant and most of the men put spurs to their horses; the others followed, and they rode back five miles until they were within our patrolled lines; then they bivouacked, supposing of course the Lancer had followed them. But he hadn't: he never joined them all next day, and likely as not he had done his best to get through that strange country by night, alone, and had tried to carry his despatches to the detachment. They knew they must tell a straight story or be severely punished. They were twelve against one when it came to evidence, as the sergeant pointed out, and so they agreed on the one that sent him to Coventry.

"Some of the Lancer officers got hold of this and swore they believed it true; but meantime the government had had the devil's own time in tiding his lordship the general over the numerous blunders he had made in the campaign, and the Lancers were summarily ordered off elsewhere. There was no one left to take up poor Archie's cause at home, and the thing died out."

"By the Lord Harry, Mr. Ewen, it wouldn't die out here! We Yankees would resurrect such a thing if it were old as a mummy."

"Sometimes I think old Maitland would be glad of the chance to do it, even broken as he is; sometimes, Mrs. Cowan says, he walks the floor all night and holds Archie's last letter in his hands. *She* thinks he charges himself with having driven the boy to suicide."

"Does Miss Maitland never revisit the old home?" asked Perry, after a moment's thought.

"She goes with her father—everywhere. He is never here more than twice a year, and seldom for more than six weeks at a time. Were it not for her, though, he would settle down here, I believe. He went to Cape Colony and tried to find the men who gave out that story, but one of them was dead and the other had utterly disappeared. There were still six survivors of that escort, the sergeant among them, and he was a man of some position and property. They stuck to the original story, and said the two men who started the sensation were mere blackmailing vagrants. Maitland advertised everywhere for the missing man, but to no purpose. I think he and Miss Gladys have finally abandoned all hope of ever righting Archie's name. She was only a child when it all happened, but she worshipped him, and never for an instant has believed the story of his having funked. She's out here riding somewhere this morning, by the way."

"Who! Miss Maitland?" exclaimed Perry, with sudden start, and a flash of eager light in his blue eyes.

Ewen smiled quietly as he answered, "Yes. She needed exercise, and wanted to come down to the gate and meet Dr. Quin. She went on up the valley; and I wonder she is not back."

The bright light faded quickly as it came; the glad blue eyes clouded heavily. Ewen looked at the young soldier, surprise in his florid face,—surprise that quickly deepened into concern, for Perry turned suddenly away, as though looking for his comrades of the hunt.

"I think they're coming now," said the manager, peering up the valley under the shading willows. "Yes! Won't you stop a bit?"

"Not now," was the hurried reply. "Thank you for that story: it has given me a lot to think about. I'll see you again." The last words were almost shouted back; for, urged by sudden dig of the spur, Nolan indignantly lashed his heels, then rushed in wrathful gallop towards the eastern bluffs. It was no wilful pang his rider had inflicted on his pet and comrade; it was only the involuntary transmission of the shock to his own young heart,—a cruel, jealous stab, that came with those thoughtless words, "She wanted to come down to the gate and meet Dr. Quin, and went on up the valley." He would not even look back and see her riding by that man's side.

XII.

To use the expression of Mr. Dana, "Ned Perry seemed off his feed" for a day or two. The hunt had been pronounced a big success, despite the fact of Perry's defection,—he had not even joined them at luncheon,—and it was agreed that it should be repeated the first bright day after muster. That ceremony came off on Monday with due pomp and formality and much rigidity of inspection on the part of the post commander. It was watched with interest by the ladies, and Mrs. Belknap even proposed that when the barracks and kitchens were being visited they should go along. Dana had been her devotee ever since the day of the hunt, and announced his willingness to carry her suggestion to the colonel, but Belknap declined. She wanted a few words with Perry, and did not know how to effect her purpose. When he stopped and spoke to her after parade on Saturday evening and would have made peace, she thought to complete her apparent conquest by a show of womanly displeasure at his conduct, and an assurance that, thanks to Mr. Dana, the day had been delightful and *his* failure to accompany her had been of no consequence at all. The utterly unexpected way in which he took it was simply a "stunner" to the little lady. So far from being piqued and jealous and huffy, as she expected, Mr. Perry justified the oft-expressed opinion of her sisterhood to the effect that "men were simply past all comprehension" by brightening up instantly and expressing such relief at her information that for a moment she was too dazed to speak. By that time he had pleasantly said good-night and vanished; nor had he been near her since, except to bow and look pleased when she walked by with Dana. She never thought of him as an actor before, but this, said Mrs. Belknap to herself, *looks* like consummate acting. Had she known of, or even suspected, the existence of a woman who had interposed and cast her into the shade, the explanation would have occurred to her at once; but that there was a goddess in the shape of Gladys Maitland within a day's ride of Rossiter she never dreamed for an instant. Believing that no other woman could have unseated her, Mrs. Belknap simply *could* not account for such utter—such unutterable—complacency on the part of her lately favored admirer in his virtual dismissal. All Sunday and Monday she looked for signs of sulking or surrender, but looked in vain. Perry seemed unusually grave and silent, was Parke's report of the situation; but whatever comfort she might have derived from that knowledge was utterly destroyed by the way he brightened up and looked pleased whenever they chanced to meet. Monday evening he stopped to speak with her on the walk, holding out his hand and fairly beaming upon her: she icily received these demonstrations, but failed to chill them or him. Then she essayed to make him suffer the pangs of the jilted by clinging to Dana's arm and smiling up in Dana's face, and then she suddenly started: "Oh, Mr. Dana! How could I have been so thoughtless?—and this is your wounded side!" Dana protested that her slight weight was soothing balm, not additional pain, and Perry promptly asseverated that if he were Dana he would beg her not to quit his arm, and her eyes looked scorn at him as she said, "How can you know anything about it, Mr. Perry? You've never been in action or got a scratch, while Mr. Dana"—and now the dark eyes spoke volumes as they looked up into those of her escort— "Mr. Dana is one of the heroes of the fighting days of the regiment." Even *that* failed to crush him; while it had the effect of making Dana feel mawkish and absurd. Perry frankly responded that he only wondered the women ever could find time to show any civility whatever to fellows like him, when there were so many who "had records." She was completely at a loss to fathom him, and when tattoo came on Monday night, and they were all discussing the project of a run with the hounds for the coming morrow,—a May-day celebration on new principles,— Mrs. Belknap resolved upon a change of tactics.

Dana was officer of the guard and over at the guard-house, but nearly all the other officers were chatting about the veranda and the gate of the colonel's quarters. Thither had Captain Belknap escorted his pretty wife, and she was, as usual, the centre of an interested group. Perry came strolling along after reporting the result of tattoo roll-call to the adjutant, and Captain Stryker called to him and asked some question about the men on stable-guard. The orders of the colonel with regard to watching the movements of the men after the night roll-call were being closely observed, and when the trumpets sounded "taps," a few moments later, several of the troop-commanders walked away together, and this left a smaller party. It was just at this juncture that Mrs. Belknap's sweet voice was heard addressing the commanding officer:

"Oh, colonel! Ever since Thursday I have been telling Captain Belknap about those lovely albums of yours; and he is so anxious to see them. *Could* he have a look at them to-night?"

"Why, certainly!" exclaimed the colonel, all heartiness and pleasure. "Come right in, Belknap, come in,—any of you,—all of you,—where it's good and light." And he hospitably held open the screen door. Perry had seen the albums a dozen times, but he was for going in with the others, when he felt a little hand-pressure on his arm, and Mrs. Belknap's great dark eyes were gazing up into his with mournful, incredulous appeal.

"Don't you know I want to see you?" she murmured so that only he could hear. "Wait!"

And, much bewildered, Mr. Perry waited.

She stood where she could look through the screen door into the parlor beyond, watching furtively until the party were grouped under the hanging lamps and absorbed in looking over one another's shoulders at the famous albums; then, beckoning to him to follow, she flitted, like some eerie sprite, on tiptoe to the southern end of the veranda, where clustering vines hid her from view from the walk along the parade. Perry began to feel queer, as he afterwards expressed it, but he stalked along after her, declining to modulate the thunder of his heavy heels upon the resounding gallery. She put her finger to her lips, and, after a nervous glance around, looked at him warningly, beseechingly.

"What on earth's the matter?" was all the perplexed and callow youth could find to say, and in a tone so utterly devoid of romance, sentiment, tenderness,—anything she wanted to hear,—that in all her experience—and she had had not a little—pretty, bewitching little Mrs. Belknap could recall nothing so humiliating.

"How *can* you be so unkind to me?" at last she whispered, in the tragic tremolo she well knew to be effective: it had done execution over and again. But big, handsome Ned Perry looked only like one in a maze; then he bent over her in genuine concern:

"Why, Mrs. Belknap! What *has* happened? What has gone wrong? What *do* you mean by unkindness?"

She faced him, indignantly now: "Is it possible you profess not to know?"

"By all that's holy, Mrs. Belknap, I haven't an idea of what you mean to charge me with. Tell me, and I'll make every amend I know how."

He was bending over her in genuine distress and trouble: he had no thought but to assure her of his innocence of any conscious wrong. She was leaning upon the balcony rail, and he rested one strong hand upon the post at the shaded corner, above her head, as he bowed his own to catch her reply.

For a moment she turned her face away, her bosom heaving, her little hands clasping nervously, the picture of wronged and sorrowing womanhood. His blunt, rugged honesty was something she had never yet had to deal with. This indeed was "game worth the candle," but something of a higher order than the threadbare flirtations she had found so palatable heretofore. She had expected him to be revealed by this time as the admirer who had only been playing a part in his apparent acceptance of the situation of the last two days; she expected to be accused of coquetting with Dana, of neglect, coldness, insult towards himself; and this she would have welcomed: it would have shown him still a victim in her toils, a mouse she might toy and play with indefinitely before bestowing the final *coup de grâce*. But instead of it, or anything like it, here stood the tall, handsome young fellow, utterly ignoring the possibility of her having wronged him, and only begging to be told how he had affronted her, that he might make immediate amends. It was simply exasperating. She turned suddenly upon him, hiding her face in her hands, almost sobbing:

"And I thought we were such—such friends!"

Even that suggestive tentative did not lay him prostrate. Fancy the utter inadequacy of his response:

"Why, so did I!" This was too much. Down came the hands, and were laid in frantic appeal upon his breast. He did not bar the way; she could have slipped from the corner without difficulty; but the other method was more dramatic.

"Let me go, Mr. Perry," she pleaded. "I—I might have known; I might have known." The accents were stifled, heart-rending.

"Don't go yet, Mrs. Belknap; *don't* go without telling me what— what I've done." And poor Ned imploringly seized the little hands in both his and held them tight. "Please tell me," he pleaded.

"No, no! You would not understand; you do not see what I have to bear. Let me go, I beg,—please. I cannot stay." And her great dark eyes, swimming in tears, were raised to his face, while with faint—very faint—struggles she strove to pull her hands away, relenting in her purpose to go the moment she felt that he was relaxing the hold in which they were clasped, but suddenly wrenching them from his breast and darting from his side, leaving Perry in much bewilderment to face about and confront the doctor.

A little opening had been left in the railing at the south end of the veranda,—the same through which the post surgeon had passed the night Mrs. Lawrence had shown to Perry the answering signal-light: it was the doctor's "short cut" between the colonel's quarters and his own side-door, and soft, unbetraying turf lay there between. Absorbed in her melodrama, Mrs. Belknap had failed to note the coming of the intruder; absorbed in his own stupefaction and his fair partner' apparent depth of woe, Ned Perry heard nothing but her soft word and softer sighs, until a deep voice at his shoulder—a voice whose accen betrayed no apology for the discovery and less sympathy for the dis covered—gave utterance to this uncompromising sentiment:

"Mrs. Belknap, this is the thirtieth—not the first—of April."

"And what has that to do with your sudden appearance, Dr. Quin? answered the lady, with smiling lips but flashing eyes. She rallie from the shock of sudden volley like the veteran she was, and took th brunt of the fight on her own white, gleaming shoulders, needing n aid from the young fellow who stood there, flushing, annoyed, yet to perturbed to say a word even had there been a chance to get one i edgewise. Blunt as he was, he could not but realize the awkwardnes of the situation. And to be so misjudged by such a man as Dr. Quin All this was flashing through his mind as the doctor answered,—

"Nothing with *my* appearance, Mrs. Belknap: it was *yours* I re marked upon. You seemed to think it All Fools' Day."

"Far from it, doctor, when I thought you miles away."

"Well, well, Mrs. Belknap," said Quin, shrugging his broa shoulders and laughing at her undaunted pluck, "I've known yo fifteen years, and never have found you at a loss for a sharp retort."

"In all the years you *have* known me, doctor, as child, as maid, a woman, you are the only man in the army who ever put me on th defensive. I see clearly that you would taunt me because of this inter view with Mr. Perry. *Honi soit qui mal y pense*, Dr. Quin! You ar the last man in this garrison—cavalry and all—who can afford to throv stones."

"Whew-w-w!" whistled the doctor. "What a little spitfire yo always were, to be sure!—Mr. Perry," said he, turning suddenly on th young officer, "let me at once apologize for a very misleading observa tion. When I spoke of having known Mrs. Belknap fifteen years sh instantly thought I meant to make her out very much older than sh is; and hence these recriminations. She always objected to me becaus I used to tease her when she was in her first long dresses,—the pretties girl at Fort Leavenworth,—and she's never gotten over it. But he father and I were good friends, and I should like to be an honest on to his daughter. Good-night to you both."

"One moment, Dr. Quin," said Perry, springing forward. "Yo

have seen fit to make comments and insinuations that have annoyed Mrs. Belknap at a time when she was under my escort——"

"Oh, Mr. Perry, no! no!" exclaimed Mrs. Belknap, laying her hand on his arm. "Not a word of that kind, I implore! *Hush!* here comes my husband."

"Ah, Belknap," said the doctor, blandly, as the big captain came hurriedly forth with searching glance along the dark gallery, "here you find me, as usual, trying to be devoted to Mrs. B. whenever I can get you out of the way. Why the jeuce can't you stay?"

"Oh, it's you, is it, doctor?" answered the captain, in tones of evident relief. "It is far too chilly for this young woman to be sitting here without a wrap, is it not? Come inside, Dolly. Come, doctor.—Halloo! what's that?"

A cavalry trumpeter came springing through the gate and up on the veranda.

"Is Captain Stryker here?" he panted.

"No. What's the matter?" demanded Perry.

"Trouble at the stables, sir. Sergeant Gwynne's assaulted again."

Perry sprang from the veranda and went tearing across the dark level of the parade as fast as active legs could carry him, leaving the doctor far behind. As he passed the company quarters he noted that several men were leaping from their broad galleries, some just pulling on a blouse, others in their shirt-sleeves, but all hastening towards the stables, where dim lights could be seen flitting about like will-o'-the-wisps. One of these troopers came bounding to his side, and would have passed him in the race. He recognized the athletic form even in the darkness, and hailed him:

"That you, Sergeant Leary? What's gone wrong?"

"It's thim blackguards from below, sir. Who else could it be?"

"Those people at the ranch?"

"The very ones, sir. No one else would harm Sergeant Gwynne. Sure we ought to have wound 'em up the one night we had a chance, sir."

Breathless, almost, they reached the stables. The horses were all snorting, stamping, and plunging about in their stalls, showing every indication of excitement and alarm. From the stables of the adjoining companies other men had come with lanterns, and a group of perhaps half a dozen troopers was gathered about the form of a cavalry sergeant who was seated, limp and exhausted, at the western door-way. One soldier was bathing his face with a sponge; the first sergeant of the troop was bending over and trying to feel the pulse.

"Stand back, you men!" he said, authoritatively, as he caught sight of the lieutenant's shoulder-straps. "Leave a lantern here.—Now, Gwynne, here's Lieutenant Perry. Can you tell him who it was?"

Gwynne feebly strove to rise, but Perry checked him.

"Sit down! The doctor is coming; don't attempt to move," panted the young officer. "Tell me what *you* know about it, Sergeant Hosmer."

"Nothing but this, sir. I was in the office, when Trumpeter Petersen ran in and said they were killing Sergeant Gwynne. I sent him for the captain and grabbed my revolver and ran here as hard as I could. He was lying just outside the door when I got here, and not another soul in sight. Sergeant Ross, of F Troop, and Sergeant Fagan, of B, came with their lanterns from the stables next door; but they had not even heard the trouble."

"Where was the stable-guard?"

"Inside, sir, and he's there now. He heard the scuffle, he says, and ran to give the alarm and to protect the sergeant, but the men scattered when he came, and he saw none of them."

"Tell him to come here. Let some of these men go in and quiet the horses. The captain will be here in a minute, and he will want to see that stable-man. Who is it?"

"Kelly, sir."

By this time Dr. Quin came lumbering heavily up the slope to the stable door. His manner was very quiet and very grave as he bent over the injured man and carefully studied his face by the light of the sergeant's lamp. Gwynne partially opened his eyes and turned his head as though the glare were too painful. The doctor spoke gently:

"You know me, sergeant?—Dr. Quin. Can you tell me what struck you? Are you hurt elsewhere than in the head?"

Gwynne made no reply for a moment, then faintly answered,—

"Stunned, mainly, and one or two kicks after I was knocked down."

Then came a deeper voice, quiet but authoritative, and the group that had begun to close in again about the doctor and his patient fell back as Captain Stryker strode into their midst.

"Sergeant Hosmer, send all these men of the troop back to their quarters at once, and permit no more to come out.—Is he much hurt doctor?"

"Somewhat stunned, he says. I've made no examination yet."

The captain looked about him. Except one sergeant holding a lantern, the other troopers, obedient to his order, were slowly fading back into the darkness on their way to the barracks. Only the doctor, Mr. Perry, and the sergeant remained by the side of the injured man. Then came the question,—

"Who did this, Gwynne?"

No answer. A deeper shade of pain and trouble seemed to pass over the young sergeant's face. He made an effort to speak, hesitated, and at last replied,—

"I cannot say, sir."

"You know, do you not?"

Again pained silence and embarrassment. At last the sergeant leaned slowly forward and spoke:

"Captain, the men were masked, the voices disguised. I could not see the dress in the darkness. I was struck on the head almost the instant I got outside the door, and it would be impossible for me to identify one of them."

"Do you think it was the same gang you had the trouble with at Dunraven?"

"I—could not say, sir."

"Do you suspect any of our own men?"

"I—would not say that, sir."

"Where is the stable-guard?" asked Stryker. "Send him here."

And presently Trooper Kelly—a wiry little Irishman, with a twinkling eye and an expression of mingled devilment and imperturbability in his face—came forth from the stable door and stood attention, awaiting his examination.

"Where were you when this assault took place, Kelly?"

"At the far end of the stables, sir," replied Kelly, with prompt and confident tone.

"Then of course you saw and know nothing of it."

"Not a wor-rad, sir."

"Why did you let a gang from that English ranch come here and beat your sergeant before your very eyes?"

Kelly reddened at the very idea:

"I'd ha' died first, sir! Sure they'd niver dared——" And then

Kelly stopped short. His Celtic pride had been touched to the quick, and had it not proved too much for even Irish wit?

"How did they get the sergeant out of the stable at this hour of the night?"

"Sure they called him out, sir."

"And the sergeant happened to be down there by the door at the time?"

"No, sir: he was in his room, beyant,—up there by the forage."

"That's a long distance from this door, Kelly; and if he could hear it in his room you could hear it farther away."

"I wasn't farther away thin, sir: I was down here when they axed for him."

"Then why didn't you open the door and see who was making such a racket, shouting for Sergeant Gwynne after taps?"

"Sure they didn't shout at all at all, sir; they axed for him quiet and respectable like, an' I wint and told him."

"Ah, yes, I see. And then, having told him, you went away to the far end of the stable."

"Yis, sir,—just so, sir; an' the moment I heard the scrimmidge, sir, I ran as hard as I could."

"Of course you considered it was none of your business what people might want with the stable-sergeant at night."

"No, sir. If he wanted me he had a right to tell me to come."

"We differ on that point, Kelly," said the captain, quietly. "For a guard, you displayed a lack of curiosity that is simply fatal.—Relieve him, Sergeant Hosmer," he continued, placidly, and then, taking Perry by the arm, led him to one side. There was a few minutes' low-toned talk between the officers while Gwynne was being led away by the doctor, and when on the following morning Colonel Brainard looked over the report of Captain Stryker's troop he was surprised to note in the column of remarks explanatory of the alterations from the status of the previous day,—

"Sergeant Gwynne from daily duty as stable-sergeant to sick in hospital, Sergeant Leary from duty to arrest, and Private Kelly from duty to confinement."

XIII.

Notwithstanding the fact that there was an atmosphere of suppressed excitement over the garrison this May-day morning, Mrs. Belknap's hunt came off according to plan, and the three heroines of the previous run rode forth with but slight change of escort. Captain Stryker felt constrained to remain in garrison: he had a quiet investigation to make, and was observed to be in close conversation with Dr. Quin as the gay party assembled in front of Colonel Brainard's quarters. Mr. Perry appeared in his captain's stead, and very politely requested the honor of being escort to Mrs. Lawrence, who accepted, yet looked a trifle embarrassed as she did so. Indeed, not until she had stolen an appealing glance at her husband and heard his cordial "By all means, dear: Perry can guide you far better than I, and perhaps you'll win another mask," did she thankfully say "Yes." Dana rode with Mrs. Belknap, as before, and it was the colonel himself who suggested to Stryker that Mr. Perry should accompany Mrs. Lawrence this day, and that he, the colonel, should ride with Mrs. Sprague.

Perry had eagerly lent himself to the proposition: he figured that now he could have an uninterrupted chat with Mrs. Lawrence and hear what she had to tell about Dunraven. Just before starting he sought Captain Lawrence, laughingly told him the terms of their agreement, and begged that he would relax his marital injunction and permit her to give him such details as she happened to be in possession of. "Indeed, Captain Lawrence," he said, "I ask from no idle curiosity. I have been to the ranch, as you now know, and have good reason for asking." To his surprise, the captain replied substantially that, while he had regretted Mrs. Lawrence's impulsive revelations, he had thought it all over and decided that the best way out was that Perry should be told the whole story and be able to see how very little there was to it. He had decided, therefore, to tell him himself; "and this evening, Perry, if you will dine with us informally, we'll talk it over afterwards. Meantime, I prefer Mrs. Lawrence's name should not be mentioned in connection with any story there may be afloat: so oblige me by saying nothing to her on the subject."

This was one matter for reflection, and something of a surprise; but there was still another, and even greater one. That very morning, just before guard-mount, and while he was dressing, Perry shouted, "Come in," responsive to a knock at his sitting-room door, and in came Captain Stryker. The object of his early call was explained in very few words.

"Perry," said he, "I have been over to see Sergeant Gwynne this morning, and the doctor walked back from hospital with me and told me of your threatened disagreement of last night. If it had not been for that sudden call to the stables I fancy there might have been a quarrel. Now, I think you know I'm one of the last men to let an officer of my regiment—especially my troop—be placed in a false position, and—you can afford to leave this matter in my hands, can you not?"

"Certainly, Captain Stryker."

"Then I want you to say nothing to Quin on the subject, and to treat him, as far as possible, as though nothing had happened. His relations with the lady's father and family were, and are, such that she ought to treat him with respect and deference, and to accept his advice even though it be given in a style that Carlyle, his favorite author, is mainly responsible for."

"There was absolutely nothing in—in that—— Well, captain," stammered poor Ned, "I don't know how to say what I want to say." He wanted to say there was nothing in that interview which could possibly be criticised, but it suddenly occurred to him that, on the contrary, there was a good deal. Then he desired to assure his captain that, so far as *he* was concerned, there wasn't a suspicion of wrong-doing; but—heavens and earth!—that was equivalent to saying the lady was doing all that was open to remark, and nothing would ever induce him to "give away a woman," as he would have expressed it. Perry stammered and reddened all the more, and at last gave it up in despair, Stryker sitting there the while with a quiet grin on his bronzed face, and mechanically slashing his boot-legs with a riding-switch.

"I think I understand the situation, Perry, and there's no great harm done. Only, let the matter drop,—so far as the doctor is concerned, I mean: I do not presume to obtrude advice upon you as to anything else."

And, though he had meditated a different course, and had fully intended hunting up Dana and sending him with a note to call upon the doctor for an "explanation," he was glad to have a man of Stryker's standing cry halt. All the same he was sore incensed against Dr. Quin,—mainly because of the jealous pain he suffered at the knowledge of his being so welcomed by Gladys Maitland when he saw fit to visit the ranch; and this pain gnawed all the more angrily now at thought of the embarrassing—even suspicious—situation in which that very man had found him on the previous evening. Pressing duties and hurried preparations kept him from brooding too much upon these sore points, but the youngsters all rallied him upon his preoccupation while at their merry breakfast-table. He had resolved that there was one thing he could and would bring to an issue with Dr. Quin, and was all impatience for the coming of evening, that he might hear from the lips of Captain Lawrence the actual stories that had been in circulation concerning Dunraven Ranch. He never went out to a hunt so utterly indifferent to the fortunes of the day, so eager to have it all over and done with. And yet—and yet—never had there opened to him a day so radiant with glorious possibility; never before in all his young life had nightfall proved so unwelcome when it finally came.

The first rabbit was started before they were a mile from Rossiter, and the hounds tumbled over him nearly a league away down the valley of the Monee. It was while they were watering their horses in the stream that Mrs. Belknap rode up beside them and laughingly addressed Mrs. Lawrence:

"That was too much of a straight-away for either of us, Mrs. Lawrence; but what wager shall we have on the first mask after this?"

"Why, Mrs. Belknap! I can never hope to rival you. It was mere accident, and good guiding on the part of some of the officers who were kind enough to stay by me, that enabled me to be 'in at the death' the other day."

"You have Mr. Perry to lead you to-day. Surely with such a guide you ought to be inspired.—Am I to see *anything* of you to-day?" she almost whispered to him, as her stirrup brushed his riding-boot.

"Certainly," he answered, quietly, and looking her over with frank blue eyes that were rather too clear and calm for her mood. "If Mrs. Lawrence will excuse me a few moments by and by, it will be a pleasure to come and ride with you. I'll ask her."

"Indeed you shall not," was the low-toned reply, while the dark eyes fairly snapped with indignation. "I do not borrow other women's escort. If you know no other way, that ends it."

And then Mrs. Sprague's cheery voice had hailed them as her eager horse came splashing into the stream; no opportunity occurred for further impressive remarks, but as the "field" rode out upon the prairie again and the dogs spread their yelping skirmish-line along the front, Mrs. Belknap felt confident that before they returned to Rossiter she would have her big, simple-hearted admirer in some shape for discipline. Two capital runs added to her self-satisfaction, for in one of them she was side by side with the foremost rider at the finish, and in both she had left the other women far in rear. Then came a third, and with it a revelation to one and all.

It was almost noon, and from a point well out on the prairie to the northeast of Dunraven the "field" was hunting slowly homeward, horses and hounds pretty well tired out, and the riders quite content with their morning's sport. Up to this time Perry had been in constant attendance on Mrs. Lawrence, and had made no effort to join Mrs. Belknap. Now, however, he could not but see that every little while her eyes sought his with significant glance and that she was riding well out to the left of the party, Dana faithfully hovering about her. The colonel with Mrs. Sprague ranged alongside just then, and a general conversation ensued, in the course of which Perry found himself a trifle in the way. If there was one thing fastidious Nolan did not like, it was to be crowded by horses for whom he had no particular respect; and, as a number of riders were grouped about Mrs. Lawrence at the moment, it resulted that Nolan's teeth and heels began to make play, and Perry laughingly resigned his position at her side, in order, as he expressed it, "to give you other fellows a chance." Even then, as he fell to the rear, it was with no thought or intention of joining Mrs. Belknap. But, once clear of the merry group, his eyes sought the distant outlines of Dunraven Ranch, glaring in the noonday sun beyond the Monee, and between him and that mysterious enclosure whither his thoughts were so constantly wandering there rode the dainty lady, the Queen of the Chase, so far as that day was concerned at least, and she was signalling to him with her riding-whip. Oddly enough, when Perry rode up to obey her summons, Mr. Dana presently found means to excuse himself and join the main body.

"Mr. Perry," she said, as soon as Dana was out of hearing, "Mrs Page will be with us to-night, or to-morrow morning at latest."

"Will she?" answered he, unconscious, forgetful, and with an air of pleased anticipation. "How pleasant for you! I'll come and pay my respects the very first thing."

"You do not understand," was the reproachful response. "You do not care, I presume; but this means that you and I will have no more long talks and happy times together."

"I'm awfully sorry, Mrs. Belknap, but I'm blessed if I can see why we shouldn't."

"No," despairingly, "it is plain enough that you see nothing. Ah, well!"—and the sigh was pathetic-profound, and the look from the dark eyes was unutterable in its sadness, "I suppose it is better so,—better so." She was silent a moment, and Perry's puzzled faculties took refuge in a long look over towards Dunraven again: he fancied he saw figures moving down the slope on the southern side.

"One thing I want you to promise me," she presently said, sad and soft and low. There was no reply. Looking up, she saw his head was averted. Was he feeling the sting, then, after all? Was he actually suffering a little pang after this affectation of nonchalance?

"One thing you must promise, for my sake," she repeated.

And still no answer came. How odd! He was bending over in the saddle as though turning from her,—perhaps to hide his face from her and from them all. He had shifted the reins into his right hand, and was apparently fumbling at the breast of his riding-coat with the left. Was it the handkerchief he needed? Were there starting tears in those blue eyes that he dared not let her see? She could not lose that luxury! Out went the little hand and touched his arm. Her tone was sweet, thrilling, appealing, yet commanding: she *would* see his face.

"Mr. Perry,—*Ned! Look* at me."

"Eh! oh! What! I *beg* your pardon, Mrs. Belknap, but I was trying to make out who that was in the timber yonder. Looks—looks almost like a woman on horseback, doesn't it?"

But when he appealed to her for confirmation of his timid, half-credulous vision he was aghast at the look in her face.

"You were not listening! You were not even *thinking* of what I was saying!" she began, her white teeth set, her soft lips livid with wrath; but she suddenly controlled herself,—none too soon, for Dana came trotting up.

"Say, Perry, what do you make that out to be down there in the valley? Colonel Brainard and I feel sure it's a lady on horseback."

And, looking at Perry, Mrs. Belknap saw that he had flushed to the very temples,—that an eager, joyous light had sprung to his eyes; but before she could say a word there came a shout from the huntsman, a yell from the leading line, a simultaneous yelp from the curs and mongrels among the "irregulars," and her horse leaped at the bit and went tearing off towards the Monee, foremost in mad pursuit of a wildly careering "jack."

"Come!" she called, as she glanced over her shoulder; but the sight was one that only added to her wrath. Nolan, plunging and

K*

snorting, was held to the spot, while his rider, sitting like a centaur, was still eagerly gazing over into the distant cottonwoods. The next instant she realized that all the field were thundering at her heels, and the instinct of the sportsman came to her aid. She *could* not be beaten in the chase.

For half a mile Bunny shot like a streak of light straight away southwestward, the hounds bunched in a slaty, sweeping cloud not thirty yards behind the bobbing tuft of his tail. Then he began a long circle towards the stream, as though to head for a "break" that extended some rods back from the line of bluffs. Another minute, and he had reached its partial shelter and darted in. For the next minute he was lost to sight of his human pursuers, but presently flashed into view again down in the creek-bottom and "streaking it" up along the northern bank, with the whole pack at his heels. The bluffs were steep just here, some of the riders a trifle timid, and all the "field" reined in a little as they made the descent; Dana, Mrs. Belknap, Parke, Mrs. Lawrence, Graham, the colonel, and Mrs. Sprague straightened out for their pursuit in the order named the instant they reached the level of the valley. The hounds were far ahead by this time, and the two light troopers in charge of them close at their heels; but who—what was the figure that flashed into view between those huntsmen and the field, darting like arrow from the fringe of willows and dashing straight in wake of the quarry? Thirty yards ahead of the foremost riders of the Rossiter party a superb English hunter, the bit in his teeth, his eyes afire and his head high in air, fresh, vigorous, raging with long-imprisoned passion for the sport of the old island home, gaining on the hounds at every stride, and defying the utmost efforts of his rider, leaped from the covert of the timber into sight of one and all, bearing a lovely but most reluctant victim on his back.

In vain with might and main she leaned back and tugged at the reins: though checked in his speed, the horse still tore ahead, keeping straight for the hounds, leaping in his easy stride every little gully or "branch" that crossed his path. Bunny took a sudden dive into the timber, fairly flew across a narrow, gravelly rapid, and darted up on the opposite bank; the hounds veered in pursuit, the huntsmen wavered and sought along the bank for a better place to cross, but the mettlesome English bay lunged through in the very wake of the hounds, crumbling the sandy banks and crashing through the pebbly stream-bed. Out on the southern slopes went Bunny, close followed by the hounds; out on their trail went the big hunter, but his rider's hat has been brushed away in the wild dash though the timber, and now a flame of beautiful golden hair—a great wave of light—flies on the wind over his glossy back, and, though she still leans over the cantle tugging hard at the reins, she is plainly losing strength. Some of the Rossiter party burst through the timber in pursuit; some still ride hopefully up the north bank, and these are rewarded, for once again poor, badgered, bewildered Bunny makes a sudden swerve, and, throwing half the hounds far behind, darts a second time to the shelter of the banks, with the other half closer at his heels than before. Those who are watching see the big hunter make a long, circular sweep, then once again bring up in the wake of the leaders, once more go leaping, plunging, crashing through the stream, and, in another minute, rabbit, hounds, huntsmen, the "field," and the fair incognita are all strung out in chase along the northern shore, and all eyes can see that *she* is an English girl and wellnigh exhausted. Still, no man can catch that hunter and lay hands on the rein. She is riding with the very foremost now, leading the troopers, even, and still Bunny spins along in front, the hounds gnashing not six feet behind him. A little point of bluff juts out just ahead; the stream winds around its base and takes a turn northward for a dozen rods. Bunny shoots the turn like the pilot of the lightning express, the hounds strain to make it without loss of vantage gained, the big hunter sways outward to the very verge of the steep and crumbling bank, and a groan goes up from the breathless pursuers; but he rallies and straightens once more in the track, and the golden hair, streaming in the advance, is the *oriflamme* of the chase. Then as they round the point Dana gives a shout of joy. Straight down the slopes, straight and swift as rode the daring hussar from whom he got his name, when he bore the fatal message like arrow-flight from the Sapouné crest at Balaklava, down the bluffs to the right front comes Nolan, with Ned Perry on his back,—Perry with set, resolute, yet almost frenzied face,—Perry with eyes that flash blue fire in the intensity of their gaze,—and Nolan's vigorous strides have brought him in circling sweep, in just ten seconds more, close to the hunter's quarter, close behind the fluttering skirt. Just ahead there is another sudden turn to the left: the stream goes one way, the bluffs another, and between them lies a five-acre patch of level prairie thickly studded, here, there, everywhere, with tiny earthen mounds and tiny, gaping, treacherous holes,—a prairie-dog village, by all that's awful! and that runaway hunter, mad in the chase of the sweeping hounds, is in the midst of it before mortal hand can check or swerve him. Another second, and they who pursue have veered to right or left or reined up on the verge,—all save one. Never faltering, Ned Perry is at her hunter's quarter,—almost at her side. They see him spurring, they see him bending eagerly towards her, they *see* that he is shouting something to her,—Heaven knows what! Then there is a groan of misery and dread from a dozen breasts,—a groan that as suddenly bursts into the gladdest of cheers: the hunter's forefoot has caught in one of the thousand little death-traps; down he goes, plunging, heaving, quivering, rolling over and over; but Nolan leaps gallantly ahead, and Ned Perry's strong arm has lifted the girl from the saddle as her steed goes crashing to earth, and bears her, drooping, faint, frightened, wellnigh senseless, but safe and clasped tight to his thankful and exultant heart.

Another instant, and Nolan is reined in in the very midst of the tumbling hounds, and Gladys Maitland is the only woman "in at the death."

XIV.

The group that gathers there a moment later is as interested a party as the central figures are interesting. Unable to set her left foot to the ground, and still encircled by Perry's arm, Miss Maitland stands leaning heavily on his breast. She is very pale for a moment, partly from exhaustion, partly from pain, for there was no time to free her foot from the stirrup, and the ankle is severely wrenched. Nolan, riderless now and cast loose, stands with lowered head and heaving flanks a sympathetic but proudly heroic looker-on: he knows he has played his part in that rescue. The huge English hunter is plunging in misery among the mounds a few yards back, his fore-leg broken. One of the troopers has seized his bridle, and another is unstrapping the heavy English saddle. "Splendidly done!" says the colonel, as he trots carefully up, casting a glance at the fallen cause of all the mischief, "but if that saddle had been one of those three-pronged abominations he couldn't have swept her off as he did." Graham has galloped to the stream for water, and the colonel lifts Mrs. Sprague from her saddle, and together they advance to offer sympathy and aid. Mrs. Lawrence follows as quickly as she can pick her way among the prairie-dog holes. Dana has deserted Mrs. Belknap, and she alone remains mounted while all these others throng about the two who stand there for the moment, clinging to each other. And now Gladys Maitland has raised her head; blushes of shame and confusion triumph over pallor and pain; she strives to stand alone, but Perry bids her desist. The moment she sees Mrs. Sprague's sweet, womanly, sympathetic face her eyes are filled with comfort and her heart goes out to her. Most reluctantly Perry resigns his prize to the arms that open to receive her, and then come the wondering exclamations of some, and the brief, breathless explanations.

"Don't try to talk yet," pleads Mrs. Sprague. "We are only too glad it was no worse."

"Indeed, I'm not hurt," answers Gladys, bravely,—"only a little wrench, but," and she laughs nervously, trying to carry it off with all the pluck and spirit of her race, "it would have been what we call a 'nasty cropper' at home if"—and her eyes turn shyly yet with a world of gratitude to his—"it had not been for Mr. Perry."

"Oh, then you know Mr. Perry!" exclaims Mrs. Sprague, with frank delight, and Mrs. Lawrence turns in rejoicing to look first in his glowing face, then at the dark beauty of Mrs. Belknap silently listening. "Why, we had no idea——" And she concludes irresolutely.

"Oh, yes: we met at the ranch,—at home. I am Miss Maitland, you know; and that is my father's place. But we've only just come," she adds, with the woman's natural desire to explain to new-found friends why and how it was that they had not met before. And then the group is joined by a bulky young Briton in the garb of a groom, though modified to suit the requirements of frontier life: he comes cantering to the scene all elbows and consternation; he gives a groan of dismay at sight of the prostrate hunter, but rides directly to his mistress. She is paling again now, and in evident pain, and Perry's face is a study as he stands, his eyes riveted upon her; but she strives to smile and reassure him.

"You'll have to ride to Dunr—to the ranch, Griggs," she said; "and—there's no help for it—papa will have to be told. Let them send for me."

"Pardon me, Miss Maitland," interrupted Colonel Brainard. "You are almost under the walls of Fort Rossiter, and Dunraven is miles away. I have sent a swift horse for Dr. Quin and a spring ambulance. We cannot let you go home, now that you are so near us, until you have had rest and proper care."

"Indeed we cannot, Miss Maitland," chimed in both ladies at a breath. "You are to come right to my house until you are fit to travel."

"I'm not very fit just now, certainly," she answers, with a faint smile; "but I can surely wait here until they send: 'twill not be more than an hour at most."

"It will be two hours,—perhaps three,—Miss Maitland," pleaded Perry, bending eagerly forward. "*Do* listen to our ladies!"

And "our ladies" prevailed. While Griggs went sputtering off to Dunraven with the sorrowful news, the strong arms of Perry and Graham lifted and bore their English captive to the shade of a clump of cottonwoods. Mrs. Sprague and Mrs. Lawrence managed to make a little couch for her as a temporary resort. Mrs. Belknap rode up and was formally introduced, then galloped away to Rossiter to send blankets for the picnic-couch and see to the pillows of the ambulance. The colonel and Perry remained with the ladies and engrossed their attention while Graham went back and sent two pistol-bullets into the struggling hunter's brain, stilling his pain forever. Then came Dr. Quin galloping like the wind down the familiar trail, chiding "Gladys" as though his right to do so were a long-established thing, and thereby setting Perry's teeth on edge, and, long before the call for afternoon stables was sounding, the fair daughter of Dunraven Ranch was housed within the walls of Rossiter and the "ice was broken." Perry had had the joy of helping carry her into Mrs. Sprague's coolest and cosiest room. She had held forth her hand—such a long, white, beautiful hand—and let it rest in his while she said, "You know how impossible it is for me to tell you how I thank you, Mr. Perry," and he had simply bowed over it, longing to say what he thought, but powerless to think of anything else; and then he had gone to his own quarters and shut himself in. Mrs. Sprague—bless her!—had invited him to call after retreat, and he had totally forgotten the Lawrences' dinner when he said he would be only too glad to come.

At the sounding of stable-call his darky servant banged at the door and roused him from his revery. He rose mechanically and went out into the broad sunshine, glancing first along the row to see how things were looking at the Spragues', and wishing with all his heart that they were somewhere within reach of a conservatory, that he might send a heaping box of fresh and dewy roses to that sacred room where she lay. How many a time, he thought, had he strolled into some odorous shop in the cities where his "leaves" were spent, and carelessly ordered cut flowers by the cubic foot sent with his card to some one with whom he had danced the german the night before and never expected to see again! What *wouldn't* he give now for just a few of those wasted, faded, forgotten flowers! He could see that the window was raised in the room to which they had carried her, and a soft breeze was playing in the folds of the white curtain; but no one was visible. Dreamily, and with no thought or look for other beings in the little garrison, he strode across the parade. An ambulance, dusty and travel-stained, was in front of Belknap's, and a couple of trunks—unmistakably feminine property—were being unloaded. He could have seen it, had he glanced over his left shoulder, and drawn the inference that "Mrs. Page" had arrived; but his thoughts were engrossed in the other direction. Then Graham came bounding along to join him, and near the quarters stood Captain Stryker, waiting for him, and both of them were unwilling to talk of anything but his exploit of a few hours before: it was all over the garrison by this time, and so was the news that Dunraven's fair and hitherto unknown mistress was now the guest of Fort Rossiter. All his jollity and gladness seemed to have ebbed away. Perry almost wished she were back at Dunraven and that no one knew of her existence but himself and that he were kneeling beside her once again, aiding her in restoring her stricken father to consciousness. But then he thought of the sudden arrival that had so disconcerted him that night, and to-day again. *What* did it mean that Quin assumed such airs of authority? How *dare* he call her Gladys?

Stables that afternoon proved a sore trial to him. Graham had to leave and go to his own troop; Parke took his place, and was all lively enthusiasm and congratulation, yet wondering at the mood in which he found his friend. Stryker, after shaking his hand and saying a few words of quiet commendation, noted the constraint upon his usually lively subaltern, and wisely drew his own conclusions. The captain had been engaged much of the morning on an investigation of the mysterious assault on Sergeant Gwynne, and the developments had been such as to surround the case with additional interest, even though nothing tangible in the way of evidence was educed. He had purposed having a talk with Perry while at stables, but, after one or two searching glances at his face, Stryker concluded it best to postpone his proposed conference, and so allowed Perry to go on about his usual duties; but he smiled in his quiet way when he noted the evident relief with which his subaltern heard the order "Lead in!" that announced that grooming was over. It was fifteen minutes more, however, before the evening duties were complete; and when at last the men went swinging homeward in their white canvas frocks and Perry could return to his quarters to dress for his eagerly-anticipated call, the first thing that met his eyes as he came in sight of officers' row was a huge, bulky, covered travelling-carriage in front of Sprague's. Two or three ladies were there at the gate. Mr. Ewen, the English manager, was just mounting his horse; Dr. Quin, too, was there and already in saddle; and before poor Perry could get half-way across the parade, and just as the trumpets were sounding mess-call for supper, the bulky vehicle started; the ladies waved their handkerchiefs and kissed their hands, and, escorted by Ewen and the doctor, saluted by Colonel Brainard and the adjutant with raised forage-caps, Gladys Maitland was driven slowly away,—and Mrs. Belknap stood there in the little group of ladies smiling sweetly upon him as he hastened towards them. For many a long day afterwards mess-call always made him think of Mrs. Belknap's smile, and Mrs. Belknap's smile of mess-call. He shuddered at sound of one or sight of the other.

It was Mrs. Sprague who stepped forward to greet him, her womanly heart filled with sympathy for the sentiment she suspected. She had to push by Mrs. Belknap to reach him; but, this time, no consideration of etiquette stood in the way.

"It couldn't be helped," she said, in low, hurried tone, her kind eyes searching his, so clouded in the bitterness of his disappointment. "It couldn't be helped. The news of her accident—or something—brought on a seizure of some kind. Mr. Maitland was taken very ill, and they sent for her. The manager came, and with him her old nurse, Mrs. Cowan, and Dr. Quin said she could be moved without trouble: so she had to go. I hated to have her, too, for I've hardly had a word with her: Mrs. Belknap has been there most of the afternoon, even when she had a guest of her own just arrived, too." And Mrs. Sprague could not but show her vexation at this retrospect.

Perry stood in silence, looking yearningly after the retreating vehicle. It would take him but a few minutes to hasten to stables and saddle Nolan; he could easily catch them before they had gone two miles; but there was parade, and he could not ask to be excused. Not until he suddenly looked around and saw that Mrs. Belknap's dark eyes were fixed in close scrutiny upon his face did he realize how he was betraying himself. Then he rallied, but with evident effort.

The colonel was standing but a few paces away, chatting with Mrs. Lawrence and his faithful adjutant. Mrs. Sprague stepped quickly towards him and spoke a few words in a low tone, while Mrs. Belknap remained looking straight into Perry's eyes. Before the young fellow could gather himself, Colonel Brainard, as though in reply to a suggestion of Mrs. Sprague's, suddenly started, exclaiming, "Why, by all means!" and then called aloud,—

"Oh! Perry, why not gallop down and overtake the Dunraven carriage and say good-by? Here's my horse all saddled now right in the yard. Take him and go: *I* would."

There was something so hearty and genial and sympathetic in the colonel's manner that Perry's face flushed despite his effort at nonchalance. The thought of seeing her again and hearing her sweet voice was a powerful incentive. He longed to go. The colonel's invitation was equivalent to an excuse from parade. There was no reason why he should not go. He was on the very point of thankfully accepting the tempting offer, when Mrs. Belknap's words arrested him. Clear and cutting, but still so low that none but he could hear, she spoke:

"Take my word for it, you are not wanted,—nor any other man,—when Dr. Quin is with her."

Perry's hesitation vanished. "Thank you, colonel. I believe I don't care to go," he answered, and, raising his cap to the ladies, turned on his heel and hurried to his quarters. Mrs. Belknap stood watching him one moment, then calmly rejoined the party at the gate.

"Well," said she, with the languid drawl that her regimental associates had learned to know so well, "this has been a day of surprises, has it not? Only fancy our having a beautiful English heiress here within reach and never knowing it until to-day!"

"But you had a surprise of your own, had you not?" interposed Mrs. Sprague, who was still chafing over the fact that her lovely and dangerous neighbor should have so monopolized the guest she considered hers by prior right, and who meant to remind her thus publicly of the neglect of which she had been guilty.

"Mrs. Page, you mean?" responded Mrs. Belknap, with the same languid, imperturbable manner. "Yes,—poor Jennie! She is always utterly used up after one of those long ambulance-journeys, and can only take a cup of tea and go to bed in a darkened room. All she wants is to be let alone, she says, until she gets over it. I suppose she will sleep till tattoo and then be up for half the night. You'll all come in and see her, *won't* you? *Au revoir.*"

And so, calmly and gracefully and victoriously, the dark-eyed dame withdrew, leaving her honest-hearted antagonist only the sense of exasperation and defeat.

It was full quarter of an hour after parade, and darkness was settling down on the garrison, when Captain Lawrence's orderly tapped at the door of Mr. Perry's quarters, and, being bidden "Come in," pushed on to the sitting-room, where he found that young officer plunged deep in an easy-chair in front of the fireplace, his attitude one of profound dejection.

"Beg pardon, lieutenant," said the man, "but Mrs. Lawrence and the captain's waitin' dinner for you."

XV.

Two days passed without event of any kind. Socially speaking, the garrison was enlivened by the advent of Mrs. Page, and everybody flocked to the Belknaps' quarters in order to do her proper homage. When Perry called he asked Parke to go with him, and, when the latter seemed ready to leave, the former, disregarding a very palpable hint from the lady of the house, picked up his forage-cap and went likewise. For two days the one subject under constant discussion at the post was the event of Miss Maitland's sudden appearance, her perilous run, and her daring and skilful rescue. Everybody maintained that Perry ought to be a very proud and happy fellow to have been the hero of such an occasion; but it was very plain that Perry was neither proud nor anything like happy. No one had ever known him so silent and cast down. The talk with Lawrence had helped matters very little.

In brief, this was about all the captain could tell him, and it was all hearsay evidence at best. The officers of the Eleventh and their ladies had, with a few exceptions, taken a dislike to Dr. Quin before Belknap and Lawrence with their companies of infantry had been ordered to Fort Rossiter. The feeling was in full blast when they arrived, and during the six or eight months they served there together the infantry people heard only one side of the story,—that of the Eleventh,—for the doctor never condescended to discuss the matter. After he was forbidden to leave the post by his commanding officer, and after the announcement of the "blockade" of Dunraven, it was observed that signals were sometimes made from the ranch at night: a strong light thrown from a reflector was flashed three times and then withdrawn. Next it was noted, by an enterprising member of the guard, that these signals were answered by a light in the doctor's windows, then that he mounted his horse and rode away down the valley of the Monee. He was always back at sick-call; and, if any one told the commanding officer of his disobedience of orders, it was not done until so near the departure of the Eleventh that the doctor was not afterwards actually caught in the act. Things would undoubtedly have been brought to a crisis had the Eleventh been allowed to remain.

Now as to the story about Mrs. Quin and her going. It was observed during the winter that she was looking very badly, and the story went the rounds in the Eleventh that she was stung and suffering because of her husband's conduct. Unquestionably there was some fair enchantress at Dunraven who lured him from his own fireside. She had no intimates among the ladies. She was proud and silent. It did not seem to occur to them that she was resentful of their dislike of her husband. They were sure she was "pining" because of his neglect —or worse. When, therefore, without word of warning, she suddenly took her departure in the spring, there was a gasp of gossip-loving cronies in the garrison: all doubts were at an end: she had left him and taken her children with her.

"The more I think of it," said Lawrence, "the more I believe the whole thing capable of explanation. The only thing that puzzles me now is that Quin hides anything from your colonel, who is one of the most courteous and considerate men I ever served with. Perhaps he *has* told him, by this time: we don't know. Perhaps he thought he might be of the same stamp as his predecessor, and was waiting to find out before he made his confidences. As to Mrs. Quin's going away when she did, it may have been simply that her health was suffering, she needed change, and went with his full advice and by his wish, and he simply feels too much contempt for garrison gossip to explain. Very probably he knows nothing of the stories and theories in circulation: I'm sure *I* did not until a very few weeks ago. You know, Perry, there are some men in garrison who hear and know everything, and others who never hear a word of scandal."

But Perry was low in his mind. He could not forget Quin's sudden appearance,—his calling *her* Gladys; and then he hated the thought that it was Quin who saw him having that confounded tender interview with Mrs. Belknap. Was there ever such a streak of ill luck as that? No doubt the fellow had told her all about it! Perry left Lawrence's that night very little comforted, and only one gleam of hope did he receive in the two days that followed. Mrs. Sprague joyfully beckoned to him on Wednesday afternoon to read him a little note that had just come from Miss Maitland. Her father had been very ill, she wrote; his condition was still critical; but she sent a world of thanks to her kind entertainers at Rossiter, and these words: "I was sorry not to be able to see Mr. Perry again. Do not let him think I have forgotten, or will be likely to forget, the service he—and Nolan—did me."

Of Dr. Quin he saw very little. With the full consent and knowledge of Colonel Brainard, the doctor was spending a good deal of time at Dunraven now, attending to Mr. Maitland. Indeed, there seemed to be an excellent understanding between the commandant and his medical officer, and it was known that they had had a long talk together. Upper circles in the garrison were still agitated with chat and conjecture about Gladys Maitland and her strange father; Perry was still tortured with questions about his one visit to Dunraven whenever he was so incautious as to appear in public; but all through "the quarters," everywhere among the rank and file, there was a subject that engrossed all thoughts and tongues, and that was discussed with feeling that seemed to deepen with every day,—the approaching court-martial of Sergeant Leary and of Trooper Kelly.

As a result of his investigation, Captain Stryker had preferred charges against these two men,—the one for leading and the other for being accessory to the assault on his stable-sergeant. Gwynne was still at the hospital, though rapidly recovering from his injuries. Not a word had he said that would implicate or accuse any man; but Stryker's knowledge of his soldiers, and his clear insight into human motive and character, were such that he had readily made up his mind as to the facts in the case. He felt sure that Leary and some of the Celtic members of his company had determined to go down to Dunraven and "have it out" with the hated Britons who had so affronted and abused them the night of Perry's visit. They knew they could not get their horses by fair means, for Gwynne was above suspicion. He was English, too, and striving to shield his countrymen from the threatened vengeance. They therefore determined, in collusion with Kelly, to lure him outside the stables, bind and gag him, get their horses, having once rifled Gwynne of the keys, ride down to the ranch, and, after having a Donnybrook Fair on the premises, get back to Rossiter in plenty of time for reveille and stables. No sentries were posted in such a way as to interfere with them, and the plan was feasible enough but for one thing. Gwynne had made most gallant and spirited resistance, had fought the whole gang like a tiger, and they had been unable to overpower him before the noise had attracted the attention of the sergeant of the guard and some of the men in quarters. An effort, of course, was made to show that the assaulting party were from without, but it was futile, and Stryker's keen cross-questioning among the men had convinced them that he knew all about the matter. There was only one conclusion, therefore,—that Gwynne must have "given them away," as the troopers expressed it. Despite the fact that he had been assaulted and badly beaten, this was something that few could overlook, and the latent jealousy against the "cockney sergeant" blazed into a feeling of deep resentment. Garrison sympathy was with Leary and his fellows: they had simply done their best to wipe out a brutal insult to their officer and their regiment, and they would have succeeded, too, but for the interference and stubborn resistance of this bumptious Englishman. It arrayed all the rank and file of the —th for the defence, and there was every prospect that when the court convened—and they well knew it would be ordered—there would be some "tall swearing."

Thursday came, and Sergeant Gwynne returned to light duty, though his face was still bruised and discolored and he wore a patch over one eye. He resumed charge of the stables in the afternoon, after a brief conversation with his captain, and was superintending the issue of forage, when Perry entered to inspect the stalls of his platoon. Nolan was being led out by his groom at the moment, and pricked up his tapering ears at sight of his master and thrust his lean muzzle to receive the caress of the hand he knew so well. Perry stopped him and carefully and critically examined his knees, feeling down to the fetlocks with searching fingers for the faintest symptom of knot or swelling in the tendons that had played their part so thoroughly in the drama of Monday. Satisfied, apparently, he rose and bestowed a few hearty pats on the glossy neck and shoulder, and then was surprised to find the stable-sergeant standing close beside him and regarding both him and the horse with an expression that arrested Perry's attention at once.

"Feeling all right again, sergeant?" he asked, thinking to recall the non-commissioned officer to his senses.

"Almost, sir. I'm a trifle stiff yet. Anything wrong with Nolan, sir?"

"Nothing. I gave him rather a tough run the other day,—had to risk the prairie-dog holes,—and, though I felt no jar then, I've watched carefully ever since to see that he was not wrenched. I wish you would keep an eye on him too, will you?"

There was no answer. Perry had been looking over Nolan's haunches as he spoke, and once more turned to the sergeant. To his astonishment, Gwynne's lips were twitching and quivering, his hands, ordinarily held in the rigid pose of the English service,—extended along the thigh,—were clinching and working nervously, and something suspiciously like a tear was creeping out from under the patch. Before Perry could recover from his surprise, the sergeant suddenly regained his self-control, hastily raised his hand in salute, saying something half articulate in reply, and turned sharply away, leaving his lieutenant gazing after him in much perplexity.

That night, just after tattoo roll-call, when a little group of officers was gathered at the colonel's gate, they were suddenly joined by Dr. Quin, who came from the direction of the stable where he kept his horse in rear of his own quarters. Colonel Brainard greeted him warmly and inquired after his patient at Dunraven. Every one noted how grave and subdued was the tone in which the doctor answered,—

"He is a very sick man, colonel, and it is hard to say what will be the result of this seizure."

"You may want to go down again, doctor, if that be the case,—before sick-call to-morrow, I mean; and you had better take one of my horses. I'll tell my man to have one in readiness."

"You are very kind, sir. I think old Brian will do all the work needed. But I would like to go down at reveille, as we have no men in hospital at all now. And, by the way, is Mr. Perry here?"

"I am here," answered Perry, coldly. He was leaning against the railing, rather away from the group, listening intently, yet unwilling to meet or hold conversation with the man he conceived to be so inimical to his every hope and interest.

"Mr. Perry," said the doctor, pleasantly, and utterly ignoring the coldness of the young fellow's manner, "Mr. Maitland has asked to see you; and it would gratify him if you would ride down in the morning."

Even in the darkness Perry feared that all would see the flush that leaped to his face. Summoned to Dunraven Ranch, by her father, with a possibility of seeing *her!* It was almost too sweet! too thrilling! He could give no reply for a moment, and an awkward silence fell on the group until he chokingly answered, "I shall be glad to go. What time?"

"Better ride down early. Never mind breakfast. Miss Maitland will be glad to give you a cup of coffee, I fancy."

And Perry felt as though the fence had taken to waltzing. He made no answer, striving to regain his composure, and then the talk went on. It was Stryker who was speaking now:

"Has the ring been found, doctor?"

"No! That is a most singular thing, and one that worries the old gentleman a great deal. It had a history: it belonged to Mrs. Maitland's father, who was from Ireland,—indeed, Ireland was her country, as it was my father's,—and that ring she had reset for her son Archie and gave it to him when he entered service with the Lancers. It was sent home with his watch and other property from South Africa,—for he died there,—and old Maitland always wore it afterwards. Archie was the last of three sons; and it broke his heart."

"And the ring was lost the night of Perry's adventure there?" asked the colonel.

"Yes. Mr. Perry remembers having seen it on his hand when the old gentleman first came down to receive him. It was missed afterwards, and could easily have slipped off at any time, for his fingers were withered with age and ill health. They have searched everywhere, and could find nothing of it. It could easily have rolled off the veranda on to the grass during his excitement at the time of the row, and somebody may have picked it up,—either among the ranchmen or among the troopers."

"I hate to think that any of our men would take it," said the colonel, after a pause.

"I do not think any of them would, with the idea of selling it," said Stryker; "but here is a case where it was picked up, possibly, as one of the spoils of war. I have had inquiry made throughout the troop, but with no result so far. Do you go down again to-night, doctor?"

"Not if I can avoid it. I am going now to try and sleep, and will not ride down till daybreak unless signalled for. Good-night, colonel; good-night, all."

Unless signalled for! Instinctively Perry edged closer to Lawrence, who had stood a silent listener to the conversation, and Lawrence turned and saw him and knew the thought that must be uppermost in his mind. Others, too, were doubtless struck by the doctor's closing words, and were pondering over their full significance. There was a moment of perfect silence, and then Lawrence spoke:

"Does anybody know what the signal is?"

"Certainly," said Colonel Brainard, promptly. "He has explained the whole thing to me. Those were signals for him that we saw the night you were all on my gallery. It was an arrangement devised by their old nurse,—she who came up with the carriage for Miss Maitland the other day. She had a regular old-fashioned head-light and reflector, and, when Mr. Maitland was so ill as to need a doctor, used to notify Quin in that way. He sometimes failed to see it, and I have given orders to-day that the guard should wake him when it is seen hereafter."

"Then *that* was what those mysterious night lights meant that we have heard so much about during the last three weeks?" asked Mr. Dana.

"Certainly," answered Brainard. "What on earth did anybody suppose they meant?"

To this there was no response for a moment. Then Lawrence burst out laughing.

XVI.

Late that night Mr. Perry left his quarters and strolled out on the walk that bounded the parade. He could not sleep; he was feverishly impatient for the coming of another day, that he might start forth on his ride to Dunraven. Few as were the words in which Dr. Quin had conveyed the message of invitation, they were sufficient to set his heart athrob and his pulses bounding with eagerness and delight. Then, too, the annihilation of one portion, at least, of the "mystery" that surrounded the doctor's night visits to Dunraven, the utterly matter-of-fact way in which the colonel had shattered that story by his announcement, and the kind and friendly tone in which the doctor had spoken to him, all had served to bring about a revulsion of feeling and to remove a great portion of the weight of suspicion and dread with which he had been burdened. He and Lawrence had walked home together, the captain ever and anon bursting into renewed peals of laughter over the utterly absurd *dénouement* so recently presented to their view. The colonel and the officers with him had, of course, asked the cause of his sudden and apparently unaccountable merriment, and, when he could sufficiently control himself, Lawrence had begged the indulgence of his post commander, saying it involved a long story,—a garrison yarn, in fact,—and one he could hardly retail just then; but, said he, "it reminds me of something we studied in our school-boy days,—'*parturiunt montes,*' and '*nascitur ridiculus mus.*' Of course I'll feel bound to tell you the facts, colonel, but I want to ask a question or two first. The story is a relic of your predecessor's, sir, and, if I haven't got a big joke on the Eleventh, may I be transferred to them forthwith." And the captain's laughter broke forth again.

But he was in more serious mood when he reached his gate and turned to say good-night to Perry:

"It all goes to show what infernal gossip can spring up out of next to nothing, Perry, and I hope you'll try and forget that Mrs. Lawrence's curiosity or womanly weakness got the better of her that night at the colonel's. It will be a lesson to her,—if people ever do profit by lessons in such matters," he added, with rather a rueful smile.

And then, though he had gone home with lighter heart and ashamed of his jealous suspicions, Perry could not sleep. There were still some things in Quin's relations with the Maitlands that required explanation and that gave him cause for painful reflection. The morrow might unravel it all and give him glad relief from every dread; but would the morrow never come?

He heard the sentries at the storehouses calling half-past eleven, and, throwing aside his pipe, he impulsively hurried out into the open air. A "spin" around the parade or out on the starlit prairie might soothe his nerves and enable him to sleep.

All lights were out in the quadrangle, save those at the guard-house. Even at Belknap's quarters, where the veranda had been thronged with officers and ladies only an hour before, all was now silence and darkness. Unwilling to attract attention by tramping up and down on the board walk, he crossed the road and went out on the broad level of the parade, but took care so to direct his steps as not to come within hailing-distance of the guard-house. It would be awkward work explaining the situation to the sergeant of the guard in case the sentry were to see or hear and challenge him. Then, too, Graham was officer of the guard, and Graham would be sure to chaff him mercilessly at the mess-table about this entirely new trait of night-prowling. Giving heed to all this, he edged well over to his left as he walked, and so it happened that he found himself, after a while, opposite the northeast entrance to the post, and close to the road on which stood the commissary and quartermaster storehouses. There was a sentry posted here, too, and it would not do to be challenged by him, any more than by "Number One."

Stopping a moment to listen for the sentry's foot-fall, Perry's ear was attracted by the sound of a door slowly and cautiously opened. It was some little time before he could tell from which one of the neighboring buildings, looming there in the darkness, the sound proceeded. Then he heard muffled footsteps and a whispered consultation not far away, and, hurrying on tiptoe in the direction of the sound, he presently caught sight of two or three dim, shadowy forms moving noiselessly along the porch of the company quarters nearest him. Stryker's troop —that to which he belonged—was quartered down beyond the guard-house on the lower side of the parade; these forms were issuing from the barracks of Captain Wayne's troop, and before Perry could realize the fact that they were out, either in moccasins or their stocking-feet, and presumably, therefore, on some unlawful enterprise, they had disappeared around the corner of the building. He walked rapidly thither, turned the corner, and they were nowhere in sight or hearing. Stopping to listen did not help matters at all. He could not hear a sound; and as for the shadows of which he was in pursuit, it was simply impossible to tell which direction they had taken. They had vanished from the face of the earth, and were lost in the deeper gloom that hung about the scattered array of wooden buildings—storehouses, fuel-sheds, and cook-sheds—at the rear of the post.

Had it been his own troop he could have roused the first sergeant and ordered a "check" roll-call as a means of determining at once who the night-prowlers might be; but Captain Wayne had his peculiarities, and one of them was an unalterable and deeply-rooted objection to any interference on the part of other officers in the management of his men. Perry's first thought, too, was of the stables and Sergeant Gwynne. Were they meditating another foray, and had the feeling spread outside their own company? No time was to be lost. He turned his face eastward to where the dark outlines of the stables could be dimly traced against the sky, and hastened, stumbling at times over stray tin cans and other discarded rubbish, until he crossed the intervening swale and reached the low bluff along which the crude, unpainted structures were ranged. All was darkness here towards the northern end, and the one sentry who had external charge of the entire line was slowly pacing his post: Perry could see his form, dimly outlined, as he breasted the slope, and it determined him to keep on in the hollow until he got to a point opposite the stables of his own troop. If there was to be any devilment it might be well to see whether this soldier, too, would turn out to be in league with the conspirators. Listening intently as he hurried along, but hearing nothing, Perry soon found himself at the pathway leading to his own domain, and the next minute was gazing in surprise at a light burning dimly in the window of the little room occupied by Sergeant Gwynne: there was not a glimmer elsewhere along the line.

Striding up to the window, he tapped lightly, and Gwynne's voice sternly challenged from within, "Who's there?"

"Lieutenant Perry, sergeant. Come around and open the stable door for me."

"One moment, sir," was the answer, and he heard the sergeant bounding, apparently, off his bed. Then a hand drew aside the shade, and Gwynne's face appeared at the window, while a small lantern was held so as to throw its rays on the face without. "All right, sir," he continued. "I thought I could not be deceived in the voice."

Perry walked around to the front again, taking another survey of the sleeping garrison as he did so, and listening once more for footsteps; but all was still. Presently the little panel in the big door was unlocked from within, and the lieutenant bent low and entered, finding Gwynne, lantern in hand, standing in his uncompromising attitude of "attention" at the entrance.

"Everything been quiet here to-night?" he asked, as he straightened up.

"Perfectly so, sir."

"Come into your room a moment; I want to speak to you," said Perry, after a moment's reflection.

They passed along the broad gangway between the rows of sleepy horses, some lying down in their stalls, others still afoot and munching at their hay. The stable-guard stood at his post and faced them as they turned into the dark and narrow passage leading into Gwynne's little sanctuary. The lamps along the line of stalls burned low and dim, and, the ports being lowered, gave no gleam without the walls. Once more, however, a bright light shone from the window of the stable-sergeant's room,—brighter than before, could they only know it, for this time there was no intervening shade. After his brief inspection of the lieutenant's face, Gwynne had left it drawn.

The sergeant set his lantern on a wooden desk, and respectfully waited for his superior to speak. Perry looked him well over a moment, and then began:

"Did you tell Captain Stryker the particulars of your rough treatment down there at the ranch?"

"The rough treatment,—yes, sir."

"Would you mind telling me where you were taken?—where you saw Dr. Quin?"

The sergeant hesitated one moment, a troubled look on his face. His one available eye studied his lieutenant's features attentively. Something in the frank, kind blue eyes—possibly some sudden recollection, too—seemed to reassure him.

"It was to Mr. Cowan's little house, sir. He interposed to save me from a worse beating at the hands of three brutes who were employed there and had some grudge against this garrison of which I was ignorant. They attacked me without a word of warning. It was he, too, who called in Dr. Quin."

"Have you—did you see any of the people at Dunraven besides this young man?"

"I saw his mother, sir. She is a nurse there, and has been in the family for years, I am told."

Perry was silent a moment. Then he spoke again:

"Have you heard any further threats among the men here since the arrest of Sergeant Leary?"

Gwynne hesitated, coloring painfully:

"It is something I hate to speak of, sir. The talk has not alarmed me in the least."

"I know that, sergeant. All the same we want to prevent a recurrence of that performance; and it was that, mainly, that brought me over here. I saw some men stealing out of M Troop's quarters awhile ago, and lost them in the darkness. I thought they might be coming over here, and—got here first."

Gwynne's face lighted up. It touched him to know his officers were on the lookout for his safety.

"I have heard nothing, sir. The men would hardly be apt to speak to me on the subject, since the affair of the other night. What I fear is simply this,—that there is an element here in the regiment that is determined to get down there to the ranch and have satisfaction for the assault that was made on you and your party. They need horses in order to get there and back between midnight and reveille, and are doubtless hatching some plan. They failed here; now they may try the stables of some other troop, or the quartermaster's. Shall I warn the sentry that there are prowlers out to-night?"

"Not yet. They will hardly make the attempt while your light is burning here. What I'm concerned about just now is this: we all know that there is deep sympathy for Leary in the command, and it is not improbable that among the Irishmen there is corresponding feeling against you. I don't like your being here alone just now; for they know you are almost the only witness against him."

"I have thought of that, sir," answered Gwynne, gravely, "but I want nothing that looks like protection. The captain has spoken of the matter to me, and he agreed, sir, that it would do more harm than good. There is one thing I would ask,—if I may trouble the lieutenant."

"What is it, sergeant?"

"I have a little packet, containing some papers and a trinket or two, that I would like very much to have kept safely, and, if anything should happen to me, to have you, sir, and Captain Stryker open it, and—the letters there will explain everything that is to be done."

"Certainly. I will take care of it for you,—if not too valuable."

"I would rather know it was with you, sir, than stow it in the quartermaster's safe," was Gwynne's answer, as he opened a little wooden chest at the foot of his bunk, and, after rummaging a moment, drew forth a parcel tied and sealed. This he handed to the lieutenant.

"Now I will go back and notify the officer of the guard of what I have seen," said Perry; "and I want Nolan, saddled, over at my quarters right after morning stables. Will you see to it?"

"I will, sir, and thank you for your kindness."

All was darkness, all silence and peace, as Perry retraced his steps and went back to the garrison, carrying the little packet in his hand.

He went direct to the guard-house, and found Mr. Graham sulky over being disturbed in his snooze by the sentry's challenge.

"What the devil are you owling around this time of night for?" was the not unnatural question. "I thought it was the officer of the day, and nearly broke my neck in hurrying out here."

But Perry's brief recital of the fact that he had seen some men stealing out of the quarters of M Troop in their stocking-feet or moccasins put an end to Graham's complaints. Hastily summoning the sergeant of the guard, he started out to make the rounds of his sentries, while Perry carried his packet home, locked it in his desk, and then returned to the veranda to await developments.

Sergeant Gwynne, meantime, having lighted his young officer to the stable door, stood there a few moments, looking over the silent garrison and listening to the retreating footsteps. The sentry came pacing along the front of the stables, and brought his carbine down from the shoulder as he dimly sighted the tall figure, but, recognizing the stable-sergeant as he came nearer, the ready challenge died on his lips.

"I *thought* I heard somebody moving around down here, sergeant. It was you, then, was it?"

"I have been moving around,—inside,—but made no noise. Have you heard footsteps or voices?"

"Both, I thought; but it's as black as your hat on this beat to-night. I can't see my hand afore my face."

"Keep your ears open, then: there are men out from *one* of the quarters, at least, and no telling what they are up to. Who's in charge at the quartermaster's stables?"

"Sergeant Riley, of the infantry; some of the fellers were over having a little game with him before tattoo, and I heard him tell 'em to come again when they had more money to lose. He and his helper there were laughing at the way they cleaned out the cavalry when they were locking up at taps. The boys fetched over a bottle of whiskey with 'em."

"Who were they?"

"Oh, there was Flanagan and Murphy, of M Troop, and Corporal Donovan, and one or two others. *They* hadn't been drinkin'."

"But Riley had,—do you mean?"

"He was a little full; not much."

"Well, look alive now, Wicks. It's my advice to you that you watch that end of your post with all your eyes." And with this Sergeant Gwynne turned back into the stable, picked up his lantern, and returned to the little room in which he slept. A current of cool night-air, blowing in through the open casement, attracted his attention. Odd! He knew he had pulled aside the shade to scan the features of the lieutenant when he tapped at the pane, but he could not recall having opened the sash. It swung on a hinge, and was fastened by a loosely-fitting bolt. Perhaps the rising wind had blown it in. He set his lamp down as before, closed the sash, and then closed and locked the lid of his chest. That, too, was open. Wicks, the sentry, well up to the north end of his post and close to the entrance of the quartermaster's corral, was bawling, "Half-past twelve o'clock, and a-all's well," when the light went out in Gwynne's little room, and all the line of stables was wrapped in darkness.

Perry fretted around the veranda until one o'clock, then sought his room. He was still too excited to sleep, and it seemed an interminable time before he dozed off. Then it seemed as though he could not have been in dream-land five minutes before a hand was laid upon his shoulder, shaking him vigorously, and a voice he well knew was exclaiming, in low but forcible tones,—

"Wake, lieutenant, wake! Every horse is gone from the quartermaster's corral. There must be twenty men gone down the valley. I've Nolan here for you at the gate."

In ten minutes Lieutenant Perry and Sergeant Gwynne were riding neck and neck out over the eastern prairie,—out towards the paling orient stars and the faintly-gleaming sky,—before them, several miles away, the dark and threatened walls of Dunraven, behind them the stir and excitement and bustle consequent upon a night alarm. The colonel, roused by Perry with the news, had ordered the instant sounding of the assembly, and the garrison was tumbling out for roll-call.

XVII.

At the head of a score of his own men, Captain Stryker rode forth some fifteen minutes later. His orders from Colonel Brainard were to go to Dunraven, and, if he found the marauders there, to arrest the entire party and bring them back to the post. From all that could be learned from hurried questioning of the sentries and the dazed, half-drunken sergeant at the corral, the troopers engaged in the raid must have selected a time when the sentry was walking towards the south end of his post to lift one of their number over the wall of the enclosure in which were kept the wagons and ambulances. This man had unbarred from within the gate leading eastward to the trail down which the "stock" was driven daily to water in the Monee. Riley admitted that "the boys" had left a bottle with him which he and his assistant had emptied before turning in, and so it happened that, unheard and unseen, the raiders had managed to slip out with the dozen horses that were kept there and had also taken six mules as "mounts" for those who could not find anything better. Eighteen men, apparently, were in the party, and the sentry on Number Three heard hoof-beats down towards the valley about half-past two o'clock, but thought it was only some of the ponies belonging to the Cheyenne scouts. There was one comfort,—the men had taken no fire-arms with them; for a hurried inspection of the company quarters showed that the carbines were all in their racks and the revolvers in their cases. Some of the men might have small-calibre pistols of their own, but the government arms had not been disturbed. Half the party, at least, must have ridden bareback and with only watering-bridles for their steeds. They were indeed "spoiling for a fight," and the result of the roll-call showed that the missing troopers were all Irishmen and some of the best and most popular men in the command. Whatever their plan, thought Stryker, as he trotted down to the Monee, it was probably carried out by this time: it was now within a minute of four o'clock.

Only a mile out he was overtaken by Dr. Quin, who reined up an instant to ask if any one had been sent ahead. "Thank God for that!" he exclaimed, when told that Perry and Sergeant Gwynne had gone at the first alarm; then, striking spurs to his horse, pushed on at rapid gallop, while the troopers maintained their steady trot. A mile from Dunraven, in the dim light of early morning the captain's keen eyes caught sight of shadowy forms of mounted men on the opposite shore, and, despite their efforts to escape on their wearied steeds, three of them were speedily run down and captured. One of them was Corporal Donovan, and Donovan's face was white and his manner agitated. Bidding him ride alongside as they pushed ahead towards the ranch, Stryker questioned him as to what had taken place, and the corporal never sought to equivocate:

"We've been trying for several nights, sir, to get horses and go down and have it out with those blackguards at the ranch. We took no arms, sir, even those of us who had pistols of our own. All we asked was a fair fight, man against man. They wouldn't come out of their hole,—they *dasn't* do it, sir,—and then they fired on us. We'd have burned the roof over their heads, but that Lieutenant Perry galloped in and stopped us. I came away then, sir, and so did most of us. We knew 'twas all up when we saw the lieutenant; but there was more firing after I left. This way, captain. Out across the prairie here. We cut down the fence on this side." And, so saying, Donovan led the little troop to a broad gap in the wire barrier, and thence straight across the fields to where lights were seen flitting about in the dark shadows of the buildings of the ranch. Another moment, and Stryker had dismounted and was kneeling beside the prostrate and unconscious form of his lieutenant. Some misguided ranchman, mistaking for a new assailant the tall young soldier who galloped into the midst of the swarm of taunting Irishmen, had fired the cruel shot. There lay Nolan dead upon the sward, and here, close at hand, his grief-stricken master had finally swooned from loss of blood, the bullet having pierced his leg below the knee. Beside him knelt the doctor: he had cut away the natty riding-boot, and was rapidly binding up the wound. Close at hand stood Gwynne, a world of anxiety and trouble in his bruised and still discolored face. Grouped around were some of the assailing party, crestfallen and dismayed at the unlooked-for result of their foray, but ashamed to attempt to ride away, now that their favorite young officer was sore stricken as a result of their mad folly. Mr. Ewen, too, had come out, and was bustling about, giving directions to the one or two of his hands who had ventured forth from the office building. The big frame house under whose walls the group was gathered was evidently used as a dormitory for a number of men, and this had been the objective point of the attack, but not a soul had issued from its portals: the occupants were the men who made the assault on Perry the night of his first visit, and now they deemed it best to keep within. Everything indicated that Perry had got to the scene just in time to prevent a bloody and desperate fracas, for the few ranch-people who appeared were still quivering with excitement and dread. Ewen was almost too much agitated to speak:

"Go to Mr. Maitland as soon as you can, doctor: this has given him a fearful shaking up. Mrs. Cowan is having a room made ready for Mr. Perry. Ah! here's young Cowan now.—Ready?" he asked.

"All ready. Mother says carry the gentleman right in.—She wants
L*

you to come too," he added, in lower tone, to Sergeant Gwynne, but the latter made no reply.

And so, borne in the arms of several of his men, Lieutenant Perry was carried across the intervening space and into the main building. When he recovered consciousness, as the morning light came through the eastern windows, he found himself lying in a white-curtained bed in a strange room, with a strange yet kind and motherly face bending over him, and his captain smiling down into his wondering eyes.

"You are coming round all right, old fellow," he heard Stryker say. "I'll call the doctor now: he wanted to see you as soon as you waked."

And then Quin came in and said a few cheery words and bade him lie still and worry about nothing. The row was over, thanks to him, and he and poor Nolan were the only victims; but it had been a great shock to Mr. Maitland and rendered his condition critical.

Perry listened in silence, asking no questions. For the time being he could think of nothing but Nolan's loss. It was such a cruel fate to be killed by those he came to save.

All that day he lay there, dozing and thinking alternately. He wondered at the tenderness and devotion with which the kind old Englishwoman nursed him and seemed to anticipate his every want. Quin came in towards evening and dressed his wound, which now began to be feverish and painful. He heard his colonel's voice in the hallway, too, and heard him say to the doctor that somebody at Rossiter was eager to come down and take care of him. "Bosh!" said the blunt surgeon; "I've a far better nurse here,—and a reserve to fall back upon that will be worth a new life to him." And, weak and feverish though he was, Perry's heart thrilled within him: he wondered if it *could* mean Gladys. Two days more he lay there, the fever skilfully controlled by the doctor's ministrations, and the pain of his wound subdued by Mrs. Cowan's cooling bandages and applications. But there was a burning fever in his heart that utterly refused to down. He strained his ears listening for the sound of her voice or the pit-a-pat of her foot-fall in the corridor. At last he mustered courage and asked for her, and Mrs. Cowan smiled:

"Miss Maitland has been here three times to inquire how you were; but it was while you were sleeping, Mr. Perry, and she rarely leaves her father's bedside. He is very ill, and seems to be growing weaker every day. I don't know what we would have done if we had not found Dr. Quin here: he has pulled him through two or three bad seizures during the past year."

"Where had you known the doctor before?" asked Perry, with an eager light in his eyes.

"Nowhere; but it was as though one of his own kith and kin had suddenly appeared here to welcome Mr. Maitland. The doctor is a first-cousin of Mrs. Maitland's: she was from Ireland, and it was from her family that the ranch was named. Lord Dunraven is of the peerage of Ireland, you know," added Mrs. Cowan, with the cheerful confidence of the Englishwoman that every person of any education or standing must be familiar with the pages of Debrett.

"How should I know anything about it?" laughed Perry. He felt in merry mood; another page in his volume of suspicion and dread was being torn away, and Quin's relations with the household were turning out to be such as made him an object of lively interest, not of jealous doubt.

Then came callers from the garrison. It seemed as though all of a sudden the blockade had been raised and that no people were so warmly welcomed at Dunraven as the very ones who had been especially proscribed. Mr. Maitland, weak and ill as he was, had asked to be allowed to see Colonel Brainard on the occasion of that officer's second visit; Stryker, Dana, Graham, and Parke had all been allowed to come up and see Perry a few moments, but Mrs. Cowan was vigilant and remorseless, would allow them only a brief interview, and, with smiling determination, checked her patient when he attempted to talk. The third day of his imprisonment Dr. Quin came scowling in along in the afternoon, manifestly annoyed about something, and said a few words in a low tone to Mrs. Cowan, and that usually equable matron fluttered away down-stairs in evident excitement.

"It's Mrs. Belknap," explained the doctor, in answer to Perry's inquiring look. "She has ridden down here with Dana and sent her card up to Gladys,—who can't bear the sight of her; I don't know why; intuition, I suppose."

Presently Mrs. Cowan reappeared: "Miss Gladys has asked to be excused, as she does not wish to leave her father at this moment; and the lady would like to come up and see Mr. Perry."

"Tell her *no!*" said Quin, savagely. "No,—here: I'll go myself." And down went the doughty medical officer, and straightway the rumbling tones of his harsh voice were heard below: the words were indistinguishable, but Mrs. Cowan's face indicated that there was something in the sound that gave her comfort. She stood at the window watching the pair as they rode away.

"Miss Gladys shuddered when she had to shake hands with her that day when we came away from Mrs. Sprague's," said she. "I hope that lady is not a particular friend of yours, Mr. Perry?"

"We have been very good friends indeed," said he, loyally. "To be sure, I have hardly known Mrs. Belknap a month, but both she and the captain have been very kind to me." All the same, down in the bottom of his heart he did not wonder at Miss Maitland's sensations. He was beginning to despair of ever seeing her, and yet could get no explanation that satisfied him.

"You know she can walk only with great pain and difficulty even now," said Mrs. Cowan. "Her ankle was very badly wrenched, and she hardly goes farther than from her own to her father's room. You ought to feel complimented that she has been here to your door three times."

"I feel more like butting my brains out for being asleep," muttered Perry in reply. "I wish you would wake me next time, Mrs. Cowan. I shan't believe it until I see it, or hear her voice at the door."

She had excused herself to Mrs. Belknap, and the doctor had denied that lovely woman her request to be allowed to come up and see Mr. Perry; and yet, the very next day, when the big four-mule ambulance from Rossiter came driving up to the front door, and Mrs. Sprague and Mrs. Lawrence, escorted by the colonel and Captain Stryker, appeared on the veranda, how did it happen that the ladies were speedily ushered up-stairs to Miss Maitland's own room, and that, after an animated though low-toned chat of half an hour with her, they were marshalled down the long corridor by Mrs. Cowan in person, and, to Perry's huge delight, were shown in to his bedside? It looked as though Quin were showing unwarrantable discrimination. Stryker and the colonel, too, came in to see him, and the latter told him that both Mr. Maitland and Mr. Ewen had begged that the arrested soldiers might not be punished. Including Sergeant Leary and Kelly, there were now twenty men under charges more or less grave in their character, and he had asked that a general court-martial be convened for their trial. The colonel deeply appreciated the feeling displayed by the stricken proprietor and his overseer; he was touched that even in his extreme illness and prostration Mr. Maitland should intercede for the men who had made so hostile an invasion of his premises and brought upon the inmates of Dunraven a night of dread and anxiety; but discipline had to be maintained, he replied, and the ringleaders in the move had been guilty of a flagrant breach which could not be overlooked.

But on the following day—the fourth of Perry's stay—the doctor came down with a face full of gloom and distress. Both nurse and patient noted it, and inquired the cause. For a time Quin avoided any direct reply: "something had ruffled him up at the post," he answered: "can't tell you about it now. I'll do it by and by. I want to think." He examined Perry's leg, dressed and rebandaged the wound, and then went back to Mr. Maitland's room. They could hear his voice in the hall after a while, and Perry's heart began to throb heavily: he was sure the low, sweet tones, almost inaudible, that came floating along the corridor, were those of Gladys. When Mrs. Cowan spoke to him on some ordinary topic, he impatiently bade her hush,—he could not bear to be disturbed,—and, far from being hurt at his petulance, Mrs. Cowan smiled softly as she turned away.

Then Quin came back, and, after fidgeting around a moment, abruptly addressed his patient:

"Perry, do you remember that morning you rode down here right after reveille and met me on the trail,—or at least would have met me if I hadn't dodged and gone over to the other side of the valley?"

"Certainly I do, doctor."

"I may as well explain that singular performance first. You may have heard that I didn't get along amicably with your predecessors of the Eleventh. Their colonel was ass enough to totally misconstrue the purpose of my visits here, and I was ass enough to make no explanation. The Maitlands went away; I was not called for again while the Eleventh remained; and therefore I said no more about it. Mr. Maitland returned unexpectedly soon after you came, and the first I knew of it was the signal-lights telling me he was there, ill, and that I was wanted. It was the night of the colonel's dinner-party. I couldn't explain then, and decided to go at once and explain afterwards. When I met you all of a sudden the next morning, the first impulse was to get away out of your sight, and I obeyed it simply because of the unpleasant experiences I had been having with your fellow-cavalrymen. I did not want to have to answer questions. See? I was ashamed of it, but too late to turn back."

Perry nodded. "I understand it—now," he said.

"Well, what I want to ask is about Sergeant Gwynne. Did you meet him before you got back?"

"Yes,—a mile or so out from the post."

"You stopped and talked with him, didn't you?"

"Yes,—for several minutes."

Mrs. Cowan's needle-work had fallen in her lap. She was seated near the window, and had been busily sewing. Now she was looking up, eager and intent.

"You've known him a long time, haven't you?"

"Yes,—ever since he joined. He's one of the best sergeants I ever knew."

"You would hardly think him guilty of any dishonesty, would you?"

Mrs. Cowan was rising from her chair; the needle-work had fallen to the floor.

"Dishonesty! Not by a—good deal!" was the reply that bade fair to be even more impulsive, and was checked only in deference to the presence of a woman.

"Well, neither would I, from what I've seen of him; and yet Mr. Maitland's seal ring was found on him last night."

"My God! Of course he could explain it in some way?"

"He couldn't,—or wouldn't. He simply stood there, white as a sheet except where those bruises made him green and blue. He had denied the charge flatly when accused; and yet there it was in his chest. I never saw any man so taken aback as Captain Stryker: he said he would have sworn to his innocence."

"So would I!—so I do, by Jupiter! It's some foul plot!—it's——"

But he got no further. To his own amaze, to the utter bewilderment of Dr. Quin, Mrs. Cowan precipitated herself upon her patient, seized the hand that lay nearest her on the coverlet, and burst forth into half-articulate, sobbing, indignant words, mingled with kisses showered passionately on that astonished hand.

"Oh, bless him for the words! Oh, God bless you, Mr. Perry! . . . Oh, the fools! the lunatics! . . . A thief, indeed! . . . The idea of *his* being accused! . . . Oh, God! what would his mother in heaven say to this? . . . As though he had not borne far too much already! . . . It's his own—his *own* ring, I tell you! Who else should wear it? . . . Who dare take it from him now? . . . Oh, the infamy of it all!"

In her wild excitement, in her incoherent praise and lamentation and wrath and indignation, her voice, her sobs, rang through the room and out along the broad corridor. Even in their amaze the two men heard a hurried step approaching, a limping, halting, painful step, yet rapid and impulsive. Quin, absorbed in his contemplation of the excited woman, paid no attention; Perry's eager eyes were strained upon the door-way, where, the very next instant, with pallid features and startled mien, Gladys Maitland suddenly appeared and stood staring in upon the spectacle of Mrs. Cowan kissing and sobbing over Perry's hand. Already he had divined the truth, and strove to warn the tear-blinded woman of her presence; but Mrs. Cowan's excitement had increased to the verge of hysteria: she was laughing and crying now by turns, blessing her soldier patient for his faith in the accused sergeant, and then breaking forth anew in indignant expletive, "Who are his accusers? Who dare say thief to him? . . . Not one is fit to look him in the face! 'Twas the very ring his mother gave him, . . . his own! his own!"

And then the doctor seized her and turned her so that she must see Gladys,—Gladys, wild-eyed, panting, staring, tottering forward from the door-way. One sharp cry from the woman's lips, one spring towards the reeling form, and she had caught the girl in her arms:

"Gladys, Gladys, my little pet! my own baby girl! Look up and thank God! I've tried to keep my promise and his secret until he released me. I've tried hard, but it's all useless: I can't, I can't. Oh, Gladys, sweetheart, your mother's smiling down on us this day. Who do you think has come back to us, safe and strong and well and brave? Who but your own brother, your own Archie, Gladys?"

XVIII.

"Yes, certainly very pretty,—now. It's such a pity that English women grow coarse and stout and red-faced so very soon after they are married." The speaker was Mrs. Belknap, and her soft voice was tuned to a pitch of almost pathetic regret. They were talking of Miss Maitland, who had just been assisted to her saddle by the colonel, and now, followed by the faithful Griggs and escorted by Captain Stryker, was riding away homeward after a brief call at the post. Fort Rossiter, once so humdrum and placid and "stupid," as the ladies termed it, had been the vortex of sensations for a whole fortnight, and one excitement had trodden on the heels of another with such rapidity that people were growing weary.

Perhaps the happiest man in garrison was Captain Stryker: he had refused to believe in the guilt of Sergeant Gwynne when Captain Wayne came to him to say that there were men in his troop who openly accused the sergeant of having that cherished seal-ring secreted in his chest. So confident was he that he had gone with the captain and Mr. Farnham to the stables and there told Gwynne of the charge against him. Gwynne flushed hotly, denied the truth of the story, but hesitated when asked if he would allow his chest to be searched. This was quickly noted by Wayne and Farnham, and the search was insisted upon. Gwynne then said there were a few items in that chest which he allowed no one to see; he pledged his soldier word that they were nothing but a paper or two, some little photographs, and a book. These he asked permission to remove first; then they might search. But Wayne sternly refused. The sergeant turned very white, set his lips, and hesitated still, until his own captain spoke; then he surrendered his key. Wayne and Farnham bent over the chest while the troop first sergeant rapidly turned over the clothing, books, etc., with trembling hands. There was a little compartment at one side, in which were lying some small items,—a pocket-compass, a pencil-case, some keys, a locket and a neck-chain, and, among these, something wrapped in tissue-paper. This was handed to Captain Wayne, who unrolled the paper, and—there was a massive seal-ring. A crest was cut in the stone, and, taking it to the light, Wayne was able to make out the motto,—" *Quod sursum volo videre.*" It was the ring Maitland had lost.

Stryker looked wonderingly at his sergeant, who stood there as though petrified with amaze and consternation, pale as death, and unable to say a word. Asked to explain the matter, he could only shake his head, and, after a while, hoarsely mutter, "I know nothing about it. I never placed it there."

"Do you mean to tell me you never saw it before?" asked Wayne, sternly. And Gwynne was silent.

"Is this the first time you ever saw it, I say?" repeated the captain, angrily.

"No, sir: I *have* seen it before," was the answer.

"Then you must have known 'twas stolen, and you have connived at its concealment," was Wayne's triumphant conclusion; and on the report of his officers Colonel Brainard had no alternative but to order

Gwynne's close arrest. Only Stryker's appeal and guarantee saved the sergeant from confinement in the guard-house.

The next sensation was the sight of Dr. Quin galloping back to the post like mad and bolting unceremoniously into the colonel's gate. Then Stryker was sent for, and the three officers held an excited conversation. Then the orderly went at a run over to the quarters, and in five minutes Sergeant Gwynne, erect as ever and dressed with scrupulous care, looking anything but like a guilty man, was seen crossing the parade towards his colonel's house. The men swarmed out on the porches as the tidings went from lip to lip, and some of the Irish troopers in Wayne's company were remarked as being oddly excited. Just what took place during that interview none could tell, but in ten minutes the news was flying around the garrison that Sergeant Gwynne was released from arrest, and in less than half an hour, to the wonderment of everybody, he was seen riding away towards Dunraven with Dr. Quin, and for two days more did not reappear at Rossiter.

But when the story flashed from house to house about the garrison that Sergeant Gwynne was not Sergeant Gwynne at all, but Mr. Archibald Wyndham Quin Maitland, late of Her Majesty's —th Lancers, and only surviving son of the invalid owner of Dunraven Ranch and other valuable properties, the amaze amounted to almost stupefaction. It was known that old Mr. Maitland was lying desperately weak and ill the day that Quin the doctor came riding back. All manner of stories were told regarding the affecting nature of the interview in which the long-lost son was restored to his overjoyed father, but, like most stories, they were purely the offspring of imagination, for at that interview only three were present: Gladys led her brother to the room and closed the door, while good Mrs. Cowan stood weeping for joy down the long corridor, and Dr. Quin blinked his eyes and fussed and fidgeted and strode around Perry's room with his hands in his pockets, exploding every now and then into sudden comment on the romantic nature of the situation and the idiocy of some people there at Rossiter. "Joy does not kill," he said: "Maitland would have been a dead man by the end of the week, but for this: it will give him a new lease of life."

And it did. Though the flame was feeble and flickering, it was fanned by a joy unutterable. The boy whom the stricken father believed his stubborn pride and condemnation had driven to despair and suicide was restored to him in the prime of manly strength, all tenderness, all forgiveness, and Maitland's whole heart went up in thanksgiving. He begged that Brainard and Stryker would come to him, that he might thank them for their faith in his son; he bade the doctor say to Perry that the moment he could be lifted from his bed he would come to clasp his hand and bless him for being a far better friend to his son than he had been a father.

The sergeant's return to the post was the signal for a general turn-out on the part of the men, all of whom were curious to see how he would appear now that his identity was established. Of course his late assailants could not join in the crowd that thronged about him, but they listened with eagerness to everything that was told. "He was just the same as ever," said all accounts. He had never been intimate with any of them, but always friendly and kind. One thing went the rounds like lightning.

"You'll be getting your discharge now, sergeant," said Mrs. Reed, the voluble wife of the leader of the band, "and taking up your residence at the ranch, I suppose. Of course the British minister can get it for you in a minute."

"Not a bit of it, Mrs. Reed," was the laughing answer. "I enlisted to serve Uncle Sam five years, and he's been too good a friend to me to turn from. I shall serve out my time with the —th."

And the sergeant was true to his word. If old Maitland could have prevailed, an application for his son's discharge would have gone to Washington; but this the soldier positively forbade. He had eight months still to serve, and he meant to carry out his contract to the letter. Stryker offered him a furlough, and Gwynne thankfully took a week, that he might be by his father's side and help nurse him to better health. "By that time, too, the garrison will have grown a little more accustomed to it, sir, and I will have less embarrassment in going on with my work."

Two days before his return to duty there came a modified sensation in the shape of the report that a trooper of Wayne's company had deserted. He was a man who had borne a bad reputation as a turbulent, mischief-making fellow, and when Sergeant Leary heard of his going he was in a state of wild excitement. He begged to be allowed to see his captain, and to him he confessed that one of his little party of three had seen the ring drop from Mr. Maitland's finger the night of the first visit to Dunraven, had managed to pick it up and carry it away in the confusion, and had shown it to his friend in Wayne's troop when they got back. The latter persuaded him to let him take it, as the lockers of the men who were at Dunraven were sure, he said, to be searched. It was known that he had a grudge against Gwynne; he was one of the men who *was* to have gone to the ranch the night they purposed riding down and challenging the Englishmen to come out and fight, but had unaccountably failed at the last moment. They believed that *he* had chosen that night to hide the ring in the sergeant's chest: he could easily have entered through the window. And this explanation—the only one ever made—became at once accepted as the true one throughout the garrison.

During the week of his furlough the sergeant found time to spend many hours by the bedside of Lieutenant Perry, who was rapidly recovering, and who by the end of the week had been lifted into an easy invalid-chair and wheeled in to see Mr. Maitland. When *not* with Mr. Perry, the young trooper's tongue was ever wagging in his praise. He knew many a fine officer and gallant gentleman in the service of the old country, he said, and he admired many a captain and subaltern in that of his adopted land, but the first one to whom he "warmed"— the first one to win his affection—was the young cavalryman who had met his painful wound in their defence. Old Maitland listened to it all eagerly,—he had already given orders that the finest thoroughbred at Dunraven should be Perry's the moment he was able to mount again, —and he was constantly revolving in mind how he could show his appreciation of the officers who had befriended his son. Mrs. Cowan, too, never tired of hearing Perry's praises, and eagerly questioned when the narrator flagged. There was another absorbed auditor, who never questioned, and who listened with downcast eyes. It was she who seldom came near Perry during his convalescence, she who startled and astonished the young fellow beyond measure, the day the ambulance came down to drive him back to the fort, by withdrawing the hand he had impulsively seized when at last she appeared to bid him adieu, and cutting short his eager words with "Mrs. Belknap will console you, I dare say," and abruptly leaving the room.

Poor Ned! In dire distress and perplexity he was driven back to Rossiter, and that very evening he did a most sensible and fortunate thing: he told Mrs. Sprague all about it; and, instead of condoling with him and bidding him strive to be patient and saying that all would come right in time, the little woman's kind eyes shone with delight, her cheeks flushed with genuine pleasure; she fairly sprang from her chair, and danced up and down and clapped her hands and laughed with glee, and then, when Perry ruefully asked her if that was the sympathy he had a right to expect from her, she only laughed the more, and at last broke forth with,—

"Oh, you great, stupid, silly boy! You ought to be wild with happiness. *Can't* you see she's jealous?"

And the very next day she had a long talk with Dr. Quin, whose visits to Dunraven still continued; and one bright afternoon when Gladys Maitland rode up to the fort to return calls, she managed to have quite a chat with her, despite the fact that Mrs. Belknap showed a strong desire to accompany that fair English girl in all three of her visits. In this effort, too, the diplomatic services of Captain Stryker proved rather too much for the beauty of the garrison. Was it possible that Mrs. Sprague had enlisted him also in the good cause? Certain it is that the dark-featured captain was Miss Maitland's escort as she left the garrison, and that it was with the consciousness of impending defeat that Mrs. Belknap gave utterance to the opening sentence of this chapter: Mr. Perry had distinctly avoided her ever since his return.

One lovely evening late in May Mr. Perry was taking his first ride on the new horse, a splendid bay, and a perfect match for Gladys Maitland's favorite mount. Already had this circumstance excited smiling comment in the garrison; but if the young man himself had noted the close resemblance it conveyed no blissful augury. Everybody remarked that he had lost much of his old buoyancy and life; and it must be confessed he was not looking either blithe or well. Parke had suggested riding with him,—an invitation which Perry treated so coldly that the junior stopped to think a moment, and began to see through the situation; and so Mr. Perry was suffered to set forth alone that evening, and no one was surprised when, after going out of the west gate as though bent on riding *up* the Monee, he was presently seen to have made the circuit of the post and was slowly cantering down towards the lower valley. Out on the eastern prairie another horseman could be seen; and presently the two came together. Colonel Brainard took down his binocular and gazed out after them.

"I declare," said he, "those two figures are so much alike I cannot tell which of them is Perry."

"Then the other is Sergeant Gwynne, colonel," said Stryker, quietly. "Put him in our uniform, and it would indeed be hard to tell the two figures apart. Mr. Maitland told me last week that that was what so startled and struck him the first time he saw Perry."

"How is Mr. Maitland now, do you know?"

"He gets no better. After the first week of joy and thanksgiving over his boy's restoration to him, the malady seemed to reassert itself. Dunraven will have a new master by winter, I fancy."

The colonel was silent a moment. Then he suddenly asked,—

"By the way, how was it that Gwynne *wasn't* drowned? I never understood that."

"He never meant to be," said Stryker. "He told Perry all about it. He was ruined, he thought, in his profession and his own country, and he knew his father's inexorable pride: so he simply decided to put an end to Archie Maitland and start a new life for himself. He wrote his letters and arranged his property with that view, and called the steward to enable him to swear he was in his state-room after the steamer weighed anchor. Then in a jiffy he was over the side in the darkness; it was flood-tide, and he was an expert swimmer; he reached a coasting-vessel lying near; he had money, bought his passage to France, after a few days at Cape Town, and then came to America and enlisted. He got a confession out of one of the irregulars who was with him, Perry says, and that was one of the papers he was guarding so jealously. He had given others to Perry that very night."

"They seemed to take to each other like brothers from the start," said the colonel, with a quiet smile.

"Just about," answered Captain Stryker.

Meantime, Perry and Sergeant Gwynne have been riding slowly down the valley. Night has come upon Dunraven by the hour they reach the northern gate,—no longer closed against them,—and as they near the house Perry slowly dismounts. "I'll take the horses to the stable myself: I want to," says his trooper friend, and for the second time the young officer stands upon the veranda at the door-way, then holds his hand as he hears again the soft melody of the piano floating out upon the still night-air. Slowly and not without pain he walks around to the east front, striving to move with noiseless steps. At last he stands by the open casement, just where he had paused in surprise that night a month agone, and, slowly drawing aside one heavy fold of curtain, gazes longingly in at Gladys Maitland, seated there at the piano, just where he first saw her lovely face and form. Her fingers are wandering idly over the keys, playing little fragmentary snatches,

—first one melody, then another; her sweet blue eyes are fixed on vacancy,—she sees nothing in that room, or near it; she is paler than when he first looked upon her, and there are traces of deep anxiety and of some hidden sorrow in the fair, fresh face. Presently, under the soft touch of her fingers, a sweet, familiar melody comes rippling forth. He remembers it instantly; it is the same he heard the night of his first visit,—that exquisite "Spring Song" of Mendelssohn's,—and he listens, spell-bound. All of a sudden the sweet strains are broken off, the music ceases; she has thrown herself forward, bowed her queenly head upon her arms, and, leaning over the key-board, her form is shaken by a storm of passionate tears. Perry hurls aside the sheltering curtain and limps rapidly across the soft and noiseless rug. She never dreams of his presence until, close at her side, a voice she has learned to know and know well—a voice tremulous with love, sympathy, and yearning—murmurs only her name, "Gladys," and, starting up, she looks one instant into his longing eyes.

Sergeant "Gwynne" Maitland, lifting the heavy *portière* a moment later, stops short at the entrance, gazes one second at the picturesque scene at the piano, drops the *portière*, and vanishes, unnoticed.

Things seem changed at Dunraven of late years. The —th are still at Rossiter; so is Lieutenant Perry. It may be the climate, or association with an American sisterhood, or—who knows?—perhaps somebody has told her of Mrs. Belknap's prediction, but Mrs. Perry has not yet begun to grow coarse, red-faced, or stout. She is wonderfully popular with the ladies of the —th, and has found warm friends among them, but Mrs. Sprague of the infantry is the woman she particularly fancies, and her gruff old kinsman Dr. Quin is ever a welcome guest at their fireside. It was he, she told her husband long after, who undid the mischief Mrs. Belknap had been able to sow in one brief conversation. "I've known that young woman ever since she wore pinafores, Gladys. She has some good points, too, but her one idiosyncrasy is that every man she meets should bow down to and worship her. She is an Alexander in petticoats, sighing for new worlds to conquer, has been a coquette from the cradle, and—what she can't forgive in Ned Perry is that he simply did not fall in love with her as she thought he had."

Down at Dunraven the gates are gone, the doors are ever hospitably open. Ewen is still manager *de jure*, but young Mr. Maitland, the proprietor, is manager *de facto*, and, though there is constant going and coming between the fort and the ranch, and the officers of the —th ride in there at all hours, what makes the ranchman so popular among the rank and file is the fact that Sergeant "Gwynne," as they still call him, has a warm place in his heart for one and all, and every year when the date of his enlistment in the —th comes round he gives a barbecue dinner to the men, whereat there are feasting and drinking of healths and song and speech-making, and Leary and Donovan and even the recreant Kelly are apt to be boisterously prominent on such occasions, but blissfully so,—for there hasn't been a shindy of any kind since their old comrade stepped into his possessions at Dunraven Ranch.

THE END.

www.ingramcontent.com/pod-product-compliance
Lightning Source LLC
Chambersburg PA
CBHW032205230426
43672CB00011B/2523